ENCYCLOPEDIA OF POLYMER CLAY TECHNIQUES

A comprehensive directory of polymer clay techniques covering a panoramic range of exciting applications

SUE HEASER

RUNNING PRESS
PHILADELPHIA • LONDON

A QUARTO BOOK

First published in the United States in 2007 by Running Press Book Publishers.

9 8 7 6 5 4 3 2 1

Digit on the right indicates the number of this printing.

ISBN-13: 978-0-7624-3087-1
ISBN-10: 0-7624-3087-7

Library of Congress Control Number: 2007927633

Conceived, designed, and produced by
Quarto Publishing plc
The Old Brewery
6 Blundell Street
London N7 9BH

QUA: EPCT

Project editor: Michelle Pickering
Art editor: Natasha Montgomery
Designer: Lizzie B Design
Photographer: Phil Wilkins
Picture researcher: Claudia Tate
Design assistant: Jessica Wilson
Illustrator: John Woodcock
Assistant art directors: Penny Cobb, Caroline Guest

Art director: Moira Clinch
Publisher: Paul Carslake

Color separation by SC (Sang Choy) International Pte Ltd, Singapore
Printed by SNP Leefung Printers Ltd, China

This book may be ordered from the publisher.
Please include $2.50 for postage and handling.
But try your bookstore first!

Running Press Book Publishers
2300 Chestnut Street
Philadelphia, PA 19103-4371

Visit us on the web!
www.runningpress.com

CONTENTS

INTRODUCTION

Polymer clay was first invented in Germany in the 1930s for doll maker Kathe Kruse. After World War II, her daughter Fifi used the plastic clay product to create mosaics and called the clay Fifimoik, which is a combination of her name Fifi and the word mosaic. This was shortened to Fimo, the first polymer clay to be marketed and now known all over the world. Meanwhile, in the United States during the 1960s, a similar product called Sculpey was being developed.

Both these clays were primarily marketed as children's toys, but during the 1970s and 1980s, artists in several countries almost simultaneously realized the possibilities of a fine-grained, colorful product that could be baked to a permanent hardness in a home oven. Many talented artists began to experiment, and they discovered the enormous potential of what has become the most exciting new art material since the development of acrylic paint.

Today, polymer clay has established itself as an enormously versatile medium. It is used all over the world, by professionals and amateurs alike, in a wide range of genres, from jewelry and fine art to sculpture, modeling, doll making, and animation. The original two brands have been greatly expanded and new manufacturers have developed additional brands, giving today's artists a wonderfully wide choice of color, texture, and quality.

Polymer clay has a remarkably large variety of techniques, probably more than any other art material, and it would be impossible to include all of these in a single volume. However, this book covers all of the popular techniques that are tried and tested and known to be durable, as well as ideas from the cutting edge of polymer clay and recent discoveries.

Where possible, artists who have developed particular techniques are credited throughout the book. However, many techniques have been discovered and developed by different artists simultaneously all over the world, so this is often an almost impossible task. While the ownership of designs should always be sacred, techniques are only truly developed by sharing.

The techniques come from all the main polymer clay genres. Too often, artists cling to their original genre when diversification would enrich their work and give unexpected insight into new directions. This book is therefore intended to inspire both beginners and advanced polymer clay enthusiasts alike to explore and develop the myriad possibilities of this wonderful material.

Sue

POLYMER CLAY

Polymer clay is made from tiny particles of PVC plastic mixed with a pigment and a liquid plasticizer. When cured in a home oven at approximately 265°F (130°C), it becomes a permanent solid plastic. Polymer clay is made all over the world by a variety of manufacturers, and is rated as a nontoxic craft material that is safe for use in a home oven. Polymer clay is available in a variety of sizes. Whenever quantities are specified in this book, they refer to a standard 2oz (56g) block of clay.

POLYMER CLAY QUALITIES

Polymer clay has wonderful qualities that have resulted in its enormous growth as an art and craft material over the past few decades.

- Polymer clay is fine-textured, allowing excellent detail to be achieved.
- It is available in a large range of colors that can be mixed to make more colors, giving an extensive palette.
- No special tools or equipment are needed.
- The clay has a shelf life of several years and can be reworked repeatedly until baked.
- The clay is cured to a permanent hardness by baking in a home oven.
- Hardening causes negligible shrinkage and color change.
- Once hardened, the clay can be sawn, cut, sanded, polished, painted, and glued into more complex structures.
- Repeat baking will not affect the clay, so sculptures can be created in a series of consecutive hardenings.

TYPES OF CLAY

There are different types of polymer clay that are suitable for different purposes. All polymer clay normally cures to a flexible rather than a fully hard state. A thin sheet can be flexed and the stronger kinds are extremely robust. Different brands have different strengths (see page 156).

COLORED CLAY

This is the most popular kind of polymer clay and includes metallic, pearlescent, and translucent clays. The size of the color range varies according to the brand.

Lightweight clay

SPECIAL-EFFECT CLAYS

These clays have a particular quality for special effects.

- Flexible clays are flexible after baking and can be used for textile and other fiber effects.
- Mold-making clay is a version of flexible clay.
- Eraser clay is a kind of clay that bakes to make a usable eraser.
- Lightweight clay is used for making flowers and other pieces, such as puppets, where light weight is desirable but strength is still required.

Eraser clay

Mold-making clay

DOLL-MAKING CLAY

Polymer clay is used by doll artists to make one-of-a-kind dolls of astonishing realism and quality. The manufacturers have responded by developing clays that simulate human flesh in all its variety. The strength and quality of these clays vary, and it is wise to try several kinds to see which suits you best.

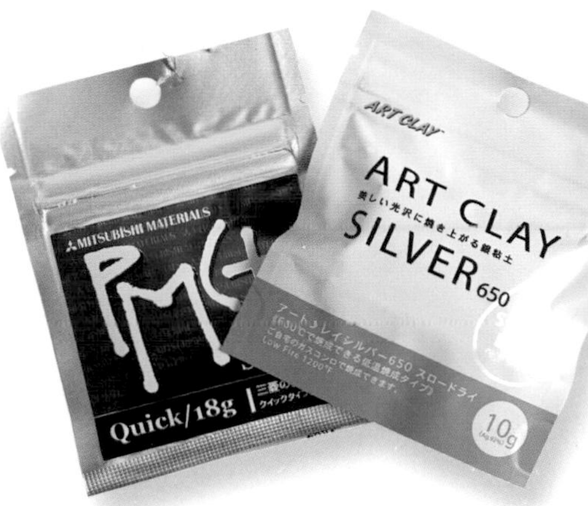

METAL CLAY

Strictly speaking, this is not a polymer clay, but it is used in the same way and can be combined with polymer clay. The most popular are the silver clays, of which two different brands are available: Art Clay Silver and Precious Metal Clay.

SCULPTING CLAY

With the increase of computer games and animated films, sculptors are using finely detailed polymer clays to make their originals (or maquettes). The most popular sculptor's clay is Super Sculpey made by Polyform Products of the US. A new Firm Gray variety of this clay has recently been introduced; its opaque gray color means that detail is easy to see and adjust.

CLAY SOFTENER

Polymer clay that has become old and crumbly can often be resuscitated with a clay softener. Sculpey Clay Softener is a liquid and Fimo MixQuick is a soft clay. Both can be used with any brand.

ARMATURE CLAY

Armature clay is the same as lightweight special-effect clay (opposite). This clay is used inside sculptures as an armature.

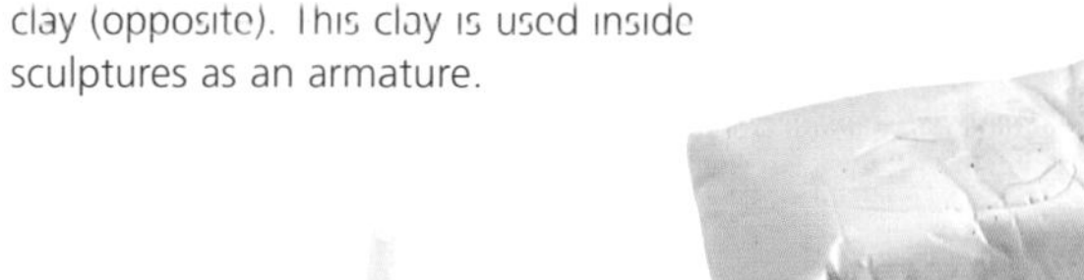

LIQUID CLAY

Now available in several brands, liquid clay can be tinted with oil paint and used for many special effects.

POLYMER CLAY SAFETY

- In the past there have been occasional alarmist reports about the toxicity of polymer clay, but recent studies by Duke University in the US have confirmed that there is little or no toxicity concerns with the material, even when ingested. This makes it safer to use than most art and craft paint products.
- It is recommended that you do not use polymer clay in contact with food because the porous clay could absorb the food and become unhygienic.
- As with any craft material, use sensible precautions when working with polymer clay. Supervise children during the baking process and wash your hands after using the clay.

OTHER MATERIALS

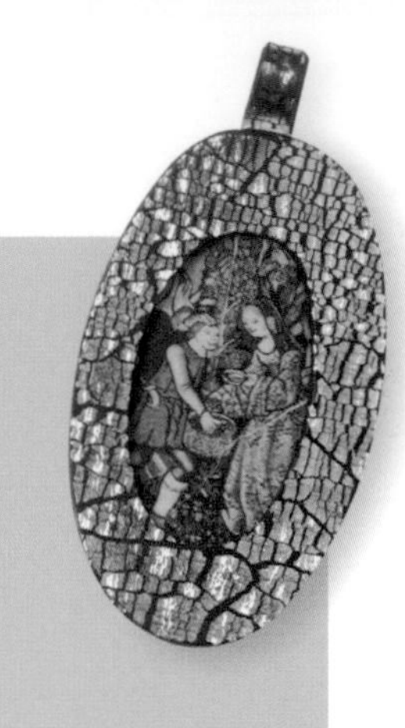

Polymer clay combines beautifully with all kinds of other materials, from paints and inks to powders, resins, and even dried herbs. The following materials are known to be stable when used with polymer clay and can enhance and embellish your work in hundreds of ways.

SURFACE EMBELLISHMENT MATERIALS

The surface of polymer clay can be embellished with all sorts of materials, from paints to powders. Be aware that all powders can be irritants, so use them in a well-ventilated room.

PAINTS

- Acrylic paint is the best paint to use on baked polymer clay. Use good-quality artist's acrylic.
- Oil paint is used to tint liquid polymer clay and resins. Do not use it to paint the surface of baked polymer clay because it may never dry properly.

INKS

- Acrylic inks are available in pearlescent as well as opaque and transparent colors from art materials suppliers.
- Stamping ink comes in a pad to use with rubber stamps. Use heat-set or permanent ink pads for polymer clay.

METALLIC POWDERS AND WAXES

- Pearlescent mica powders are sold under various brand names. They come in a huge color range, including conventional colors such as gold, pearl, and silver as well as two-tone and iridescent colors. Used to simulate metallic effects on polymer clay, they are most vivid on black clay. Brush onto unbaked clay, bake, and then varnish to protect the powder. They can also be mixed into liquid clay.
- Metallic powders are used in the same way as pearlescent powders. These are usually only available in gold, silver, and copper from art and craft suppliers.
- Leafing and gilding wax can be used to rub over baked polymer clay, and are available in both tube and cake form.

ARTIST'S PASTELS
These are available in sticks from art materials suppliers. The stick is rubbed onto paper to release the powder, which is then brushed onto clay before baking. They add subtle pastel color.

METAL LEAF
Artificial leaf is available in gold, silver, and copper as well as variegated and flakes. It is much cheaper to use than real gold and silver leaf.

METAL FOIL
Heat-set foils come in a large range of metallic colors and holographic effects. They can be applied to polymer clay sheets for wonderful metallic effects. Jones Tones and Tonertex foils are brand names.

TRANSFER PAPER
Lazertran Silk is a proprietary printing paper used to make water slide transfers.

SOLVENTS, GLUES, AND VARNISHES
It is important to use the correct types for polymer clay if you are to achieve good results.

SOLVENTS
- Alcohol in the form of methylated spirits, rubbing alcohol, surgical spirit, or even vodka is used to degrease the surface of polymer clay before painting or gluing. Alcohol is also used as a release agent for image transfer techniques.
- Acetone is used as a release for transfers and for cleaning up after using resin. Nail polish remover can be used instead.

VARNISHES
- Acrylic varnish, both gloss and matte, is water-based and the best to use. Use either artist's or crafter's acrylic varnish or the varnish sold by polymer clay suppliers. Do not use oil-based varnish, which may never dry on polymer clay.
- Polyurethane varnish and floor coatings are water-based acrylic varnishes and are durable on polymer clay. Brand names are Future in the US and Johnson's Klear in Europe.
- Alcohol-based varnish is available from some clay manufacturers and is very durable.

GLUES
- PVA glue is widely available white craft glue that has two main applications. Use it to glue soft materials to baked polymer clay, such as fabric, paper, and doll hair; and spread it over baked polymer clay to provide a key when adding soft clay.
- Cyanoacrylate glue (superglue) makes a permanent bond with polymer clay. Use it to glue two pieces of baked polymer clay together, or for attaching jewelry findings. Superglue can also be used to mend broken pieces of polymer clay almost invisibly, with the resulting join being stronger than the clay itself.
- Two-part epoxy glue is the traditional jeweler's glue and is the strongest to use for attaching jewelry findings.

MISCELLANEOUS MATERIALS

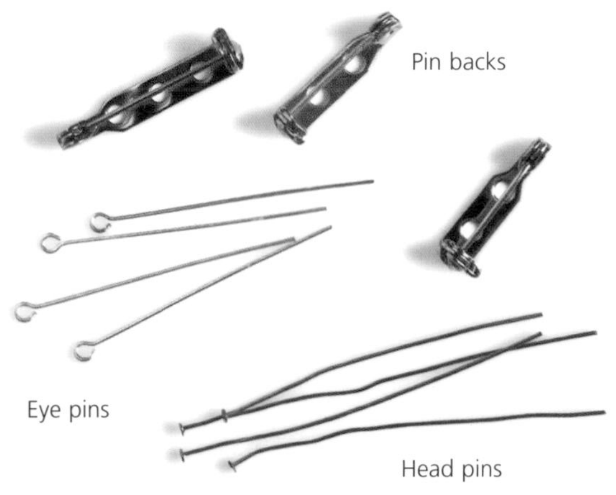

Pin backs

Eye pins

Head pins

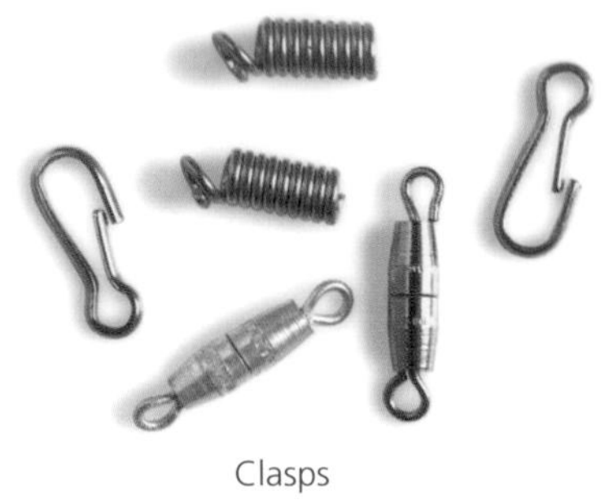

Clasps

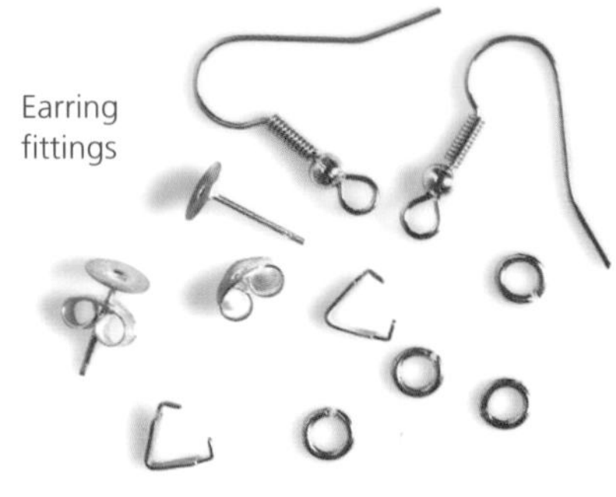

Earring fittings

Bails and jump rings

JEWELRY FINDINGS

These are the metal bits and pieces that are attached to polymer clay designs to create jewelry, including pin backs; earring fittings; clasps; eye pins and head pins for making beaded drop earrings; jump rings for joining components together; and bails for hanging pendants. Findings are widely available from jewelry-making suppliers and come in a range of finishes, from pure gold and silver to plated metal. Use epoxy glue (traditional jeweler's glue) to attach findings to baked polymer clay. Small magnets are used to make fridge magnets.

RESINS

These are used for enamel effects on polymer clay and as artificial water in natural history sculpture. Clear resin is sold as a liquid resin with a separate hardener. When mixed together, it usually has a working time of 1–2 hours and then takes about 24 hours to set hard. Clean up with acetone. Resins are widely available but some are confusing to track down because they are sold under different brand names and for different uses. The kinds to use for polymer clay are:

- Clear coating resin (brand names include Envirotex and Crystal Sheen).
- Clear embedding resin (used for embedding flowers and insects for paperweights and jewelry).
- Artificial water resins sold for miniaturists (brand name Solid Water). This type can be used for enamel techniques as well as for miniature pools.
- Cold enamels (available in a variety of colors; use the transparent colors for best effect).

DOLL-MAKING MATERIALS

Pipe cleaners and doll hair are available from doll-making suppliers. Look for viscose doll hair, which is the finest and easiest to use.

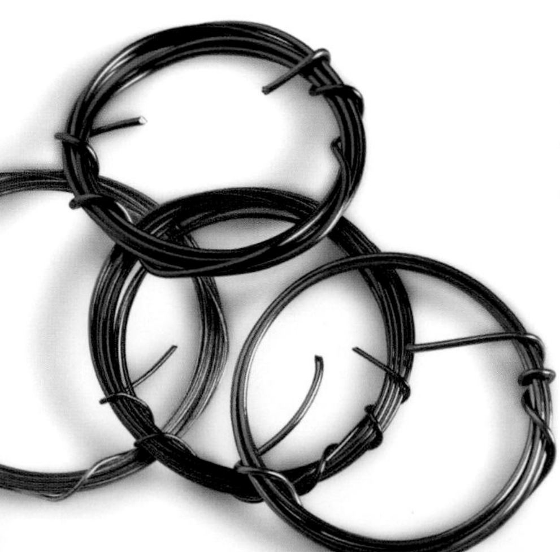

WIRE

Craft wire comes in a wide range of colors and gauges and is used for linking polymer clay beads and creating jewelry pieces. Wire is also used to make an armature to provide internal supports to sculpted polymer clay.

TOOLS AND EQUIPMENT

The basic tools and equipment required for working with polymer clay are very simple, and you will probably find that you already have everything you need in your home. The following pages list the essential tools—and suggestions for more advanced tools for when you really get hooked.

BASIC TOOLS

These are required for the majority of the techniques used with polymer clay.

WORKING SURFACE

The best surfaces for polymer clay work are wipeable and smooth. A melamine chopping board works well. Ceramic tiles are useful for working and baking on. Perspex and glass also make ideal surfaces. When a particular working surface is required for a technique, it is specified in the materials and tools list; when not specified, you can use whichever surface you prefer, regardless of what is used in the demonstrations.

CUTTING TOOLS

A craft (X-acto) knife with a curved blade is more versatile than a straight one. Long thin blades, called tissue blades or slicer blades, are used for cutting straight lines and slicing canes. Ripple blades are used for slicing clay to make special effects, such as faux abalone.

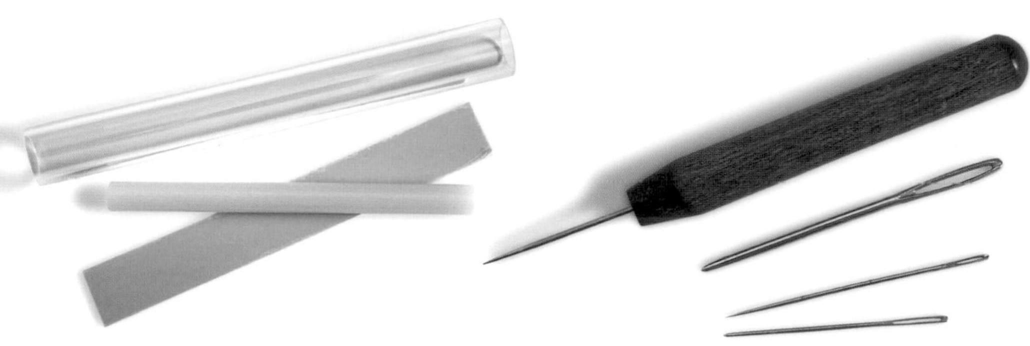

ROLLER AND ROLLING STRIPS

A clear acrylic roller is nonstick and allows you to see the clay through it. A small roller is useful for miniatures. Rolling strips are simply strips of cardboard or wood of a required thickness and are used to keep your rolling even.

PIERCING TOOLS

Darning needles and needle tools (a needle set in a handle) are best for piercing.

PASTA MACHINE

Not essential but great fun, a pasta machine is a quick way of conditioning clay, rolling even sheets, and mixing colors. Do not use a pasta machine for food after using it for polymer clay because it is impossible to clean properly.

BAKING EQUIPMENT

See page 30 for descriptions of ovens and baking surfaces.

SPECIAL TOOLS

In addition to the basic tools, you will require a selection of the following tools for particular techniques.

SCULPTING TOOLS

- Improvised tools are often the most useful, such as a tapestry needle, a ballpoint refill (dried up) with a cone tip, and a glass ball-headed pin set in a polymer clay handle and baked.
- Plastic tool sets with different tips are available from clay manufacturers. Plastic smooths polymer clay well.
- Dental tools come in many shapes; choose the ones that suit you.
- Ball-headed tools are sold for paper embossing and sculpting. They are good for sculpting faces in polymer clay.
- Clay shapers are rubber-tipped tools for shaping clay.

Improvised tools

Below, from left to right: ball-headed tool, dental tool, two clay shapers, and three plastic tools.

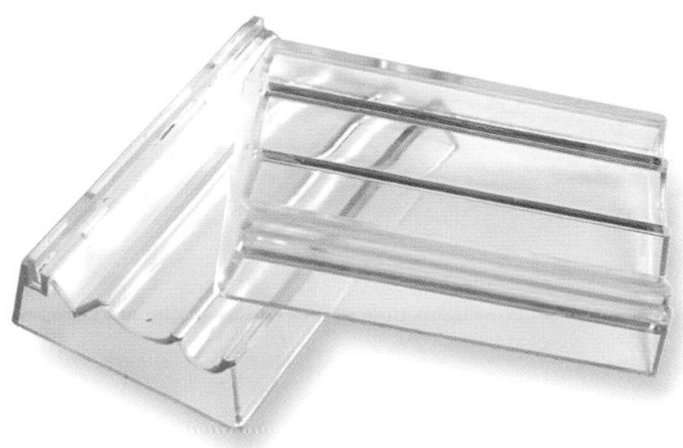

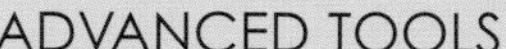

ADVANCED TOOLS

If your polymer clay work leads into a craft business, you may want to consider investing in power tools to save you time. A mini hobby drill is ideal for polymer clay and will cut, drill, and buff. If you are going into mass production, then larger tools such as a buffing wheel, a power drill with a stand for drilling holes in beads, and even a motorized pasta machine will serve you well.

BEAD ROLLERS
These are sold in a variety of designs to make even and symmetrical beads of all shapes. Beads can just as easily be made by hand, and with practice you will get them neat and even.

CLAY EXTRUDER
The best kind is one with a plunger that is screwed down; the push-down kind is hard to use with polymer clay.

SANDING, BUFFING, AND DRILLING EQUIPMENT
Foam-backed sanding pads in fine grits are ideal for polymer clay. A heavy fabric, such as denim or quilt batting, is used for polishing.

STAMPS AND TEXTURE SHEETS
Rubber stamps work beautifully with polymer clay. Choose stamps that have clear-cut designs with good relief. Wooden textile stamps and printer's metal stamps are good alternatives. Texture sheets are made of rubber or plastic.

MOLDS
There are many kinds of molds that can be used with polymer clay. The best are simple one-part push molds. Silicone push molds are mostly sold for cake decorating, while resin molds and flexible rubber molds are available from polymer clay manufacturers. Plastic vacuum-formed molds are not as detailed as the other kinds.

CUTTERS
You can use brass cutters with plungers to push out the clay shape, as well as cutters from polymer clay suppliers, kitchen equipment stores, and cake decorating suppliers.

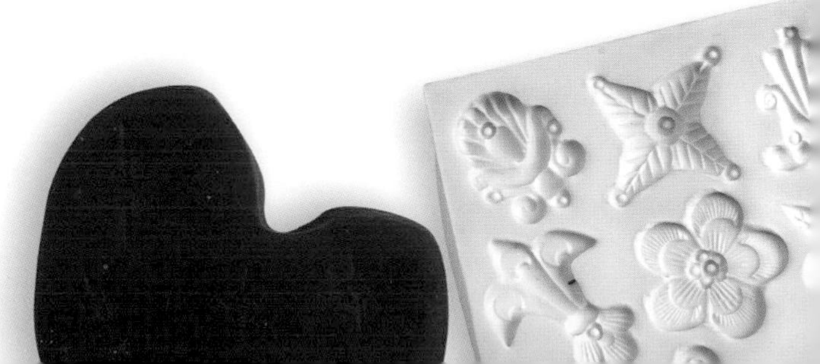

CHAPTER 1:
BASIC TECHNIQUES

Polymer clay is a very easy material for the beginner to master. Most of us have played with modeling clay as children, and simple techniques such as making logs and balls are quickly recalled.

This chapter shows all the basic skills that you need to work with polymer clay.

CONDITIONING THE CLAY

Polymer clay is a very easy material to work with because, apart from a few simple tools, all you need are your hands—and enthusiasm. Polymer clay of all brands needs a certain amount of kneading or "conditioning" to make it malleable and ready to use. The clay is affected by the ambient temperature. In hot weather, softer clays will need minimal conditioning or they will become too soft and sticky. Firmer clays will need more conditioning, especially in cold weather. Do not overcondition or you will knead air bubbles into the clay that will weaken it, and the bubbles may show in rolled-out sheets. You can condition by hand or use a pasta machine for speed.

ARTIST'S TIPS

- Work on a smooth, clean surface that you can wipe down easily, such as a melamine chopping board, a sheet of Perspex, or a ceramic tile. Small sculptures or flat-backed jewelry can be created on a ceramic tile and placed into the oven to bake on the tile, without having to move the clay piece while it is soft.
- You will not achieve a professional finish if there is dust and fluff in the clay, so keep your work area, tools, and hands clean.
- Wash your hands before using polymer clay and clean them with wet wipes between colors or if you find the clay building up on your hands. Always wash your hands when you have finished working.
- Hot, sticky hands will give disappointing results, so try to keep your hands cool while you work. Do not overwork the clay; lay a piece down to cool if it becomes too soft to use. Clay can be placed in the refrigerator or freezer for 10 minutes to cool down if necessary. You can also dust talcum powder or cornstarch onto the clay if it becomes too sticky.
- Keep your nails short; long nails will cause marks in the clay surface that are difficult to remove.

HAND CONDITIONING

Do not try to condition more than about a quarter of a 2oz (56g) pack at a time unless you have very strong hands.

STEP 1
Open the packet of clay and cut off several small pieces.

STEP 2
Squeeze the pieces of clay together with your fingers.

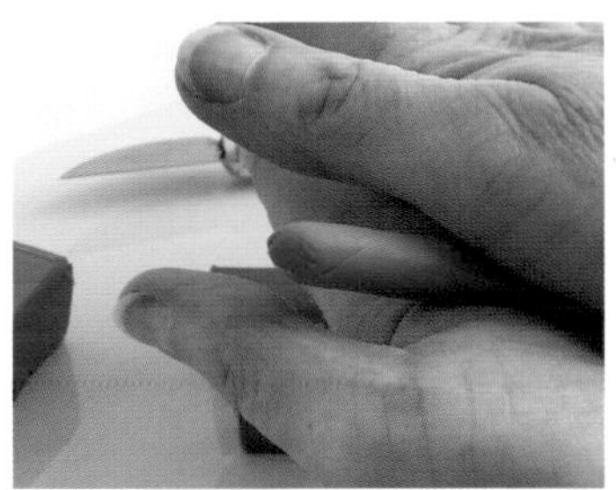

STEP 3
Roll the clay between the palms of your hands to form a log.

STEP 4
Fold the log in half, then roll it between your palms again. Repeat this process a few times until the clay is conditioned. The warmth from your hands will help to soften the clay.

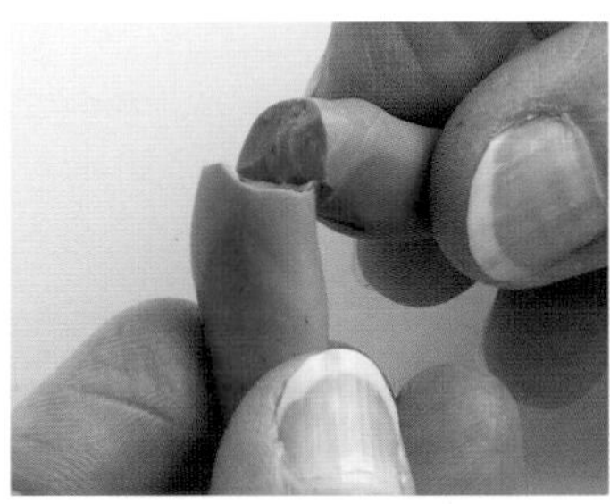

STEP 5
To tell if the clay is properly conditioned, shape it into a ½in (13mm) diameter log and bend it in half. If it cracks, it needs more conditioning.

STEP 6
If the log bends, it is properly conditioned.

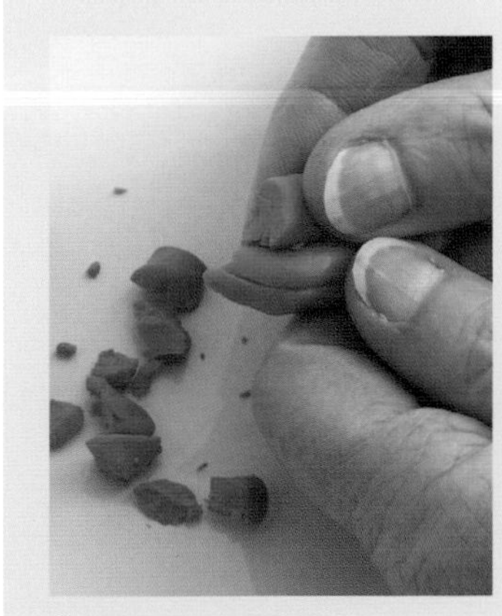

FIRM CLAY BY HAND

Knead each small piece of firm clay with your fingers, warming it as you do so. As soon as any crumbling diminishes, roll the clay into a log, folding and repeating until it becomes pliable. Now combine the smaller pieces into a larger log and repeat until the clay is conditioned.

MACHINE CONDITIONING

A pasta machine will condition polymer clay rapidly.

STEP 1
Using a tissue blade, cut the clay from the block into sheets of ¼in (6mm) thickness or less.

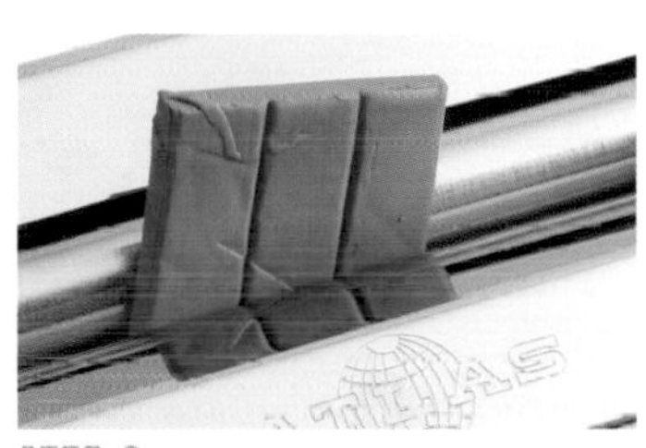

STEP 2
Set the pasta machine on the widest setting and pass each sheet through the machine.

STEP 3
Press two sheets together and pass through again, repeating until all the sheets are combined into one large sheet. Now fold the sheet in half and, placing the fold vertically to avoid trapping air in the clay, pass through again. Repeat as necessary until the clay is conditioned. Most clays need a maximum of 10 passes through a pasta machine to condition them.

FIRM CLAY BY MACHINE

If the clay is firm and crumbles a lot on the first pass through the machine, press the cut-off sheet with your fingers to warm and thin it before passing it through again.

SOFTENING HARD CLAY

Sometimes you may find that the clay is particularly dry and crumbly and, after several minutes of conditioning, is still not soft and malleable. This calls for the addition of a clay softening agent, such as the liquid Sculpey Clay Softener or Fimo MixQuick, which is a soft clay. Knead the softener into the clay a little at a time until the desired consistency is reached, following the manufacturer's instructions.

If the clay contains hard lumps that are impossible to crush, it is beyond rescuing and has probably been partly cured by overheating during storage.

FIRMING UP SOFT CLAY (LEACHING)

If the clay is too sticky and soft for working properly, you can make it firmer by "leaching" it. Polymer clay used for delicate sculpting often requires leaching for a firmer result.

STEP 1

Roll out the clay into a sheet and press it between two sheets of ordinary white printer paper.

STEP 2

After a while you will see an oily patch, which is the plasticizer being drawn out of the clay by the paper. Test the consistency of the clay and repeat as necessary; you can leave the clay to leach overnight.

STORING CLAY

Polymer clay has a shelf life of many years. The clay will slowly harden in the pack as the plasticizer evaporates, but if it is stored carefully, it will remain usable for years. Opening the pack does not affect the shelf life of the clay, but follow these tips to keep the clay in good condition.

- Store opened clay in a dustproof container, such as a cake tin.
- Small pieces of clay, such as canes, or sheets of blends can be wrapped or layered in baking parchment or waxed paper to prevent them from touching each other and sticking together.
- Do not wrap clay in plastic wrap, which can react with the plasticizer in polymer clay.
- Do not store clay in rigid plastic containers because these can be damaged by the unbaked clay.
- Keep the clay away from heat of any kind—a sunny window or a radiator can partially bake the clay.
- Cold and freezing do not adversely affect polymer clay.

Store sheets of clay separated between layers of baking parchment or waxed paper.

Roll canes for storage in baking parchment or waxed paper so that they do not touch.

2 FORMING BALLS

Simple shapes, such as balls and logs, are the building blocks of polymer clay. Fortunately, most of us have made these forms at nursery school, so it is only a matter of practicing old skills. Clay balls are used as a starting point for many projects, both in sculpting and jewelry.

ROUND BALL

With a little practice, you can make balls that are perfectly round and regular by hand (see also page 41 for bead rollers). Polymer clay projects often ask you to make a ball in a specific size. The best way to do this is to roll a log (see page 22) of the ball diameter required and then cut a length from the log of the same measurement. Rolled into a ball, this gives approximately the correct size.

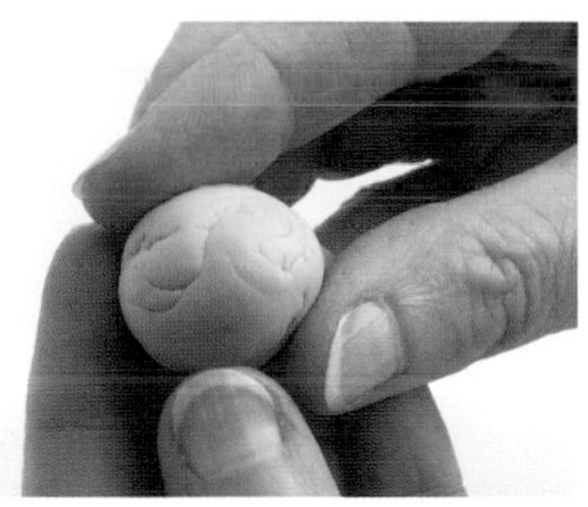

STEP 1

Take a piece of conditioned clay and shape it into a rough ball in your fingers. A ½in (13mm) size is easy to practice with.

STEP 2

Lay the ball in the palm of one hand and cover it with the palm of your other hand. Pressing firmly to start with, rotate the upper hand in a circular movement, lessening the pressure as the ball is formed. You may need to adjust the pressure, depending on the softness of the clay and the size of the ball.

STEP 3

Measuring the ball Check the ball diameter by making a measuring gauge. Mark the edge of a piece of cardboard into different lengths and cut out a slot that is deeper than the measurement. Placed over a ball, this will tell you the diameter. A plastic circle template can be used as well.

OTHER SHAPES

You can form many other shapes from a basic round ball.

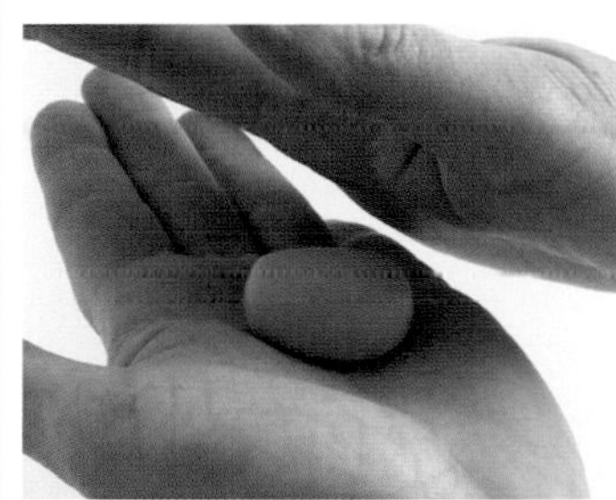

OVAL

Roll your upper hand back and forth lightly to form an oval.

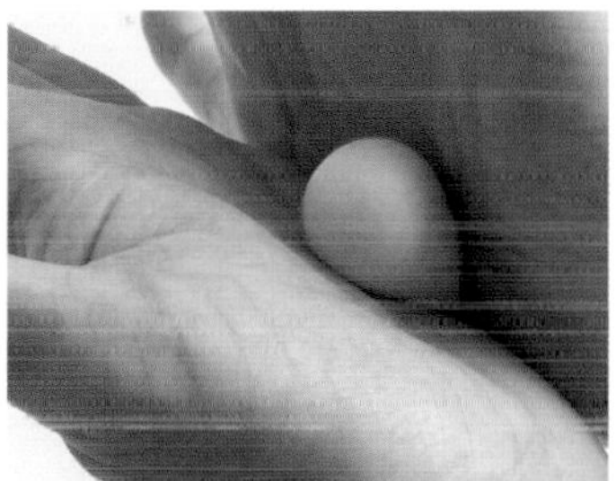

TEARDROP

Press the side of your upper palm onto one side of the ball and roll it back and forth to point that side.

PEAR

Form an oval and hold it just above the center between your forefingers. Roll back and forth to make a "waist" and create a pear shape.

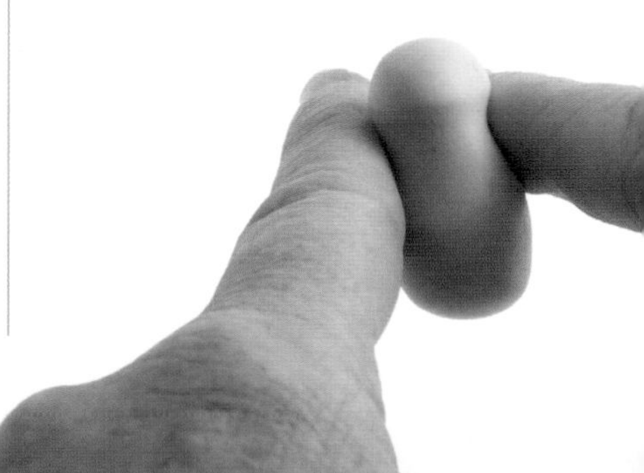

3 ROLLING LOGS

Logs are used in all forms of polymer clay work, so practice making them until you can get a smooth, even result. You can use the same measuring template suggested for balls of clay to measure the thickness of logs (see page 21). To cut a log into identical lengths, simply lay the log next to a ruler and cut at the required intervals.

BASIC LOG

The secret of rolling an even log by hand is to roll lightly and evenly, moving your fingers up and down the log as it forms. Pressure for too long on one spot while rolling will make the log irregular.

STEP 1

Form a ball of clay and roll it into an oval (see page 21). Lay the oval on a smooth work surface and roll it back and forth, with the fingers of your hand held flat and tight together.

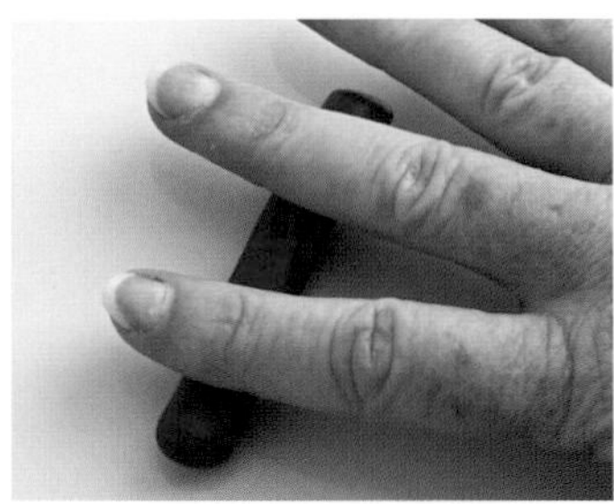

STEP 2

As the log elongates and thins, spread your fingers each time you push the log away from you, and close them as you roll the log back. This prevents any thin areas from forming. Keep the pressure light all the time.

USING A ROLLING AID

If you find it difficult to make a log of even thickness with your fingers, use a smooth piece of cardstock or (ideally) a piece of Perspex that you can see through, to roll the log back and forth instead of your fingers. This creates a beautifully even log.

THINNING THE LOG

Some projects require extremely thin "snakes" of clay—$\frac{1}{32}$in (1mm) thick or even less. You can use an extruding clay gun (see page 29) or you can roll them by hand. Use well-conditioned but cooled clay. Form a basic log, about 2in (5cm) long and $\frac{1}{4}$in (6mm) thick. Hold one end of the log in your nonworking hand and roll the other end with your working hand. As you roll, pull the clay outward from the "handle" end to extend and thin it. Continue rolling until you have the necessary length and thickness. The thicker end of the log is used to hold the clay and control it, without the heat of your hands softening and breaking the very thin log.

PIERCED LOG

A log that is formed around a hard core, such as a piece of wire or a skewer, is useful for making tube beads and for achieving logs of clay that look as though they are turned wood. Make sure that the wire or skewer is perfectly straight.

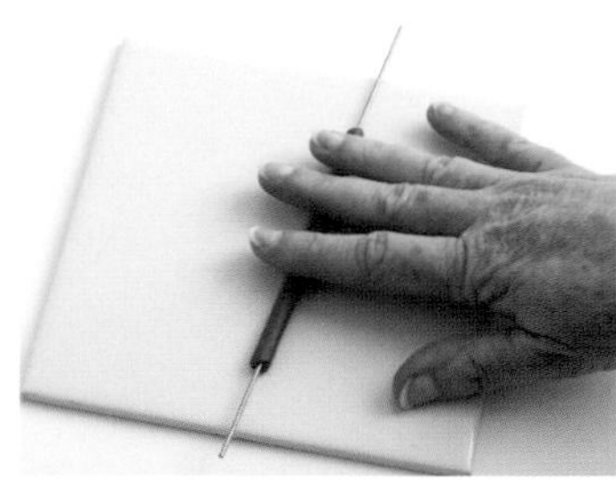

STEP 1

Form an oval as before and pierce it lengthwise with a headless skewer or wire. Roll the log back and forth, using a rolling aid if you wish. If the clay pulls away from the core, press it back on firmly all along its length and roll again.

STEP 2

Adding grooves If required, add grooves to the log by pressing a tool such as a knitting needle onto it and pushing it back and forth so that the log rotates and the needle forms a groove all around.

ROLLING SHEETS

Rolling polymer clay into sheets is the starting point of many projects. This can be done by hand or by using a pasta machine to roll out the clay quickly and evenly. Air bubbles can be a problem when rolling sheets in a pasta machine, especially with clay that is being reused, because air pockets may have become trapped inside.

HAND ROLLING

You can roll polymer clay into sheets using a smooth rolling pin. To achieve an even thickness, you will also need rolling strips. These are simply two strips of cardboard or wood of the desired thickness.

STEP 1
Flatten a piece of conditioned clay into a pancake with your hands. Lay the clay on a smooth surface and place a rolling strip on either side. Roll over the clay firmly with a rolling pin until the clay sheet is the thickness of the strips.

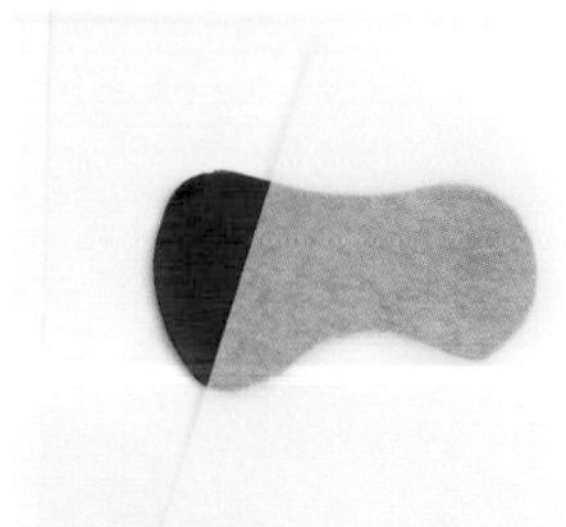

STEP 2
The rolled clay sheet will stick to the surface below, but it is easy enough to peel off the sheet unless you roll very thinly. For very thin sheets, or for rolling clay that is relatively soft and sticky, place the clay pancake between two sheets of baking parchment as you roll.

MACHINE ROLLING

Condition the clay with a pasta machine (see page 19) and then set the machine to the required thickness of sheet.

STEP 1
Fold the clay in half and insert the clay back into the rollers with the fold at the side to avoid trapping air bubbles in the clay. Wind smoothly and evenly without stopping while the clay is between the rollers.

STEP 2
Removing air bubbles If bubbles appear in the surface of the clay, fold the worst bubbles to the outside and roll again, making sure that you place the fold at the side. Repeat, so that the bubbles work to the surface and disperse.

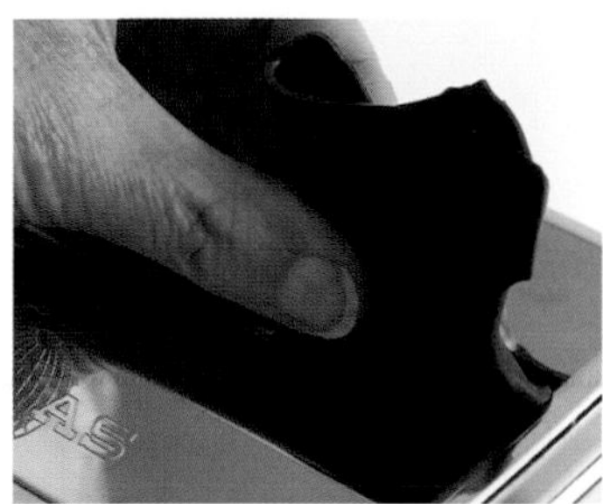

STEP 3
Squaring the sheet To stop the edges of the sheet from becoming ragged as you roll them, press one edge of the sheet against the side of the pasta machine as you roll to straighten it. Fold the sheet, rotate it, press another edge against the side, and so on.

ARTIST'S TIP

Some projects require the thinnest possible sheet of clay. The last setting on most machines usually cockles the clay (shown below), so get to know your machine and find the thinnest sheet it will roll to. To roll very thin sheets of clay, roll as thinly as possible on the machine, then lay the sheet on a piece of nonstick baking parchment and roll even thinner by hand.

5 COLOR MIXING

Polymer clay comes in a wonderful array of colors. These colors can be mixed to make new colors in the same way as artist's paints. Brands vary as to their range of colors as well as their color names. For this reason, this book refers to descriptive color names rather than those of a specific brand. Swatches of the main colors used in this book are shown here. You will need to match the colors in the brand you are using in order to obtain similar results. The exception to this rule are the color workshops that accompany techniques that require precise color mixtures, such as simulating aggregate stones. The color workshops use Premo Sculpey clay, which is one of the purest mixing clays.

Polymer clay is available in a comprehensive range of basic colors that can be mixed to create even more variety.

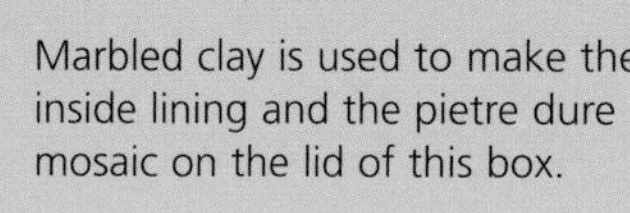

Marbled clay is used to make the inside lining and the pietre dure mosaic on the lid of this box.

MIXING COLORS

The color mixtures in this book are mostly given as how many parts of each color should be mixed together to make the new color. To measure parts, roll a log of the same thickness of each color and cut the required number of equal lengths. To mix by hand, press logs of the colors required together, then fold and roll repeatedly until the colors combine into one. A pasta machine is much quicker—roll a sheet, fold, and repeat.

BASIC POLYMER CLAY COLORS

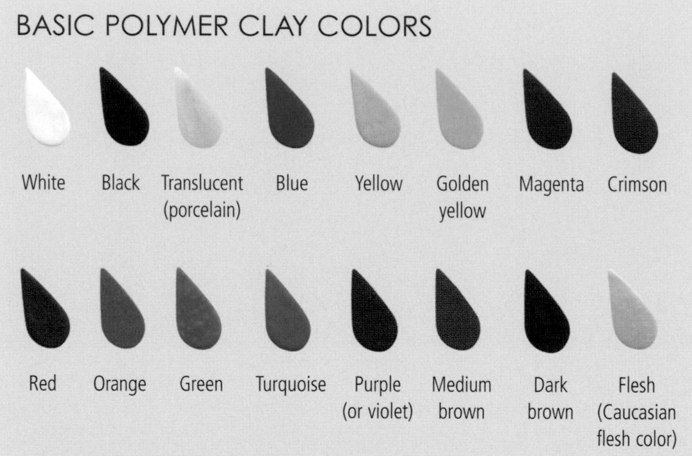

BASIC COLOR MIXTURES

You can purchase the following colors or mix them from the basic colors shown above.

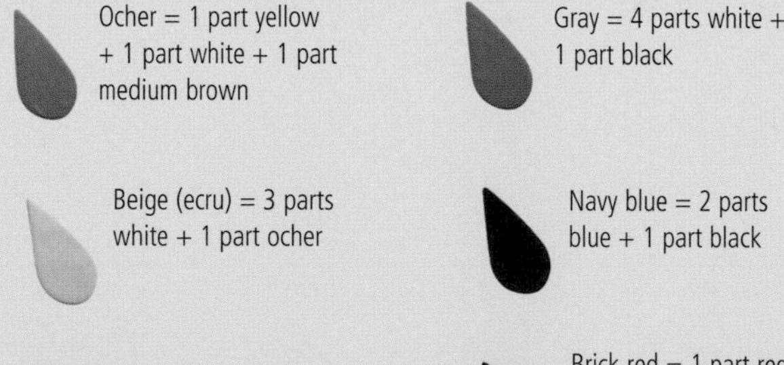

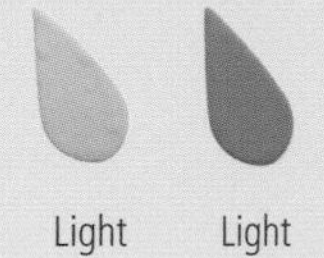

Hand marbled clay with stripes and random swirls of color.

PASTEL COLORS

Pastels can be made for any color by mixing it with white. Quantities will vary between brands, but as a general guide use 4 parts white + 1 part color.

Light green Light blue Pink

TRANSLUCENT COLORS

These are available in some brands, but it is easy to mix your own. Translucent white is a useful frosty white that resembles porcelain.
Translucent white = 16 parts translucent + 1 part white
Translucent color = 16 parts translucent + 1 part color

Translucent white Translucent red Translucent blue

MICA-BASED METALLIC COLORS

Pearlescent colors containing mica particles are available for creating mica shift and pearlescent effects.

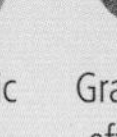

Gold Silver Pearl Copper Pearl red Pearl green Pearl blue

METALLIC AND SPECIAL-EFFECT COLORS

Some metallic clays contain glitter for sparkly effects. There are various other special-effect clays, including fluorescent colors, glow-in-the-dark clay, and simulated stone colors with inclusions.

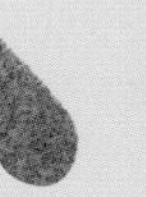

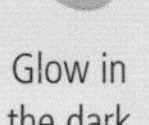

Metallic silver Metallic gold Granite effect Fluorescent pink Glow in the dark

MARBLING

Polymer clay has the wonderful ability to retain color separation within the clay body during mixing. This is used to great advantage in millefiori caning, but is also invaluable at a simpler level to create random marbled and streaking effects in the clay. For streaky marbling, it is best to marble by hand. The longer you continue mixing, the finer the streaks will become until they blend into a new color.

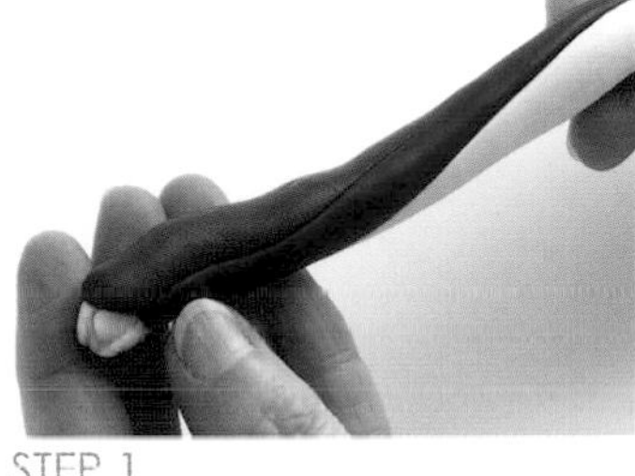

STEP 1
Press logs of contrasting colors together and roll them into a single log.

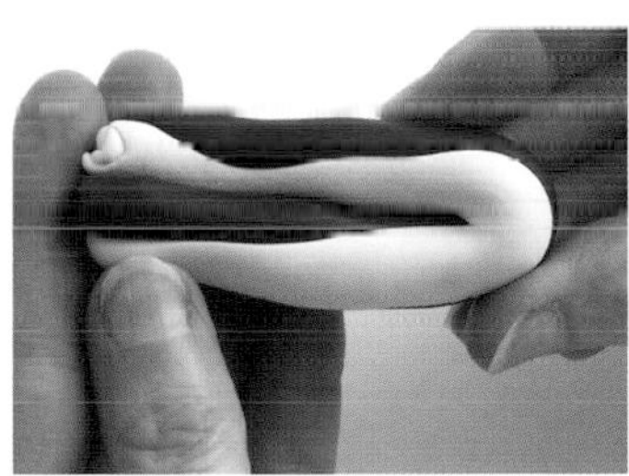

STEP 2
Fold the log in half and roll again.

STEP 3
Repeat the folding and rolling until the clay is streaked with the different colors. To produce a log with even stripes, keep the colored logs aligned carefully when you fold in half each time. For thick stripes, only fold and roll a few times; for thinner stripes, continue longer.

STEP 4
For random swirls, twist and fold the clay randomly as you mix. For the final log, twist all along its length to make attractive swirls.

Marbling in a pasta machine rather than by hand produces broad areas of color.

MAKING BLENDS

Blends are special effects created with different colored polymer clays when one color grades into another. The color change can be subtle or dramatic, abrupt or gradual. Blends are usually created in sheet form, but can then be reassembled into logs or loaves of clay for different techniques. Millefiori caning is one of the main uses of blends, but other techniques such as sculpting and mosaics also use blending.

A bracelet made from slices of a spiral millefiori cane. The cane is made by rolling two sheets of clay together, one black and one a blend of red, yellow, and blue.

SKINNER BLEND

This ingenious technique is named after the American artist who first developed it, and can be used to create blends on a large scale. The steps here show how to use a pasta machine to create the blend, but you can use a roller and rolling strips instead. Choose two contrasting colors of clay that will make a third color where they blend together.

STEP 1

Roll out a sheet of clay in each of the two colors on a medium setting on the pasta machine (use this same setting throughout). Cut each sheet into a triangle with the tip trimmed and lay next to each other to form a rectangular shape. The trimmed tips of the triangles will ensure that a strip of white and blue remain on each side of the blend.

STEP 2

Press the sheets together where they meet along the central diagonal, then fold in half.

STEP 3

Place the folded edge into the rollers of the pasta machine and pass the sheet through.

STEP 4

Fold the sheet in half again, in the same direction as before, and pass through the machine again.

STEP 5
Continue folding and rolling in this way for several more passes. The colors will form stripes where they are blending together.

STEP 6
Continue folding and rolling until you achieve the required blend.

STEP 7
Eventually, the sheet will become a continuous blend from one edge to the other.

USING BLENDS

Once you have a sheet of blended clay, you can use it in many ways.

BLENDED LOGS
Roll the blended sheet as thinly as possible and then roll it up into a log. Start with the color you want in the center of the log. For a blended log that has a slight spiral stripe effect inside it, roll up the sheet without first rolling it thin. Use for millefiori canes.

BLENDED LOAVES
Some projects require a block or loaf of clay that grades from light to dark. Roll out the clay as thinly as possible and then fold the clay into a loaf, concertina fashion. When you reach the end of the sheet, consolidate the clay in all directions by pressing it firmly into a loaf of the required dimensions for the project. If you do this without first thinning the sheet, you will get a more striped effect.

Try these...

Multicolor blend Blend together triangles of as many colors as you wish. If you trim the point of each triangle, you will have a strip of the original color dividing each area of blend.

Strip blend Some projects need a sharp gradient between colors (pietre dure mosaic, for example). In this case, simply roll together two logs of clay, folding and rolling in the usual way. The blend will occur in a small strip where the two logs meet. You can also do this with several logs of different colors.

7 CUTTERS AND TEMPLATES

Polymer clay sheets can be cut into shapes easily and quickly using cutters or templates. The resulting cutout shapes can be used in numerous ways, including: blanks for pins, earrings, pendants, and other jewelry pieces; embellishments for boxes, wall hangings, vessels, and frames; mosaic or marquetry pieces; board game pieces; and petals and leaves for polymer clay flowers cut out using sugarcraft flower cutters.

Cutout shapes in marbled and plain clays can be used to make quilting and parquetry patterns.

ARTIST'S TIP

Cutters with plungers are a mixed blessing for polymer clay. If the cutout piece lifts up with the cutter, you will need to press the plunger to push it out. This can make an unwelcome mark on the cutout piece. Open cutters are often preferable, because you can use the pad of your finger or a soft, blunt tool to push out the clay without marking it.

USING CUTTERS

All kinds of cutters are used in much the same way.

STEP 1

Roll out a sheet of clay to the thickness required and press the sheet lightly onto a ceramic tile so that it adheres. Brush the surface of the clay lightly with talcum powder or cornstarch to prevent the cutter from sticking in the clay.

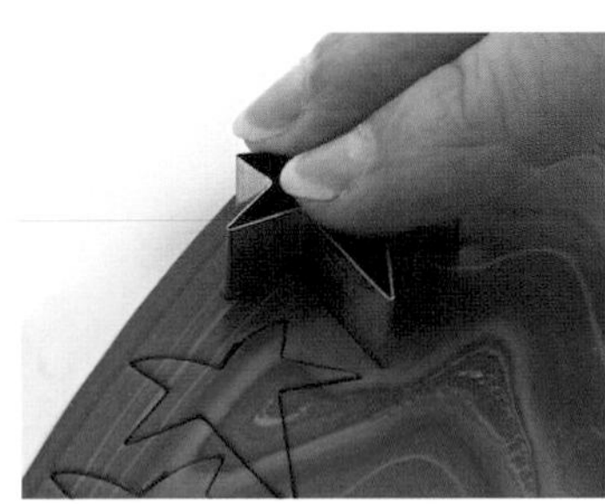

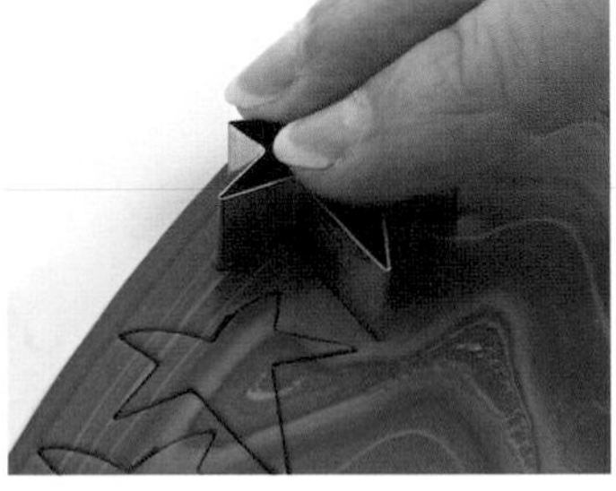

STEP 2

Press the cutter down firmly into the clay, until it contacts the tile all around. The natural stickiness of the clay should stop the pieces from being removed with the cutter; if they dislodge, press the sheet down a little.

STEP 3

Remove the cutter and pull away the scrap clay. You can bake the cutout pieces on the tile to avoid distorting them while they are soft if this suits the project. If you need to manipulate them while they are soft, slide a blade under each one to free it from the tile.

USING TEMPLATES

Proprietary templates are available from polymer clay tool suppliers and quilting shops. To make your own template, draw or photocopy a shape onto thin cardstock, then cut it out.

Lay the template on a sheet of clay that has been pressed lightly onto a tile to stick it down. Cut around the template with a craft knife; remove the excess clay and the template.

8 EXTRUDERS OR CLAY GUNS

The basic clay gun or extruder is a barrel with a metal plunger. The softened clay is inserted into the barrel and the plunger is pressed to extrude the clay through a shaped die screwed to the end. Use the extrusions fairly soon after making them so that they retain their flexibility and do not stiffen as they become cool. There are many exciting techniques for using extruded clay, including basketry, cloisonné, fantasy hair for sculptures, filigree, stained glass, millefiori canes, and fiber techniques.

Four-color striped extrusion

ARTIST'S TIPS

- Always use warmed and softened clay. Hard clay may show stress marks or tears when extruded and is much harder to push out.
- Keep the clay gun as clean as possible; wipe out the inside with alcohol or wet wipes.
- Spray the inside of the gun with silicone furniture polish to make it easier to clean.

USING A CLAY GUN

The Makin's Professional Clay Gun is now available all over the world; with its winding handle, it is easy (and painless) to use.

STEP 1

Condition the clay well, softer clay is easier to extrude. Undo the end of the clay gun barrel and insert the plug of clay. Place a die of your choice onto the end of the gun and screw down the holding collar.

WRAPPED EXTRUSIONS

Fill the barrel with one color and then add ½in (13mm) of another. Extrude the clay; after the first inch or so, the extrusion will have an interior color of the first clay wrapped in a shell of the second color.

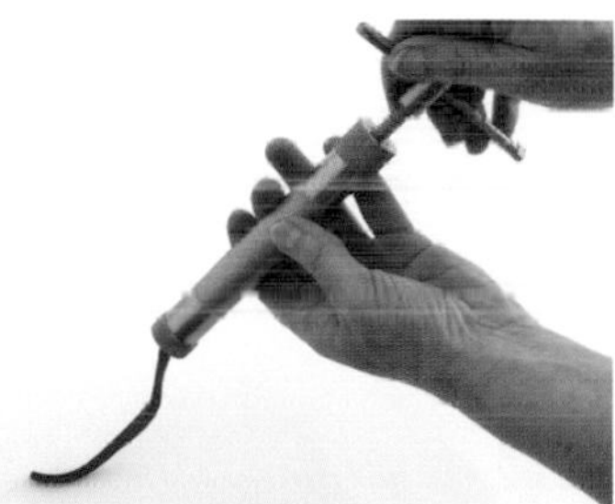

STEP 2

Wind the handle; the clay will extrude from the die.

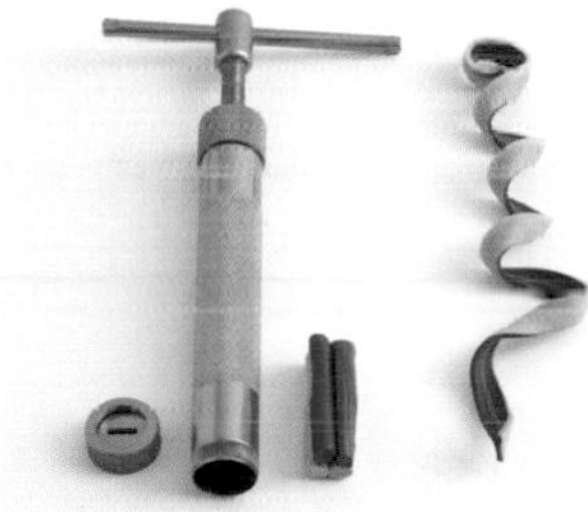

STRIPED EXTRUSIONS

Press logs of contrasting colors together and insert into the barrel. The resulting extrusion will have stripes of color that grade subtly into one another.

Experiment with various combinations of clay extruded through different-shaped dies.

BAKING

Polymer clay is a man-made plastic clay that is hardened by heating. When polymer clay is baked, the liquid plasticizer evaporates and all the tiny particles of PVC that make up the clay body fuse together into a permanent plastic. This process, sometimes called curing, is achieved by a combination of the correct temperature and baking for long enough so that the clay is heated to this temperature right through. Thicker pieces will therefore need to be baked for longer. All types of polymer clay come with the manufacturer's recommended baking times and temperatures.

SAFETY TIPS

It is safe to bake polymer clay in a home oven; all the brands of polymer clay available have been rigorously tested in every country where they are sold worldwide and have all been given a nontoxic certificate for use in a home oven. However, sensible precautions should be taken, as is normal with any craft material.

- Follow the manufacturer's instructions on the pack. The different brands have slight differences in baking requirements.
- If you accidentally bake the clay at a high temperature—above 320°F (160°C)—the clay will burn. Burning plastic can give off toxic smoke, but it smells so bad that you are unlikely to inhale enough to harm you. Turn off the oven at once and ventilate the room well.
- If you want to avoid polymer clay smells in your home oven, bake the clay inside an ovenproof pot with aluminum foil sealing the top. You may need to increase the baking time.
- If you are going into production for a small business and baking in large quantities, it is wise to invest in a small toaster oven or a dedicated oven in the garage to bake the clay. This avoids the buildup of plastic smells that can occur if you bake a lot of clay in your kitchen oven.

EQUIPMENT

All you need is a regular home oven and a suitable baking surface.

BAKING SURFACE

Bake polymer clay pieces on a baking sheet, an ovenproof dish, a ceramic tile, or even a piece of glass. The low oven temperatures will not affect these surfaces. If you want to avoid a shiny surface where the clay rests on the baking surface, cover the latter with baking parchment or a piece of ordinary paper. Place the clay on top of this and bake. This is also necessary when using a metal baking surface because it prevents the clay from scorching where it touches the metal.

ELECTRIC OVENS

These are the easiest to control when baking polymer clay. Electric fan ovens are the best of all; the dry heat circulating makes the clay very strong, but set the temperature to about 20°F (10°C) lower than recommended to allow for the hotter air. Small toaster ovens are normally fine for polymer clay, but avoid those with exposed elements that are just above the clay or the clay may scorch. Cover the clay with a tent of foil if this happens.

GAS OVENS

A setting of gas mark ¼ to ½ is usually about right for polymer clay, but it is safest to check with a separate oven thermometer. Be aware that gas ovens have a steep temperature gradient inside—they are much hotter on the top shelf.

KITCHEN RANGES

You can bake polymer clay in a cast-iron kitchen range, but you will need a separate oven thermometer so that you can check the temperature inside the oven.

BAKING THE CLAY

Bake the clay as recommended on the packet. Most polymer clay bakes at 230–270°F (110–130°C) for about 20–30 minutes, depending on the thickness. Preheat the oven to the correct temperature, place the clay on your chosen baking surface, and bake for the required time. Remove the clay from the oven and allow to cool.

BAKING BEADS

Polymer clay beads will not sag or distort during baking, so there is no need to thread them onto wires to bake. In fact, this can actually cause distortion; it is best to handle the unbaked beads as little as possible. A piece of paper or cardstock folded into a concertina shape and laid on a baking sheet will prevent the beads from rolling around when you place them in the oven.

BAKING SHEETS

Some projects require a flat sheet of baked clay. Roll out the sheet of clay and place it between two sheets of baking parchment. Lay this on a tile and place an upturned tile over it to hold it down. Bake for the usual amount of time plus about 10 minutes to allow for the tiles to heat through. This ensures that the sheet is completely flat and smooth after baking.

SUPPORTS

Polymer clay pieces that are unsupported can sag when heating up in the oven and you will need to provide support during baking for these if they do not have an internal armature. Aluminum foil is ideal for this because it can be shaped as required. You can also use cardboard or even pieces of crockery to support your work.

Miniatures baked with aluminum foil supports.

PRACTICAL TIPS

Polymer clay is not difficult to bake, but you need to get it right to make a permanent product that will last for years. See page 156 for information about clay strength.

BAKING TEST

You can use a simple baking test to check that your oven is baking at the correct temperature. Domestic ovens can often be 20–40°F (10-20°C) out, which does not affect food baking but can be a problem for polymer clay. (Note: Sculpey III cannot be used for this test because it is always brittle after baking.) Make some small pancakes of polymer clay, about 1in (25mm) diameter and 1⁄16in (1.5mm) thick. Bake in the usual way, allow to cool, and then assess the results.

- **Clay snaps easily** Oven is too cool; try increasing the temperature by 20°F (10°C) and test again.
- **Clay can be flexed into a U bend before breaking** Baking is correct.
- **Clay is shiny or sweaty-looking and the color has darkened or browned** Oven is too hot; lower the temperature.

QUENCHING

When extra baked strength is required, bake the polymer clay as usual and remove from the oven. Immediately immerse the clay in ice-cold water. This causes the plastic to contract and creates a denser and more solid product. It is also useful if any small cracks appear in a polymer clay piece; the cracks will contract and virtually disappear.

MULTIPLE BAKING

Polymer clay can be baked repeatedly without harm. This is useful for building up elaborate sculptures or for adding fresh clay to a project. Smear a little PVA or stick glue onto the baked clay surface and allow to dry. Apply the fresh clay, which will stick better to the glued area. Bake again for the time required for the added pieces.

PLAQUING

Translucent and flesh clays can develop flaws during baking, called plaquing or "half moons." This is sometimes desirable, such as when making faux stones, but can ruin items such as a doll's face. Plaquing is usually caused by too much air and moisture kneaded into the clay, so avoid overconditioning or reusing already worked clay for an important piece. Make sure that your hands are thoroughly dry before handling the clay.

This piece of flesh-colored clay intended for a doll sculpture is spoiled by plaquing.

10

CUTTING, DRILLING, AND CARVING

Incising produces lovely surface patterns that are emphasized by antiquing.

Once baked, polymer clay is a little softer than soft wood and can be cut, drilled, and carved in much the same way. This means that, unlike with ceramic clays, you are not constrained to make the entire project in the soft state. Elements can be created, baked, and then shaped further before assembly.

CUTTING

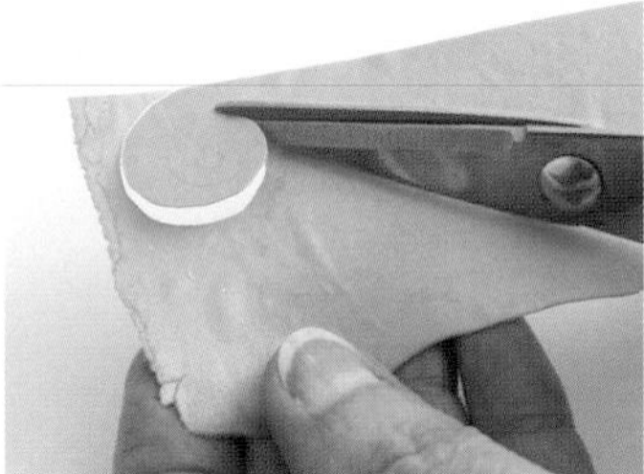

USING SCISSORS
Use scissors to cut sheets of clay to shape or to cut out shapes for inlay.

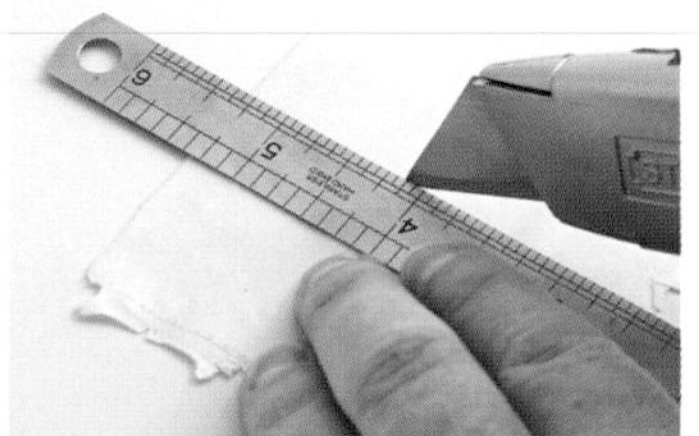

USING A KNIFE
A sharp craft knife cuts polymer clay cleanly. Warm the baked clay first to make it easier to cut. Use this method for slicing pre-baked canes and cutting out or trimming sheets.

USING A PAPER PUNCH
Cut out very thin sheets of baked clay—$\frac{1}{32}$in (1mm) thick or less—using a paper punch. The shapes can be applied to soft clay for lovely decorative effects.

DRILLING

Sometimes it is better to drill holes in polymer clay after baking to get a clean finish. This applies to holes for pendants and holes through beads. Make a pilot hole when the clay is soft so that the drill bit will cut in the right place. Baked polymer clay is soft enough so that you can simply twist a fine drill bit into the clay by hand. A small hobbyist's mini-drill can be used, but take care that it does not skid off the clay surface when drilling.

CARVING

FILING
Use a small needle file to make incised effects or to smooth rough edges on baked polymer clay.

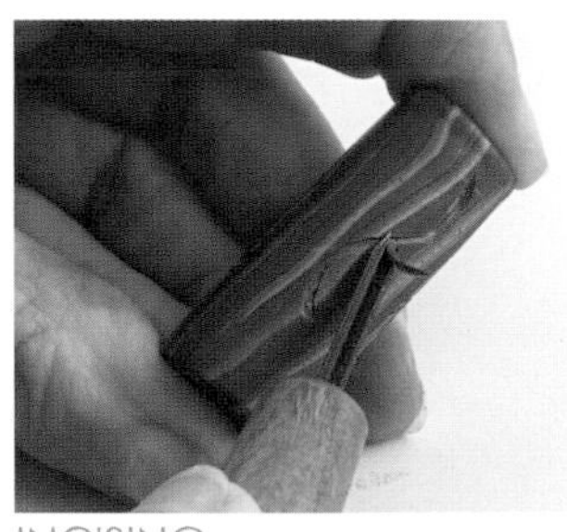

INCISING
Use a V-shaped lino-cutting tool to incise grooves into baked polymer clay. This gives a much sharper and cleaner result than if you incise the clay when it is soft.

INSCRIBING
Use a sharp needle or an engraving tool to inscribe shallow surface effects in baked clay.

11 SANDING AND BUFFING

Baked polymer clay can be sanded smooth and then buffed to give a wonderful patina. This is particularly effective with beads and faux semiprecious stones for making jewelry. Translucent polymer clay is much more transparent when the surface is buffed and sanded.

This swirled lentil bead made from marbled clay has been buffed to a high sheen.

ARTIST'S TIPS

- You can use either wet-and-dry sandpaper or foam-backed sanding pads.
- To get a really good, smooth finish, you will need three types: coarse (300–400 grit); medium (800–1000 grit); and fine (1200–1400 grit).
- Fine wire wool is also useful for smoothing baked polymer clay; use it instead of the coarse-grit sandpaper.

SANDING

Hold the baked polymer clay piece under a gently running faucet. Lukewarm water helps to soften the clay and makes sanding quicker. Sand first with a coarse sanding pad to remove the major blemishes and then progress through to medium and then fine. The running water helps to prevent the sandpaper or sanding pad from clogging.

BUFFING

BY HAND

The sanded surface will look dusty and pale in color and now needs to be buffed. A good firm rub with quilt batting, a stiff cotton fabric such as denim, or even a pair of women's nylon pantyhose will buff the surface to a shiny patina.

USING A MINI-DRILL

Polymer clay can be buffed more rapidly using a mini-drill with a cotton buffing wheel. If you have one, a bench grinder with a buffing wheel does the job even faster. Take care with power tools, because the clay piece can easily be snatched out of your hand.

12 GLUING AND EMBEDDING

The strongest glue for attaching jewelry findings to baked polymer clay is a two-part epoxy glue. Superglue is best for gluing pieces of baked polymer clay together; choose a medium-speed glue (5–10 seconds setting time) so that you can realign if necessary. Use PVA glue or Tacky glue for gluing fiber or fabric to baked clay. You can also embed part of a jewelry finding into the polymer clay before baking.

A small embedded loop provides an attachment for ear wires or a pendant bail.

Support glued items in foil or a dish of sand to keep them level while the glue dries.

GLUING

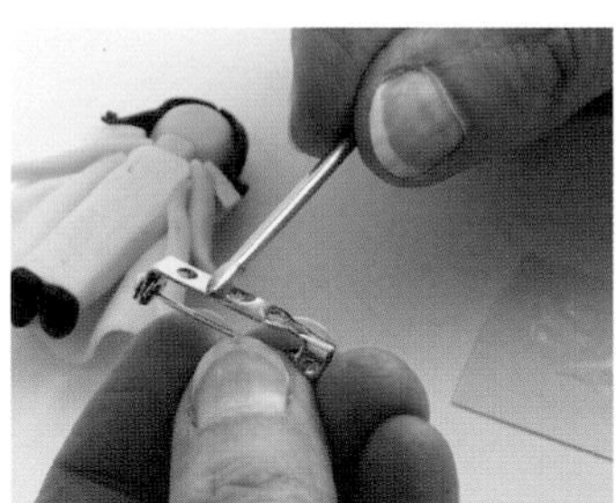

METAL TO CLAY

Clean the surfaces to be joined with a cotton swab dipped in alcohol. Squeeze out equal quantities from each of the two tubes of epoxy glue and mix them together on a piece of scrap cardstock or foil. Apply the glue to the pin back, then press the pin back onto the polymer clay.

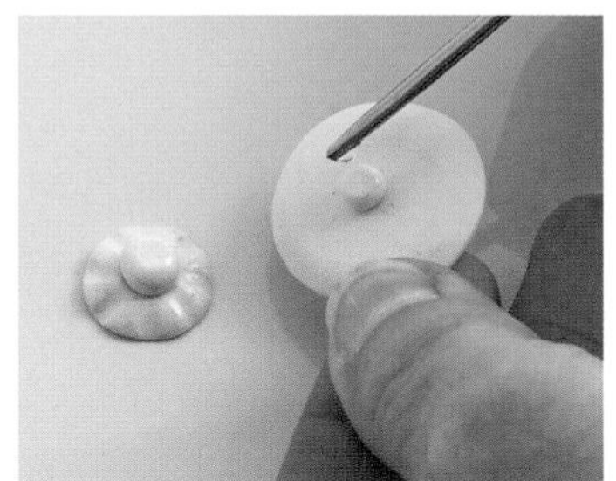

CLAY TO CLAY

Degrease with alcohol as before for the strongest bond. Pour a small pool of superglue onto a piece of foil and use a needle or small bamboo skewer to apply glue along one of the clay surfaces. Press the two pieces together and hold firmly until they bond.

FIBER TO CLAY

Pour out a small amount of PVA glue and use a needle to apply it as before. PVA glue is ideal for gluing doll hair to polymer clay dolls.

EMBEDDING

PENDANT LOOP

Form a small loop in the end of a short length of wire and make a larger loop in the other end. Press a small ball of polymer clay onto a tile and press the larger loop into it so that the small loop is just clear of the clay. Press the baked pendant or earring over the large loop so that the loop is trapped in the clay. Bake the piece again.

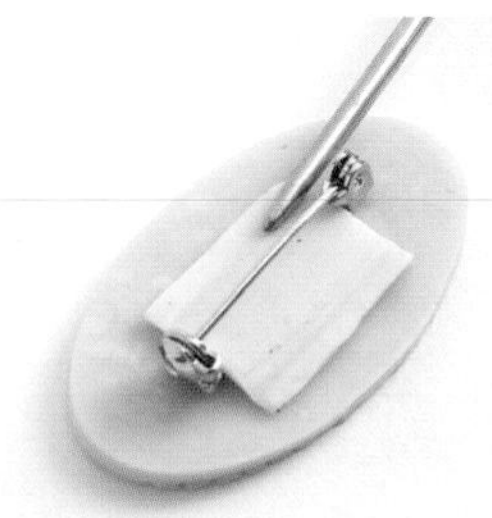

PIN BACK

Cut a small strip of clay large enough to go over the pin bar. Brush a little liquid polymer clay or PVA glue over the back of the front piece and position the pin bar. Lay the clay strip over the pin bar and press down firmly on either side. You can make this a decorative element with crimping or a small stamp. Bake.

13 VARNISHING

Baked polymer clay does not gain added strength or durability with a layer of varnish. Varnish is used simply to provide a gloss to the surface or to protect paint or other applied finishes. Varnish comes in various finishes: gloss, matte, or satin (which is somewhere between the two). Use gloss varnish when a shiny result is required, such as on beads. It is also useful for protecting and enhancing metal leaf and powders. Polymer clay is naturally matte, so use matte or satin varnishes as a protective coating on painted clay where a gloss finish is undesirable, such as a doll's face.

SUITABLE VARNISHES

The main polymer clay manufacturers all make varnish that can be used on any brand and these are proven to be compatible with the clays.

Choose:

- Water-based acrylic varnish, such as hobby varnish.
- Water-based polyurethane varnish.
- Alcohol-based varnish.
- Acrylic floor coatings, such as Future floor polish (US) or Johnson's Klear (Europe), are an economical alternative.

Avoid:

- Oil-based varnishes of any kind, which may become sticky on polymer clays when they react with the plasticizer.
- Nail polish; some can react with the clay and go sticky.
- Spray-on aerosol varnish; even if the varnish is acrylic, the propellant can react with polymer clay.

APPLYING VARNISH

Apply alcohol-based varnish directly to the clay surface after baking. To prevent beading (when a water-based varnish will not stick properly on the clay and gathers in droplets on the surface), brush the surface of the baked clay with alcohol and allow to dry before varnishing. Apply a second coat of varnish when the first is fully dry to get a higher shine. Some polymer clays can develop bleeding in the clay surrounding a painted area some time after the paint was applied. To avoid this, coat the clay with a matte varnish before painting, then seal with a top coat of matte or gloss varnish when the paint is dry. Allow to dry thoroughly before applying the top coat of varnish; this will avoid any clouding of the varnish.

UNDERCOATS
To avoid delicate paint effects from bleeding, apply an undercoat of matte varnish before painting, then finish with a top coat of the varnish of your choice.

SMALL BEADS
Thread the beads temporarily onto a piece of wire to enable you to varnish several beads at a time without them rolling about. Bend a hook in one end of the wire to hang it up until the beads are dry.

LARGE BEADS
Push a thick needle into the bead hole to steady it while you brush on the varnish.

MINIATURES
Small pieces of crockery or food are difficult to hold when varnishing, so pin them down with the point of a large blunt-ended needle as you brush on the varnish.

CHAPTER 2: SHAPING TECHNIQUES

There are many different techniques used to manipulate and shape polymer clay. The variety is quite extraordinary, from weaving baskets and rolling beads to molding buttons and building boxes. Creations can be made entirely in soft clay and then baked, or different elements made, baked, and then assembled.

14 BEADS

Beads have been made out of potter's clay for thousands of years, and beads made from polymer clay are a natural development of this ancient tradition. Polymer clay beads are easily made by hand and the glorious array of clay colors adds to the delight. Once you have mastered the basic bead shapes, you can apply all kinds of different finishes. The materials and tools required vary, depending on the type of beads you are making.

Pearlescent powders brushed onto beads before baking give wonderful effects that can look remarkably similar to real pearls. Use white clay for light-colored pearls and black clay for metallic colors.

ARTIST'S TIP

There is no need to thread beads onto wires for baking; they will not sag and setting them upright on the baking sheet will not leave a visible mark. Alternatively, use a concertina-folded piece of cardstock to prevent the beads from rolling about during baking.

ROUND BEADS

These are the basic shape from which many other bead forms are made, so it is worth practicing to make regular shaped beads (see page 21). These instructions can be adapted to make any size of round bead. For example, for ½in (13mm) beads, use a ½in (13mm) thick log and cut ½in (13mm) lengths from it. For ¼in (6mm) beads, use a ¼in (6mm) thick log and cut lengths of ¼in (6mm), and so on.

STEP 1
Roll a log of clay of the thickness required and cut plenty of equal lengths of the same thickness. Roll each length into a ball and drop each ball lightly onto the work surface. The lighter your touch, the more even the result.

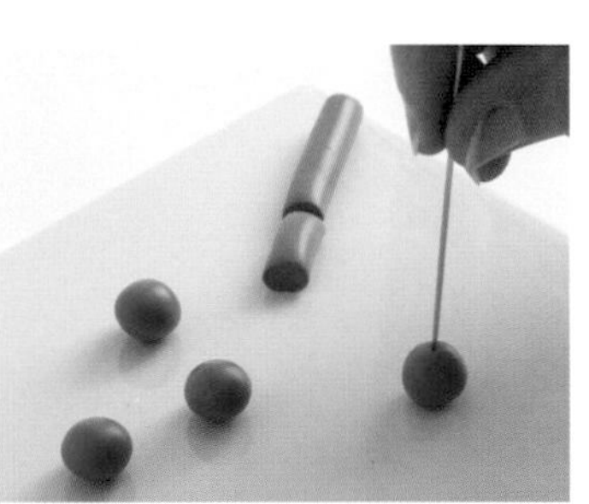

STEP 2
Using a needle tool or a sharp darning needle, pierce straight down through a bead until the needle reaches the work surface.

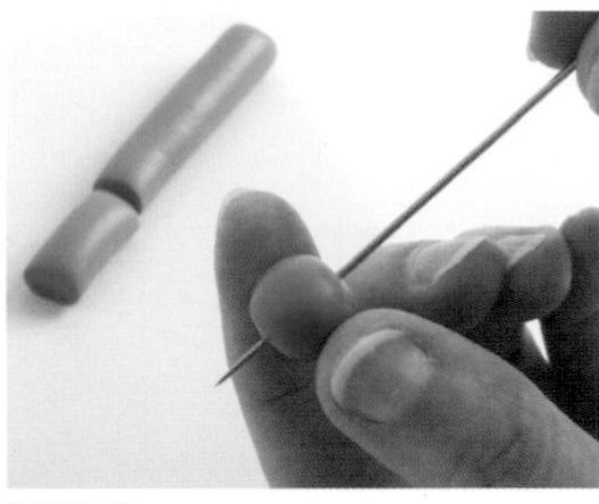

STEP 3
Lift the needle with the bead on it. Holding the bead gently, twist the needle as you push it right through the bead.

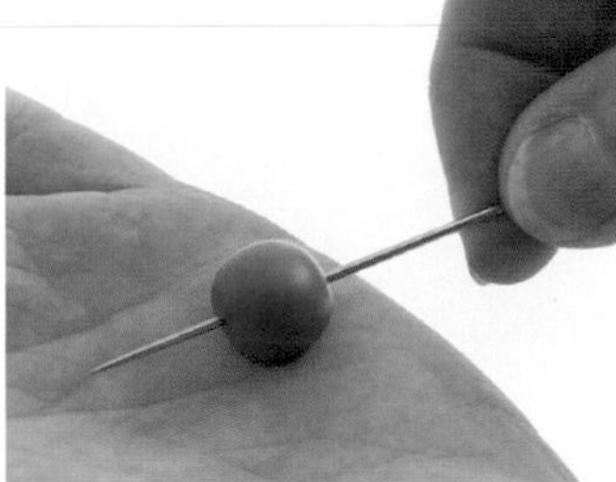

STEP 4
With the bead still on the needle, lay it on the palm of your hand and push the needle from side to side to make the bead rotate. This will enlarge the hole and round off the bead if it was distorted by the piercing. Gently place the bead, upright, onto a baking sheet covered with paper. Repeat for all the other beads.

Pebble beads knotted onto a length of linen cord make a pretty necklace.

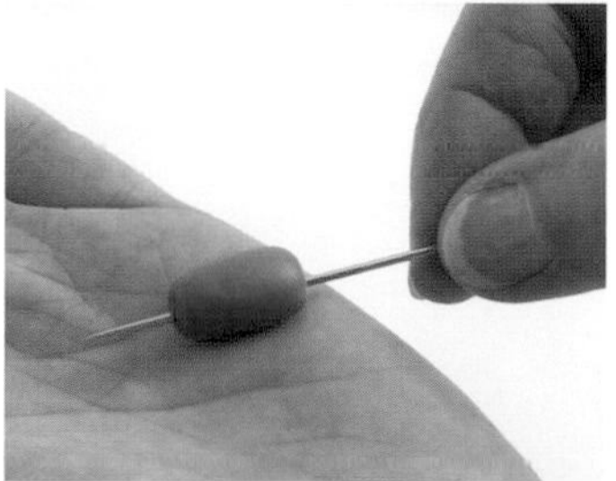

OVAL BEADS
Roll a round ball lightly back and forth in your hands to make an oval. Pierce lengthwise and finish as for a round bead.

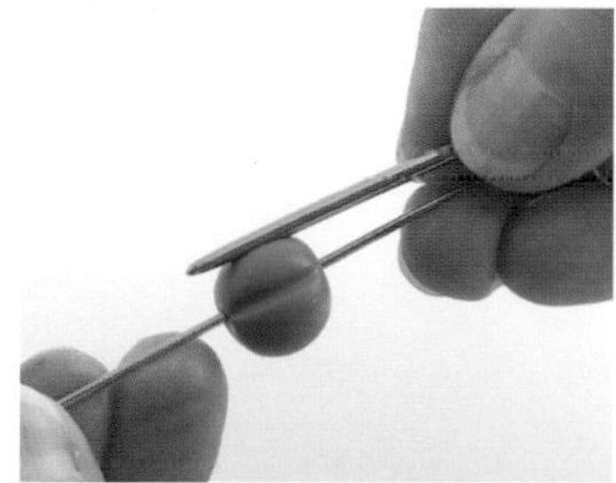

MELON BEADS
Form a round ball and pierce it, but do not roll on your palm. Hold the bead on the needle and press a second needle against the ball to make vertical indentations at regular intervals all around the bead.

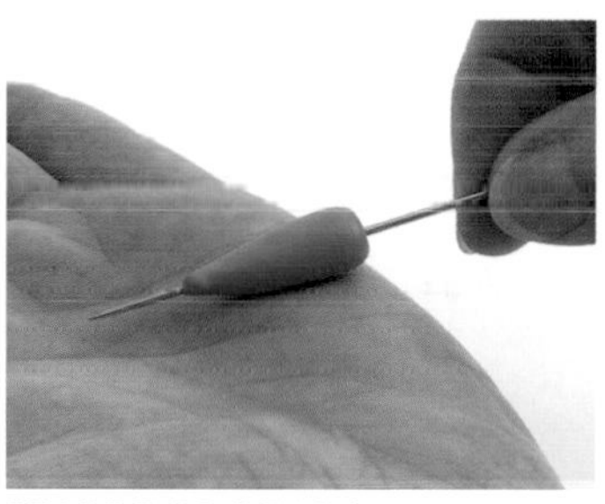

TEARDROP BEADS
Shape a ball into a teardrop. Pierce carefully lengthwise so that the hole emerges from the center of the teardrop point. Roll on your palm to shape further. Teardrop beads can also be pierced across the point.

PEBBLE BEADS
Form random round beads from marbled clay and press with a piece of quilt batting to texture. Pierce and bake.

DISK BEADS

Start with a round ball in the same way as for round beads. It should be about half the diameter of the disk bead required.

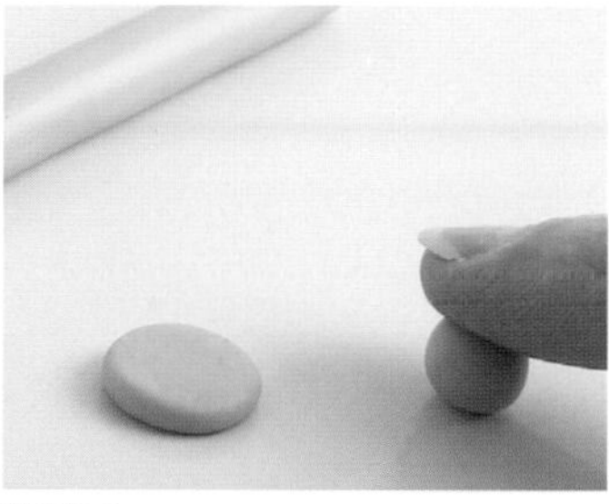

STEP 1
Place the ball on a tile and press down with the pad of your finger until it is the diameter required.

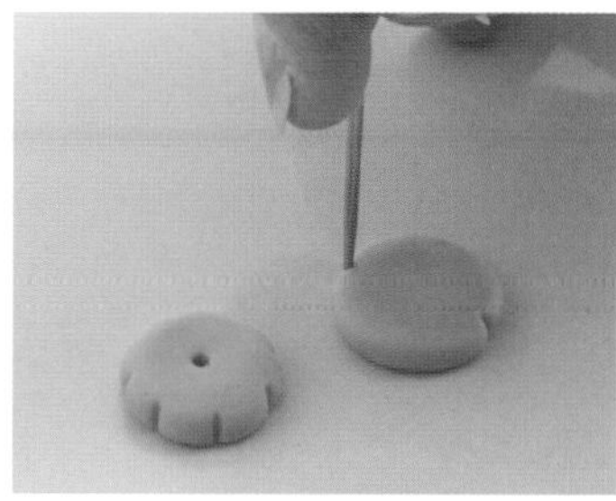

SCALLOPED DISKS
Press the side of a needle into the disks at even intervals all around before piercing.

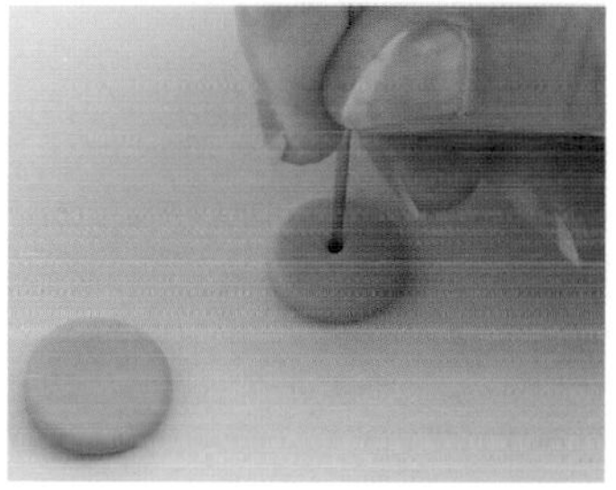

STEP 2
Pierce the center of the disk with a needle and rotate this slightly to open the hole. Bake on the tile to avoid distortion. You can also pierce disk beads horizontally.

SLICED DISKS
Make a log of clay and pierce longitudinally with a knitting needle. Bake on the needle; while the clay is still warm, remove the needle and slice the log into thin sections. A fluted log will produce a scalloped disk bead.

DONUT DISKS
Form a large ball of clay and press down onto a tile. Use a round cutter to cut out the center of the disk. Run a finger around the cut edge to smooth it and chamfer the edge. Bake on the tile.

A necklace made from bicone beads interspersed with small round beads. All of the beads have been colored with pearlescent powders to produce metallic and pearl effects.

Swirled lentil beads in different sizes threaded onto sheer ribbon with small glass beads make a striking necklace.

BICONE BEADS

Use a small piece of Perspex or glass to roll these attractive beads.

STEP 1
Make a round ball and lay it on the work surface. Cover with the Perspex and use a circular clockwise motion as though you were simply rolling a round bead.

STEP 2
The bicone shape will soon appear. You can make it more pointed or flatter by manipulating the sheet of Perspex.

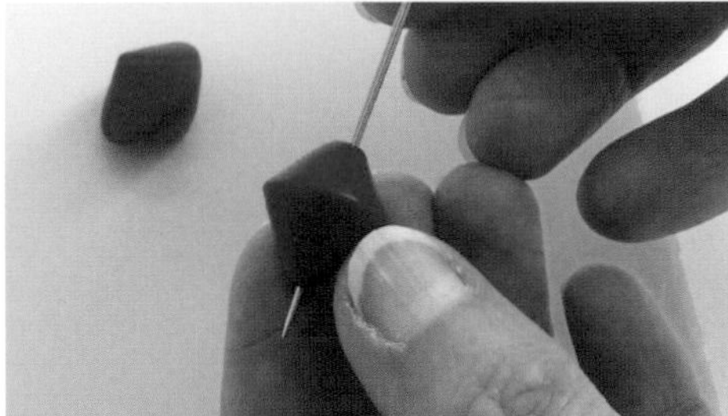

STEP 3
Allow the bead to cool in order to avoid squashing the points, and then pierce and finish as usual.

SWIRLED LENTIL BEADS

These are a delightful natural development out of a bicone bead that many artists have discovered by accident.

STEP 1
Marble two or three colors of clay together and make a round ball. Position the ball so that a junction of two or three colors is uppermost and roll with a Perspex sheet as for a bicone bead.

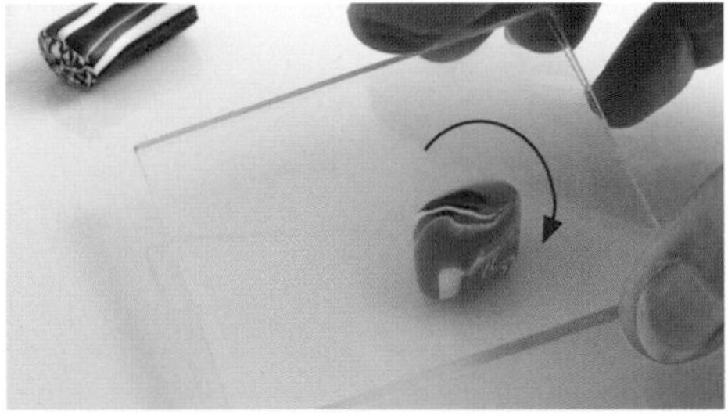

STEP 2
Always rotate the Perspex in the same direction. A swirl will begin to appear at the point of the bicone (another forms simultaneously underneath the ball).

STEP 3
Continue until the swirl is pronounced. Flatten the bead into a lentil with the Perspex and pierce across the bead for greatest effect.

TUBE BEADS

These large beads are formed from logs of clay. Marbled clay gives particularly good effects.

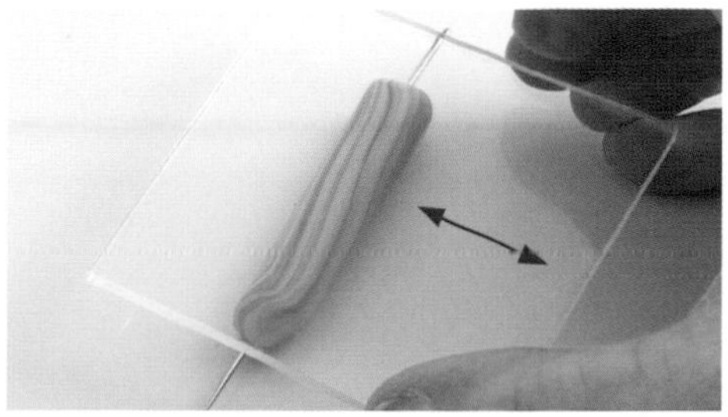

STEP 1

Single tube Roll a log of the size bead required, using a Perspex sheet or piece of glass to get the bead as even as possible. Without trimming the ends, pierce through the bead lengthwise. Bake the bead; while it is still warm, cut off the ends for a neat finish.

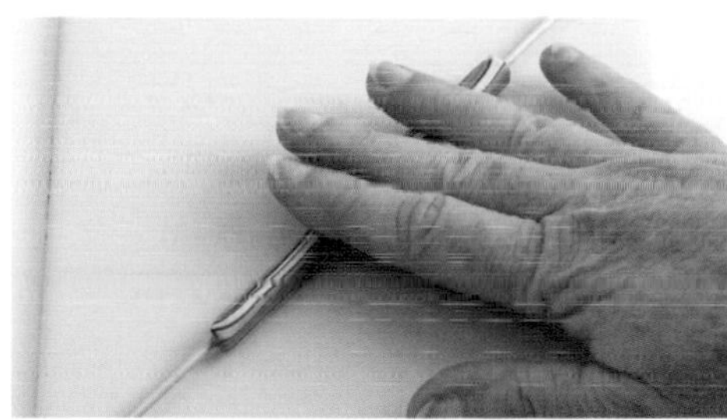

STEP 2

Multiple tubes Roll a log of clay and pierce it with a long double-pointed knitting needle. Roll the log with the needle inside it on your work surface, until the clay extends down the needle and is the required diameter.

STEP 3

If the clay begins to pull away from the needle, press it down firmly all along its length and roll again to make the log even. If you have used marbled clay, you can twist the log for a spiral effect.

STEP 4

Bake the clay on the needle. Remove the needle as soon as you take the clay out of the oven or it may become trapped as the clay cools (use oven gloves). With the clay still warm, use a sharp blade to cut the tube into lengths as required.

BEAD ROLLERS

Proprietary bead rollers are available if you find it difficult to make beads evenly by hand. They come in a variety of types to make all kinds of beads, from round and oval to bicone and tube beads.

CURVED TUBE BEADS

Roll and pierce the bead in the usual way, but thread a length of wire through the bead after piercing and then bend the bead into a curve. Bake on the wire and trim the ends after baking.

Tube beads rolled from marbled clay make wonderful feature beads for jewelry. Combine them with other small beads to make necklaces and earrings.

Place a larger rolled-up bead between a pair of smaller ones, and intersperse with small glass beads, to make a necklace.

A metallic bicone-shaped core bead with stamped decoration makes a lightweight feature bead for the center of a necklace. It is framed by clay melon beads and glass beads.

BEADS FROM SHEETS

This technique is borrowed from paper crafts. The resulting polymer clay beads are much stronger than the paper version.

STEP 1

Roll a thin sheet of gold clay and a thicker sheet of red clay. Press the two sheets together and roll or pass through a pasta machine to make a single sheet about 1/16in (1.5mm) thick.

STEP 3

With the red side uppermost and starting at the base of the triangle, roll up into a bead. Pierce to ensure that the hole has not filled, and then bake.

CORE BEADS

Polymer clay is a relatively light material, so large beads are often more comfortable to wear than those made of glass or metal. To lighten polymer clay beads further, you can form a lightweight core and wrap this in clay. Aluminum foil or Sculpey UltraLight polymer clay can be used for bead cores. Crumple the foil into a ball and roll it firmly on a work surface to compact. (Alternatively, make a core of lightweight polymer clay and bake.) Cover with a sheet of polymer clay, smoothing the joins. Pierce right through the foil. Before baking beads with cores, you can texture the bead surface or stamp the surface with rubber stamps. The hard core inside will prevent the bead from distorting.

SCULPTED BEADS

Small sculpted models can be pierced in a suitable place to make feature beads.

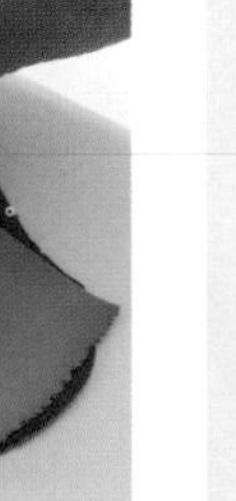

STEP 2

Using a tissue blade, cut the sheet into tall triangles.

PINWHEEL BEADS

Make a two-color sheet as before and cut out squares about 1in (25mm) across with a square cutter. Make cuts on the diagonal as shown, leaving an uncut area in the center of each square about 1/4in (6mm) across. Make the pinwheels by folding a corner of each cut section into the center and press down to secure. Pierce through one of the folds or tips.

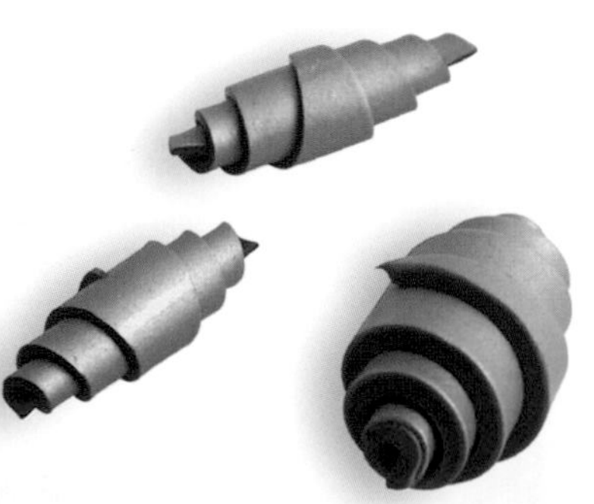

Use jump rings to attach pinwheel beads to earring findings.

15 CABOCHONS

Cabochons are easy to make from polymer clay and can be used in many different ways in jewelry. Once baked, you can mount cabochons in polymer clay bezels to make earrings, pins, and pendants. Cabochons are very effective when made with faux semiprecious stone mixtures or marbled clay. Proprietary molds are also available for cabochons, or you can make your own.

Mounted cabochon made from marbled clay.

Try these...

It is easiest to mount cabochons in polymer clay mounts after they have been baked. Smear a little PVA glue around the cabochon as a key to attach the fresh clay. Apply pearlescent or metallic powder for a faux metal effect.

Mount with hanging loop Press an extruded strip around the cabochon and add a pierced tag of clay for a hanging loop.

Rope mounts Form a long thin log of clay, fold in half, and twist to make a rope mount.

SCULPTING A CABOCHON

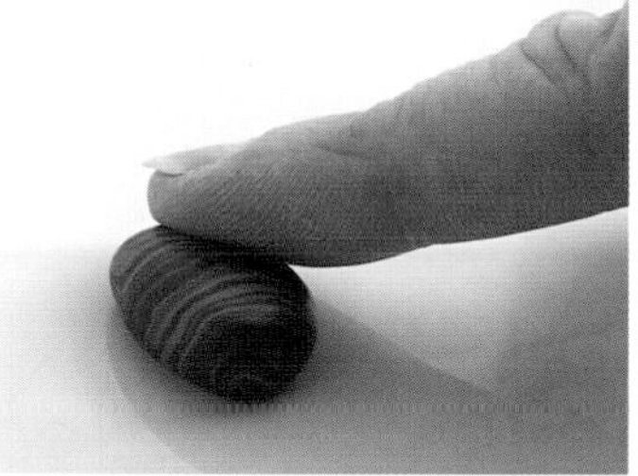

STEP 1
Form a ball of clay of the desired size and press it down onto a tile with the pad of your finger. For an oval cabochon, shape the ball into an oval. Keep pressing and smoothing until you get a semicircular cross-section.

STEP 2
Taking care to retain the rounded shape, stroke over the surface of the clay lightly with a fingertip to remove fingerprints and make the clay shine. Bake on the tile. When cool, remove from the tile and sand and buff the piece to give a realistic effect.

USING A CORE

STEP 1
You can make a cabochon by covering a scrap clay core with slices of faux stone clay or a marbled sheet. This is a more economic use of faux stone mixtures. First, make a core cabochon with scrap clay. Bake and then cover with a thin slice of the patterned clay.

STEP 2
Smooth with a finger and then bake on the tile. When cool, sand and buff in the usual way.

Cabochons made from faux semiprecious stone mixtures of clay.

16 BUTTONS

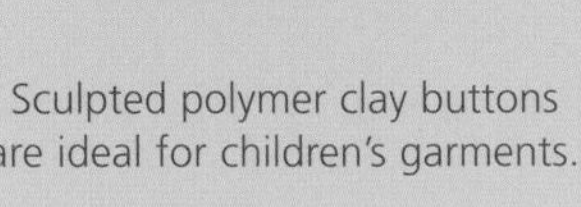

Sculpted polymer clay buttons are ideal for children's garments.

Polymer clay can be used to make fabulous buttons. The materials and tools required vary, depending on the type of buttons you are making. Choose one of the stronger clays and bake thoroughly for strength. Polymer clay buttons can be washed in a washing machine on a cool wash. If you have added powders, paint, or varnish, it is safest to hand-wash. Do not put polymer clay buttons in a tumble drier.

A simple button made from a slice of spiral millefiori cane.

A molded button with the design highlighted with gold powder.

SIMPLE BUTTONS

Quick and easy to make, these buttons can be created in any color to match an outfit.

STEP 1

Make a series of disks of equal size on a tile (see page 39). Press the center of each disk with the end of a ballpoint pen or similar tool. This provides an indented area for the holes in the button, so that the thread that stitches the button to the fabric will be protected from wear.

STEP 2

Pierce the indented area of each button with either two or four evenly spaced holes; push down with a blunt tapestry needle into the clay until it meets the tile and rotate it a little to open the hole. Bake the buttons on the tile.

CUTOUT BUTTONS

These are very easy to make and you can use marbled or textured clay for interesting effects. Roll out a sheet of clay about $\frac{1}{12}$in (2mm) thick. Lay this on a tile and use a cutter to cut out shapes. Indent and pierce as usual. This heart-shaped button has been cut out of foiled clay (see page 94).

BRAIDED BUTTONS

Extrude a length of marbled clay from a clay gun. Fold in half and twist into a rope. Coil into a spiral and indent and pierce in the usual way.

MOLDED BUTTONS

Use a proprietary mold or make your own from an antique button (see pages 56–57). If you want to add a shank rather than pierce the button, do so after the button has been baked and cooled in order to avoid distortion.

MAKING A MOLDED BUTTON

Form a log of clay and cut equal lengths that will make a button by filling the mold until the clay is a little raised above the top. You may need to use trial and error to find the right size for your chosen mold. Form a length into a ball, or roughly to the shape of an irregular shaped mold. Brush the mold lightly with talcum powder and press the clay into the mold. Ease it out carefully and lay it on a tile to bake. Here, a metal button has been used to make a mold. The raised design on the polymer clay button made from the mold has been highlighted by brushing a finger dipped in pink pearlescent powder over it before baking.

ADDING A SHANK

Adding a wire shank held on with a little clay circle makes a strong attachment point for sewing on the button. Form a simple loop in 18-gauge—1/16in (1.5mm) thick—wire and bend the ends at right angles to the loop. Roll out a 1/16in (1.5mm) thick sheet of clay and cut out a small circle with a cutter (or cut out a small square by hand). Make a slit in the center of the circle. Push the loop through the slit. Paint a little PVA glue or liquid clay onto the back of the button and press the shank on so that the clay circle covers the ends of the wire and the loop protrudes. Bake.

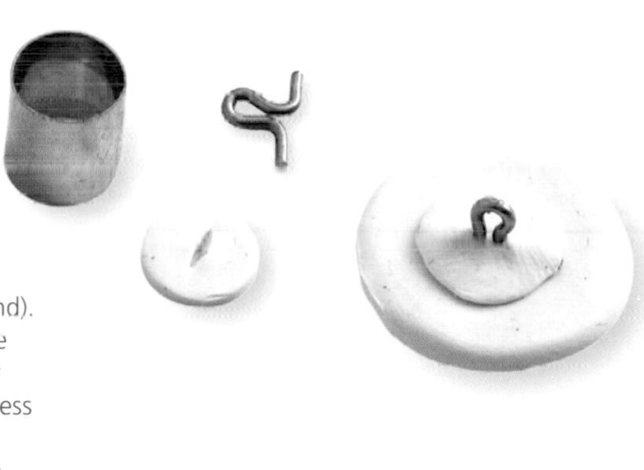

SCULPTED BUTTONS

Small sculptures, such as these frogs and owls, make delightful novelty buttons. Add the shanks after baking. The frogs have a loop of polymer clay for a shank instead of wire.

Try these...

Millefiori cane buttons Buttons made from cane slices give added sparkle to garments. Simply slice the cane evenly, about 1/12in (2mm) thick. Lay on a tile and indent with a simple round tool, such as a blunt paintbrush handle. Pierce and bake on the tile.

Faux stone buttons Cut buttons from a faux stone mixture of clay, such as agate or turquoise. Indent and pierce before baking on the tile.

17

APPLIQUÉ

This technique is rather like embroidering with polymer clay and the results are delicate and pretty. The secret is to use a knife with a curved blade like the one used here. The curve allows you to cut and place small slices of clay; any other shape of blade makes it nearly impossible to do. Use a firm variety of polymer clay or leach the clay (see page 20). When cool, you can add a mount if desired (see page 43).

Embellish the flower with more appliqué in different colors if you wish, then mount in white clay brushed with pearl powder to make a pendant.

MATERIALS AND TOOLS

- Polymer clay: ½in (13mm) ball of translucent white; small quantities of leaf green, light blue, golden yellow
- Ceramic tile
- Knife with a curved blade
- Blunt needle

FORGET-ME-NOT

There are endless ways that you can adapt this technique to build up cameos of flowers, birds, and animals.

STEP 1

Base Form a ½in (13mm) ball of translucent white and press it down onto a tile to make a cabochon (see page 43). Stroke over the surface of the clay to remove any fingerprints.

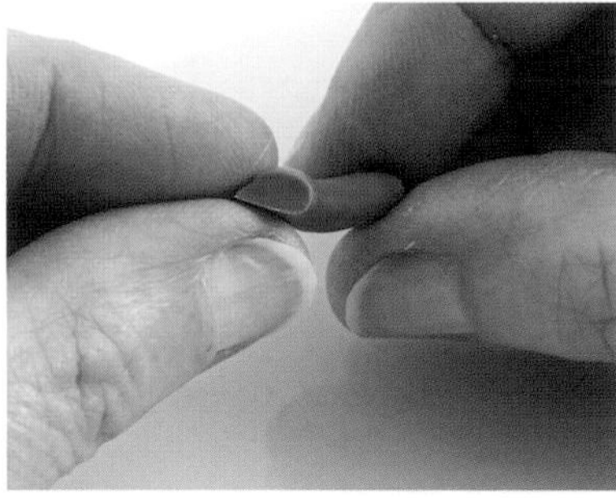

STEP 2

Leaves Form a 3/16in (5mm) log of leaf green clay and pinch it into a leaf-shaped cross-section, pointed at one side.

STEP 3

Lay the log on the work surface and cut off the end. Use the point of the blade to cut a thin slice and scoop this up onto the blade. The natural stickiness of the clay will make the slice adhere. It should be just at the point of the blade so that you can see where to place it in the next step.

STEP 4
Turn the blade over so that the slice is underneath and use the knife to press the slice onto the porcelain clay surface.

STEP 5
Cut another slice and repeat, working around in a curve to apply leaves around the base of the piece. Mark veins on the leaves with the knife.

STEP 6
Flower Now form an 1/8in (3mm) thick log of light blue clay and press it lightly onto the work surface. Do not shape the log; its natural oval cross-section will be the right shape for petals. Cut slices from this and press them over the leaves in a flower shape. You will need to turn the tile as you work around the flower, positioning each petal by placing the point of the knife at the center of the flower.

STEP 7
Make a tiny golden yellow log, about 1/12in (2mm) thick, and cut a tiny slice. Apply it to the center of the flower. Pierce the center with a blunt needle and add more flowers if required. Press over the design lightly with the pad of your finger to ensure that everything is attached well. Bake the piece on the tile.

Try these...

Daisies and butterfly Use a strip blend in white and pink (see page 27) for the petal log. Make the ferny leaves by applying thin slices from a flattened log of leaf green. Use small slices of light blue log for the butterfly wings and a thin strip of black clay for the body.

Wisteria and dragonfly Apply fern-like leaves using thin strips cut from a flattened log of leaf green clay. Apply two long thin threads of clay for the flower stalks. Make a lilac and white blend and form 1/16in (1.5mm) thick logs from the various colors of the blend. Apply darker slices to the top of the flower and lighter slices as you work down the stalk. Make the dragonfly like the butterfly above, with slices from a flattened yellow log for the thinner wings.

Fish and reeds Roll a log of leaf green very thinly and cut thin threads from this to trail over the background for the water weeds. Cut slices from a round log of orange and yellow blend for the fish scales. Apply longer thin slices in a fan shape for the fins and tail.

Japanese crane Use thin slices cut from flattened logs of white, light blue, and black clays for the feathers of the wings and tail. Start with the light blue at the bottom of the wings and work upward, overlapping the slices for the feathers.

Experiment by texturing sheets of clay using a variety of different fabrics to produce different effects.

18 TEXTILE EFFECTS

Polymer clay is excellent at simulating other materials, and textile effects in polymer clay illustrate this to perfection. Thin sheets of clay are textured with real fabric and then gathered, draped, and folded to make simulated fabrics of all kinds to use for jewelry, sculpture, and animation purposes. Bake with support if necessary so that the drapes and folds do not sag.

MATERIALS AND TOOLS

- Polymer clay: ½ block rolled into a 1/16in (1.5mm) thick sheet
- Piece of fabric, wetted and mopped dry in a towel
- Pasta machine or roller and baking parchment

A polymer clay doll with dress, lace petticoat, and ribbon bow all made in polymer clay.

ARTIST'S TIPS

- Use a strong polymer clay for simulating fabric.
- Roll the clay as thinly as you can—1/32in (1mm) thick or less is ideal. This will make the edges of the simulated fabric realistically thin and it will drape beautifully.
- Sticky clay will cause problems, so leach the clay first if necessary (see page 20).

TEXTURING THE CLAY

Choose fabric that has a definite weave and does not have a fluffy or brushed surface that may stick to the clay. Jacquard fabric, woven fabric, cotton, and linen all work well. Avoid anything with a very coarse weave unless you require that for a particular effect—it can look too coarse.

STEP 1

Using a pasta machine Roll out the clay at the thinnest setting possible without it cockling (see page 23). Lay the damp fabric onto the clay sheet.

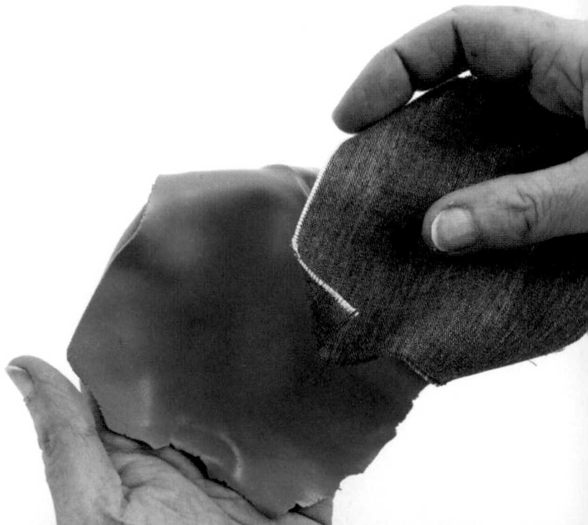

STEP 2
Pass the fabric and clay sheet together through the machine, still on the same setting.

STEP 3
Carefully peel the fabric off the clay to reveal a thin sheet of simulated fabric that you can cut to shape and use as required.

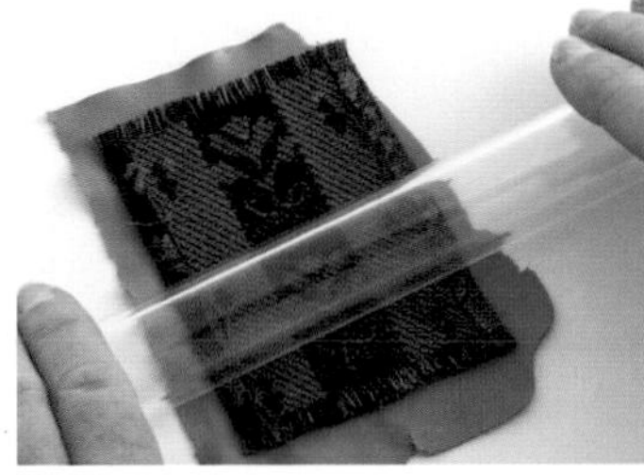

STEP 4
Rolling by hand Roll out the clay sheet as thinly as possible. Lay the clay sheet on the baking parchment and cover with the damp fabric. Roll firmly to impress the fabric texture into the clay sheet and to thin the clay at the same time.

STEP 5
Carefully peel off the fabric and paper.

PATTERNED FABRIC
Marble the clay before rolling out the sheet by machine or hand—lovely swirled and abstract patterns will result.

Try these...

Lace Use a strip of lace with a scalloped edge to impress the clay sheet. Cut out the polymer clay lace and gather it into folds.

Large-scale prints Cut slices from millefiori canes and apply them to a sheet of clay. Roll flat and texture with fabric.

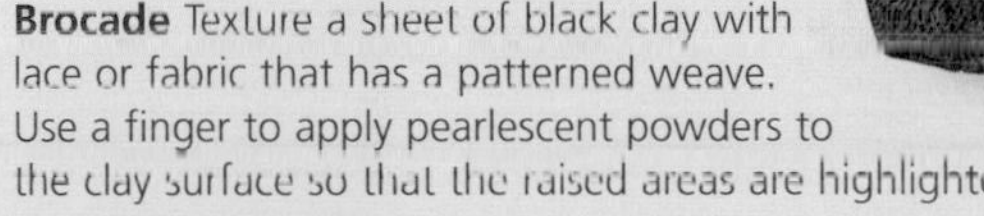

Brocade Texture a sheet of black clay with lace or fabric that has a patterned weave. Use a finger to apply pearlescent powders to the clay surface so that the raised areas are highlighted.

Ribbons Cut thin strips from a rolled out sheet of pearlescent clay. You can now loop the strip into all kinds of bows. The ends can be trailed and twirled as required and then the finished piece baked. Use bows to embellish gifts, greeting cards, polymer clay dolls, and other sculptures.

19 CORDS

When polymer clay is extruded into long strands, the resulting cords can be used in a variety of ways. Marie Segal developed this technique using a mixture of flexible and normal polymer clay for a result that is strong enough to knit.

Polymer clay cords are perfect for pendant necklaces.

MATERIALS AND TOOLS

- Polymer clay: 3 parts flexible clay + 1 part normal strong clay
- Extruder or clay gun
- Large baking sheet covered with paper or baking parchment

MAKING CORDS

Use a flexible clay, such as Sculpey Bake and Bend (Superflex), for this technique. The flexible clay should be mixed with a normal strong polymer clay, preferably of the same brand, to strengthen the strands. A mix of about 3–4 parts flexible clay to 1 part normal clay gives a result that is remarkably strong and flexible after baking. Do not make cords thinner than 1⁄16in (1.5mm) or they will be too fragile.

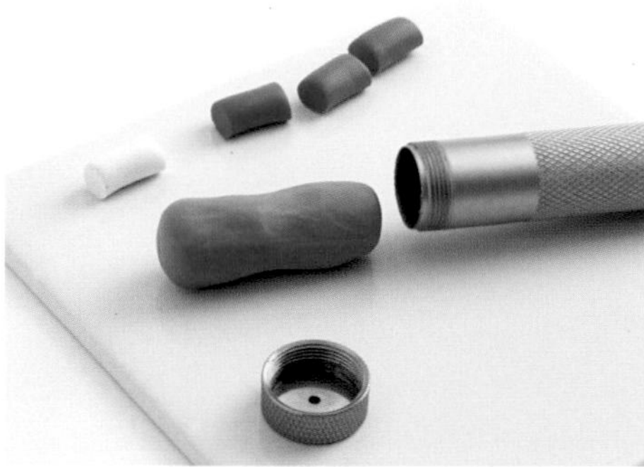

STEP 1

Thoroughly mix together the two types of clay. Place in an extruder and fit a die with a 1⁄16in (1.5mm) wide circular hole.

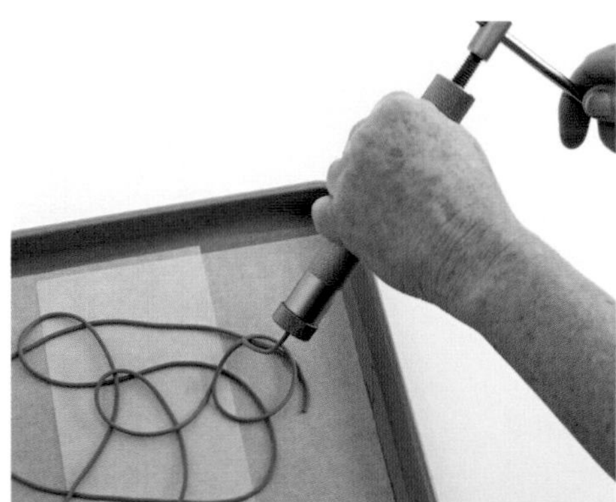

STEP 2

Extrude the clay in a long thin line, allowing it to drop onto some paper on a baking sheet. It does not matter if the strands overlap; they can be pulled apart before baking.

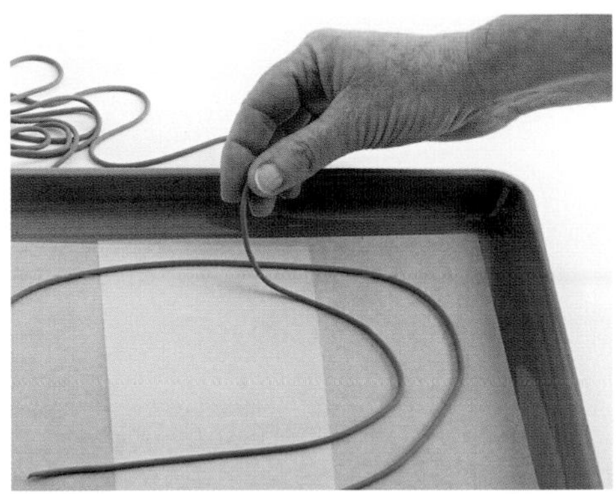

STEP 3
Arrange the cords of clay in long lines with gentle curves. You can pull them slightly when arranging them to smooth out any kinks. Bake as usual, taking care not to underbake or the cords will be fragile.

USING CORDS

The baked cords are virtually unbreakable and can be knotted, braided, crocheted, knitted, or used on their own.

COLORED CORDS FOR PENDANTS
You can make cords in colors to coordinate with your polymer clay jewelry. Add spring ends and a hook for a stylish pendant cord.

Try these...

Braided cord Braid cords before baking for the tightest result. You can also braid after baking for a more open effect.

Striped cord Press three different colored logs together and place in the extruder barrel. When you extrude the clay, the cord will emerge with the three colors in longitudinal stripes. Twist the cord along its length.

Twisted rope Extrude two or three cords using a thin die. Twist the cords together while still soft to produce a two-ply or three-ply rope and then bake.

Twisted multicolor rope Twist together two or three different colors for a multicolored twisted rope.

CROCHET AND KNITTING
This is an example of crochet using polymer clay cord. See page 154 for Marie Segal's fabulous knitted jacket. See pages 52–53 for more information on basketry and weaving.

20 BASKETS AND WEAVING

Baked flexible cords of polymer clay (see pages 50–51) can be woven into baskets using traditional basketry techniques, or the baskets can be made using soft extrusions or long logs of clay twisted together and shaped over a former. The baskets are strong and slightly flexible, provided they are made with a strong brand of clay and well baked.

Woven cords of polymer clay make an unusual hanging pendant.

Basketry techniques can be used to make normal-sized and miniature baskets.

MATERIALS AND TOOLS

- Polymer clay: total of about 1 block in 2–3 toning colors
- 3in (75mm) diameter drinking glass or glass jar
- Craft knife

SIMPLE ROUND BASKET

Choose a former that has a smooth profile with no overhangs, so that the finished basket will be easy to remove. Rolling the logs by hand gives interesting marbled streaks, but you can use a clay extruder if you prefer.

STEP 1

Marble the clay and roll some of it into a long thin log, ⅛in (3mm) thick and 12in (30cm) long. Cut the log in half and twist the two lengths together to form an even rope. The easiest way to do this is to press one end down on the surface to attach it and twist the other end, adjusting the twist until it is even all down the length.

STEP 2

Press the end of the rope onto the center of an upturned glass base. Keeping the rope twisted, coil it into a spiral, pressing each coil against the previous one to secure them together.

STEP 3

At the end of the rope, trim it at an angle and press on the end of a new rope to continue the coiling.

STEP 4
When you reach the edge of the glass base, start coiling up the sides of the glass in the same way. Keep pressing the coils together to consolidate them so that the basket will be strong after baking.

STEP 6
When you reach a sufficient height for the basket, add a final coil in a contrasting color. View the basket from the sides and check that the sides are an even height, adjusting if necessary.

STEP 5
When applying clay up the sides of the former, trim the rope each time you complete one coil and start another row. This will help keep the basket sides an even height.

STEP 7
Bake the basket on the glass. When cool, gently ease the blade of the knife between the baked clay and the glass to separate them. Push the basket off the glass.

WEAVING
Textile and fiber techniques are easily adapted to polymer clay, and weaving is no exception. As with basketry, you can weave with pre-baked cords or strips, but weaving with these in the soft state gives a softer and more cohesive result. Here, strips of marbled polymer clay have been woven into a fabric while soft.

Try these...

Openwork basket Make an openwork area in a basket by pressing on a coil in a loose scallop. Make several more regular coils above it to strengthen the rim.

Lidded basket Coil a flat lid on a tile, making it the same diameter as the basket. Make a single coil large enough to fit just inside the basket. After baking, glue this to the inside of the lid.

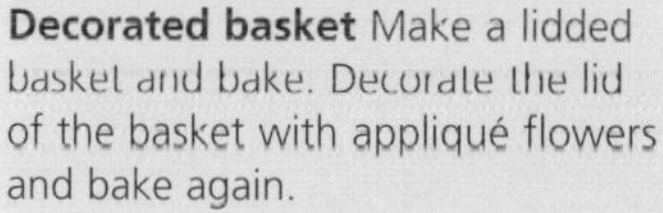

Decorated basket Make a lidded basket and bake. Decorate the lid of the basket with appliqué flowers and bake again.

Miniature picnic basket Miniature baskets are made in exactly the same way as larger baskets, but you will need to extrude or roll much thinner logs for the twisted ropes. The larger hamper was made using a foil-covered matchbox as a former.

21 MOLDING

Use pearl-colored clay and a fairy mold to make a pendant. Decorate it with pastel and pearl powders to make a sparkly necklace that any little girl would love.

The easiest way to mold polymer clay is to use a one-part push mold to make pieces that have a flat back and are ideal for jewelry or fridge magnets. These molds are produced commercially for various craft applications, such as sugarcraft and plaster casting, besides those produced specifically for polymer clay. You can also make your own molds (see pages 56–57).

MATERIALS AND TOOLS

- Polymer clay
- Rigid mold made of resin, wood, or plastic
- Talcum powder or cornstarch
- Large soft artist's paintbrush
- Craft knife
- Blunt needle

Decorate the lid of a gift box with molded multicolored pieces.

RIGID MOLDS

The technique for molding polymer clay varies slightly, depending on whether the mold is flexible or rigid.

STEP 1

Use a paintbrush to dust the mold cavity with talcum powder or cornstarch, then knock out any excess. Alternatively, lightly spray the mold with water.

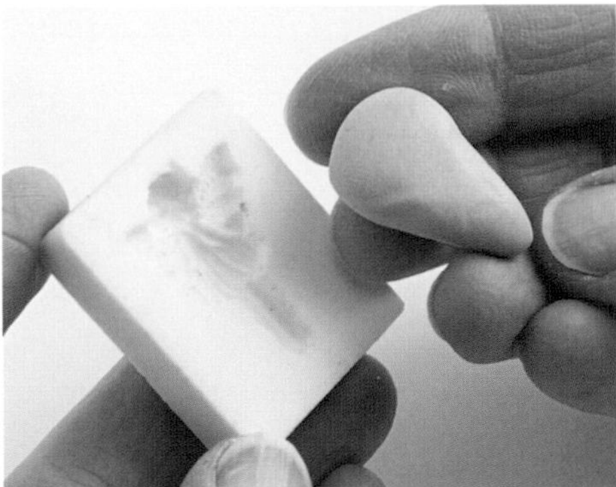

STEP 2

Form a smooth ball of clay, a little larger than the size of the cavity, and shape it roughly to fit.

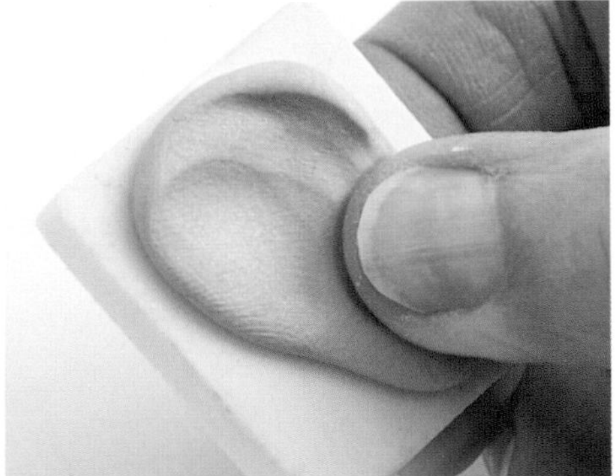

STEP 3

Press the clay firmly into the mold cavity, pushing it into the center of the cavity and then working the clay toward the edges. Be careful not to let it lift out at all or you will get a blurred impression.

STEP 4
When the clay has been firmly pressed into all areas of the mold, push the clay back from the edges a little all around. Use the excess clay to pull the molded piece gently out of the mold.

STEP 5
Lay the molded piece on a tile and cut away any excess clay.

STEP 6
For a pendant, leave a tag of clay at the top of the piece and pierce the tag to make a hanging point. Bake as usual.

FLEXIBLE MOLDS

There are some wonderful molds available from polymer clay manufacturers—Sculpey E-Z molds are some of the easiest to use because they are made from a very flexible material and the soft clay can be pushed out from the back. Silicone molds made for molding cake icing are also ideal for polymer clay, but are not quite as flexible. The basic technique is similar to using rigid molds. Flexible rubber molds do not normally need any talc to prevent sticking, unless the weather is very hot or the clay very soft.

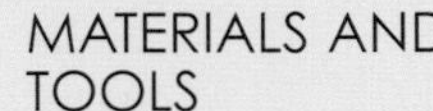

MATERIALS AND TOOLS

- Polymer clay
- Flexible mold
- Craft knife with a blunt blade

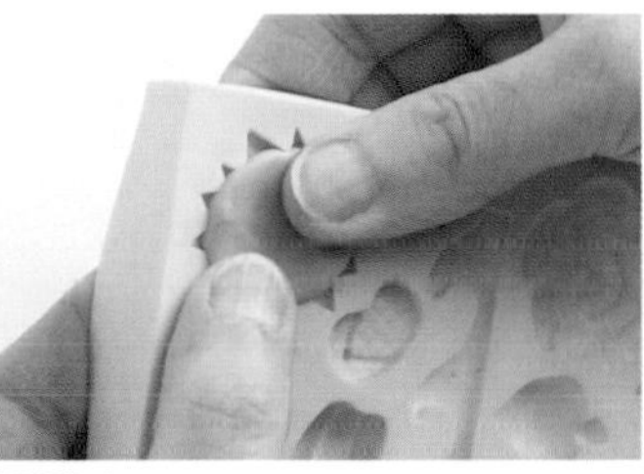

STEP 1
Using one color Fill the rubber mold cavity in the same way as for rigid molds, but only use sufficient clay to fill the cavity.

STEP 2
Trim away the excess clay until it is level with the top of the mold.

STEP 3
Place the mold in the refrigerator or freezer for about 10 minutes to cool and harden the clay. To unmold, ease the clay away from the sides of the mold cavity and push the clay out of the mold by pressing on the back of the mold. Trim if necessary and bake as usual.

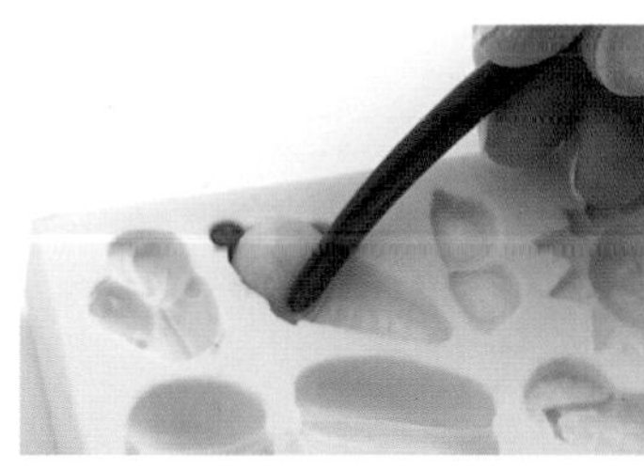

STEP 4
Using multicolors Different parts of the cavity can be filled with different colors. Treat each part of the cavity separately, filling one end with a small quantiy of clay and leveling it with the top of the cavity. Then fill the area next to it, working toward the other end of the cavity.

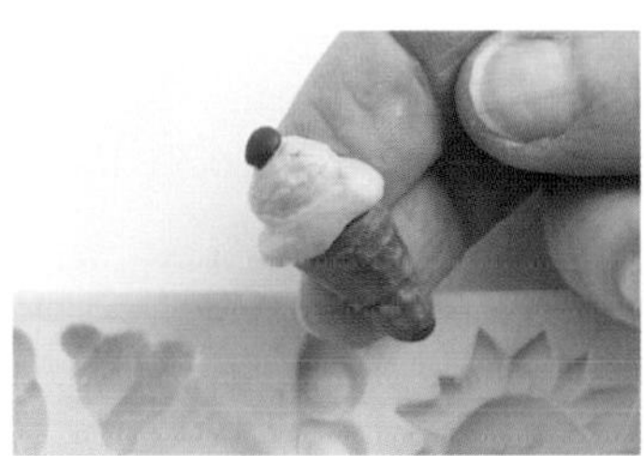

STEP 5
Cool and unmold in the same way as when using a single color of clay, then trim and bake as usual.

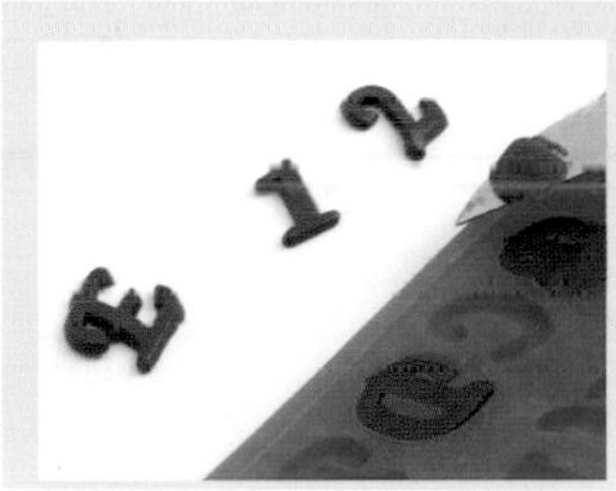

SILICONE MOLDS

These molds, made for icing sugar, are often small and detailed. Fill and trim as for the rubber molds above. When unmolding, flex the mold by bending it backward on both sides to pull out the clay. Bake as usual.

22 MAKING MOLDS

This is a very worthwhile technique to learn because you can make molds from all kinds of existing objects to add individuality and interest to your work. The best mold-making materials for polymer clay are either polymer clay itself or silicone.

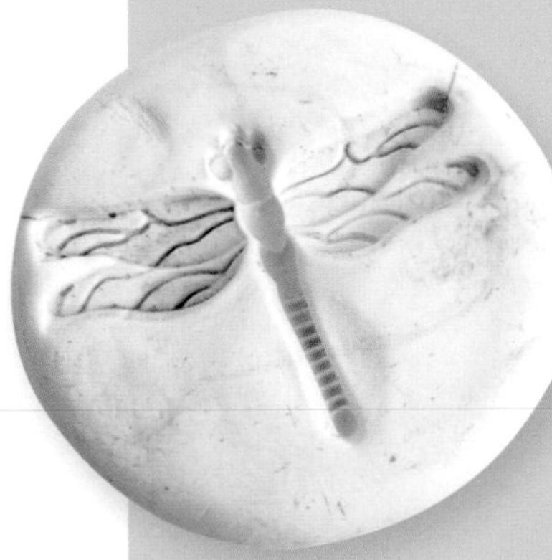

Polymer clay molds can be made from many types of originals, including sculpted models and natural objects such as shells. Decorate the molded pieces in any way you wish, from naturalistic to metallic effects.

CHOOSING ORIGINALS

You can make a simple one-part push mold from many different objects. Here are some suggestions.

- Buttons, modern or antique and made from any hard material, such as plastic, wood, metal, bone, and so on.
- Small items of jewelry, such as pendants and earrings.
- Polymer clay pieces that you have made.
- Natural objects, such as shells, leaves, seeds, and nuts.
- Small toys.
- Relief moldings on frames.
- Cameos and intaglios.

MATERIALS AND TOOLS

- Polymer clay: 1 block in white or a light color
- Original for molding
- Ceramic tile
- Talcum powder or cornstarch
- Pointed needle

ARTIST'S TIPS

- Shallow molds work best.
- Avoid undercuts or the mold will be difficult to use.
- If your original is quite thick, only press it into the molding material about halfway.

POLYMER CLAY MOLDS

Polymer clay is an extremely good mold-making material and the resulting detail can be better than silicone. It is also much less expensive. Use well-conditioned clay that is strong after baking. Some clays produce better surface impressions than others. There are also flexible polymer clays available specifically for mold making.

STEP 1

Use enough clay to make a mold about ⅜in (10mm) deep and large enough to take an impression of the original with a ¼in (6mm) border all around. Shape the clay into a ball and press this down onto a tile to make a disk. Smear the surface of the disk with talc.

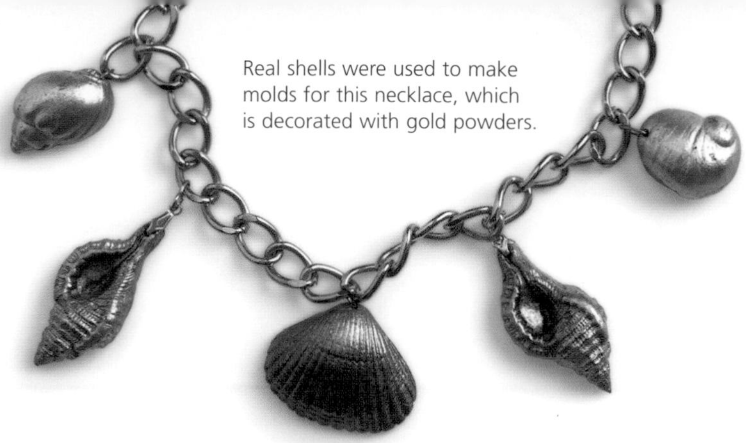

Real shells were used to make molds for this necklace, which is decorated with gold powders.

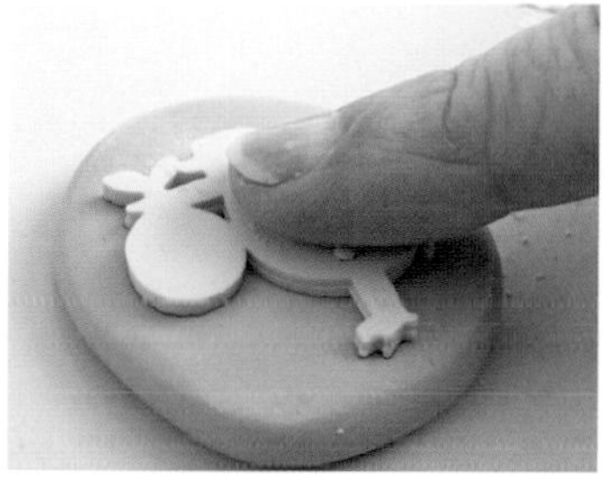

STEP 2

Press the original face down into the clay. If you are using a button, the back of the button should be level with the surface of the clay. If you are using a three-dimensional object, push it in only as far as the widest part of the object.

STEP 3

If the clay pulls away from the object at the sides, push it gently back into place.

STEP 4

Carefully remove the original from the soft clay. The point of a needle slipped under one edge will help ease it out. Take care not to make any unwanted marks in the clay.

STEP 5

Do not attempt to move the mold from the tile or you will distort it. Bake on the tile, making sure you have baked well for the strongest result.

SILICONE MOLDS

There are various types of silicone rubber available for making molds, but these instructions are for using a widely available and easy-to-use putty silicone that comes in two parts. Equal parts are mixed together to make a malleable putty that takes good impressions and cures to a flexible firmness in a short time. Always follow the instructions on the pack. The resulting molds are flexible and can be used to take impressions with a small amount of undercut because the mold can be flexed to remove the molded clay.

MATERIALS AND TOOLS

- Silicone putty mold-making material
- Original for molding

STEP 1

Mix equal quantities of the two different colored putties together until they make a uniform color.

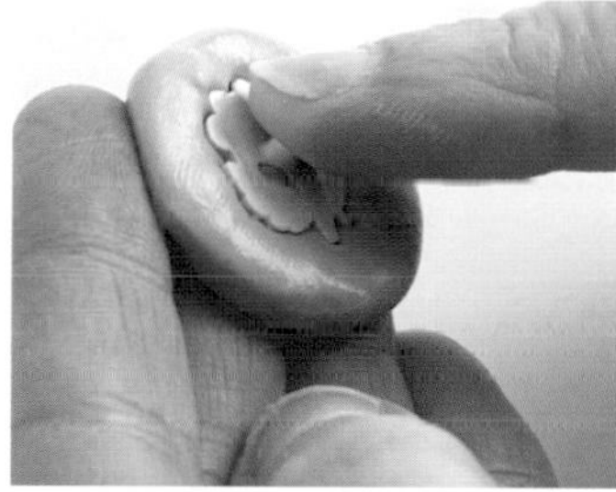

STEP 2

Roll the mixture into a ball and then press the object to be molded face down into the putty until the back is level with the surface. Push the putty toward the original around the edges if it pulls away.

STEP 3

Leave the silicone to set for about 5 minutes (or as recommended on the pack) and then remove it from the original, carefully easing it out. The mold is now ready to use.

23 FLOWERS

A rose decorated with pearlized powder made into a jewelry pin.

Polymer clay shares many of the properties of gum paste; also known as sugarcraft, this is the material used to make sugar flowers for decorating cakes. The secret of making polymer clay flowers is to use a mixture of white and translucent clays as a basic color to give a semi-translucent quality that mimics flower petals. This basic color can be tinted with any colored clay to make a wonderful range of naturalistic flower colors.

Make some tightly furled buds to go with the open harebells and leaf, and wire them together to make a pretty spray.

HAREBELLS

These delicate flowers are not difficult to make, and have many uses. They can be grouped in sprays in a vase, arranged around a cake for everlasting decorations, or even turned into drop earrings or a corsage.

MATERIALS AND TOOLS

- Polymer clay: ⅛ block each of translucent light blue and leaf green; scrap of yellow
- Cone-shaped tool; dip a pencil point in varnish to prevent it from staining the clay
- Craft knife
- Talcum powder
- Ball- or spoon-shaped tool
- Several 6in (15cm) long pieces of green coated wire for stems
- Needle
- Roller
- Real leaf
- Aluminum foil

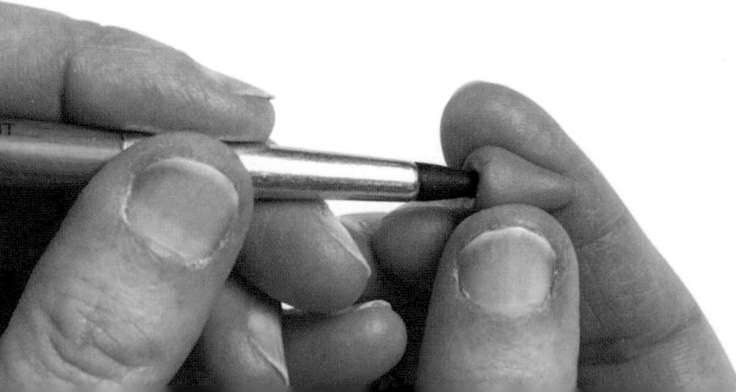

STEP 1

Flowerhead Form a ⅜in (10mm) ball of translucent light blue clay. Shape into a cone and pierce the center with a cone-shaped tool.

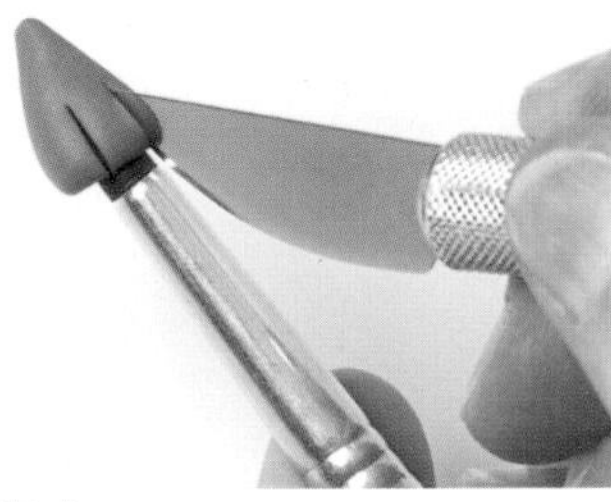

STEP 2

Make five evenly spaced cuts with a knife around the rim of the cone, cutting right through the clay onto the tool.

STEP 3

Remove the tool, pull out each petal, and pinch it into a point.

STEP 4

Lightly dust your fingers and the flower with talc and use a ball- or spoon-shaped tool to press each petal against your finger to thin and cup it. Pinch the petals into a point again and mark the outside with lines to define the petals.

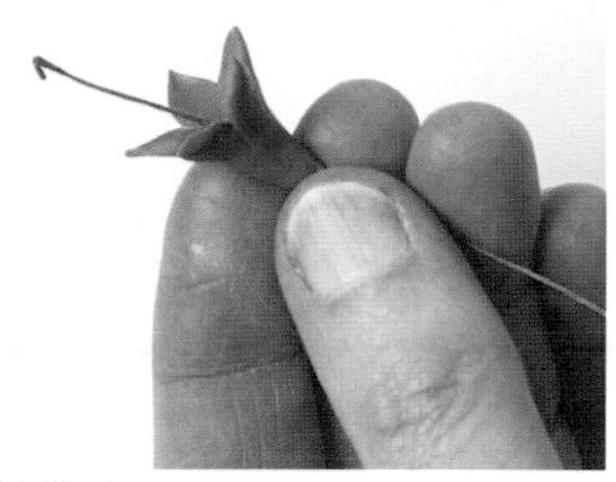

STEP 5
Curl over the end of a piece of wire and thread the other end through the flower, pulling the curled end right into the clay.

STEP 6
Insert a tiny ball of yellow clay into each flower and pierce the center with a needle.

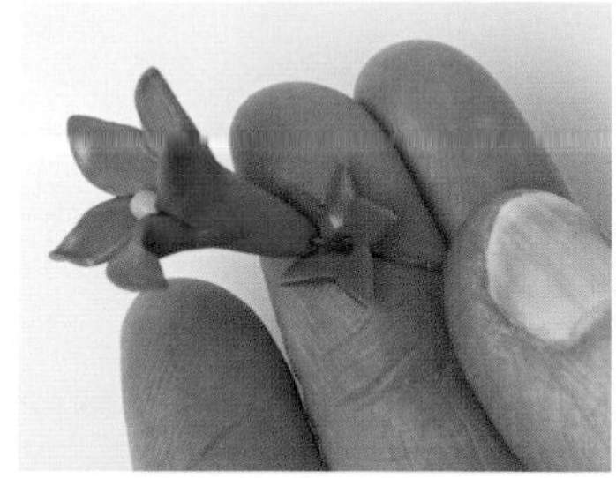

STEP 7
Calyx Cut a star shape from a thin sheet of leaf green clay and thread it onto the wire for a calyx. Press it around the base of the harebell.

STEP 8
Leaf Roll out a sheet of leaf green clay and impress it with the underside of a real leaf. Cut around the leaf shape with the knife, cutting serrations around the edge if appropriate, and pinching the edge to thin it.

STEP 9
Form a small cone of leaf green and press the end of a wire into it. Lay the base of the leaf over this. Use a tool to press along the leaf midrib to secure it. Support the leaf on a piece of foil to maintain a natural shape while baking. Bake the flowers and leaf; when cool, twist the wires together to form a spray.

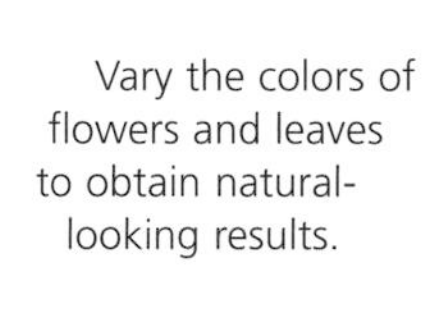

Vary the colors of flowers and leaves to obtain natural-looking results.

ROSES

Eternally popular, roses make wonderful embellishments and jewelry of all kinds.

Add a calyx to each rose or press several roses together on a pair of leaves, using the same techniques as for the harebells.

MATERIALS AND TOOLS

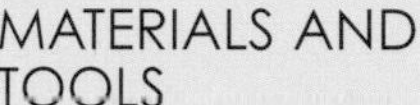

- Polymer clay: ⅛ block translucent light yellow
- Craft knife

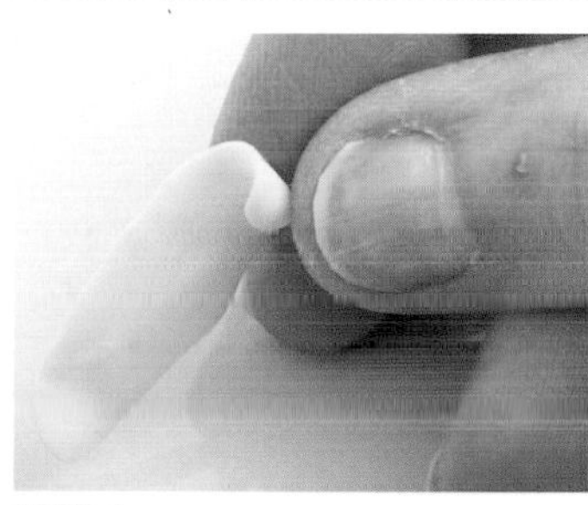

STEP 1
Form a ¼in (6mm) log of yellow and cut ½in (13mm) lengths for the petals. Shape each into an oval, then press with your fingers to flatten into a petal shape. The first petal needs to be thicker at the bottom. Roll this up with the thinner edge upward to form the rose center.

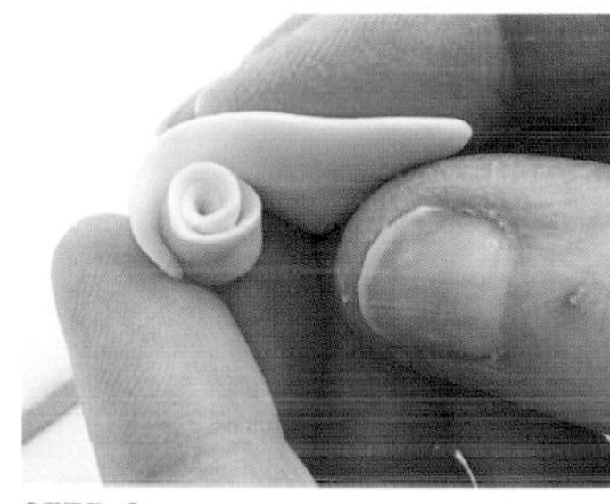

STEP 2
Flatten the other clay ovals into really thin petals about 2in (5cm) wide and 1in (2cm) high. Wrap one around the rose center.

STEP 3
Continue wrapping the petals around the rose, wrapping the top looser each time and pulling the top edge outward.

24 METAL CLAY

Developed during the past 10 years, precious metal clay has opened up an exciting new world for the polymer clay artist. While metal clay is not strictly speaking polymer clay, it uses very similar techniques and combines perfectly with the latter. The most popular is silver clay, of which two different brands are available: Art Clay Silver and Precious Metal Clay. These are made with pure silver powder, mixed with a nontoxic binder. After shaping and modeling, the clays are dried and then fired to produce 99.9% pure silver that can be hallmarked.

Oval-shaped silver clay mount with a polymer clay millefiori cane piece inserted.

Diamond-shaped silver clay mount with a polymer clay appliqué piece inserted.

PURE SILVER PENDANT MOUNT

The following technique shows how to make a pure silver mount for polymer clay designs, such as appliqué or millefiori. The polymer clay design can be safely baked inside the finished silver mount; the oven heat will not affect the silver.

MATERIALS AND TOOLS

- Silver metal clay: about ¼oz (7g)
- Ceramic tile
- Roller and rolling strips
- Shaped cutters: 1¼in (35mm) and ¾in (20mm) diamonds or other shapes of your choice
- Needle
- Tissue blade or craft knife
- Coarse-, medium-, and fine-grit sanding pads
- 1⁄32in (1mm) drill bit
- Blowtorch and fire brick (or gas hob and firing mesh for Art Clay Silver only)
- Stainless steel brush
- Polishing materials

STEP 1

Knead the silver clay lightly and roll out on a ceramic tile to about 1⁄32in (1mm) thick. Cut out a diamond with the large cutter, then remove the waste clay without moving the diamond.

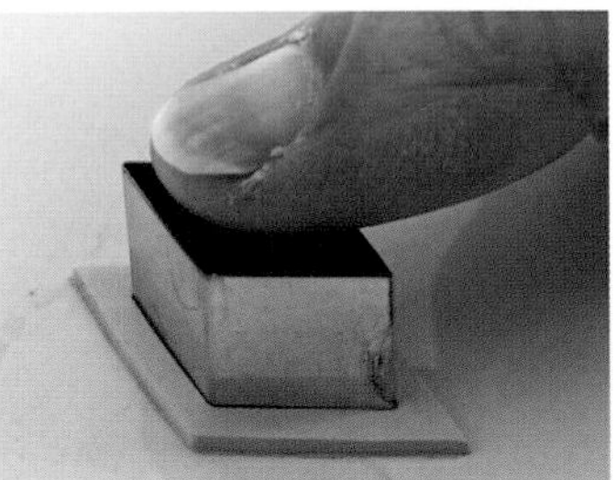

STEP 2

Cut out the center of the diamond with the small cutter to make a frame. Take care to position the small cutter centrally.

STEP 3
Use a needle to make a hole in the top for a pendant attachment. Dry the piece thoroughly by placing it in a domestic oven at 300°F (150°C) for 20 minutes or according to the manufacturer's instructions.

STEP 4
Roll out another sheet of silver clay from the scraps and brush lightly with water. Lay the dried diamond onto the dampened clay and press gently to make it stick. Trim around the diamond with a tissue blade and remove the waste clay.

STEP 5
Add water to a little silver clay and make a paste. Brush this around the edges of the piece, filling any cracks. Dry as before on the tile.

STEP 6
The clay is now in a bone-dry state but is as fragile as dried plaster, so treat it carefully. Sand the edges of the piece and twist the drill bit in the hole to make the hole larger and neatly cut.

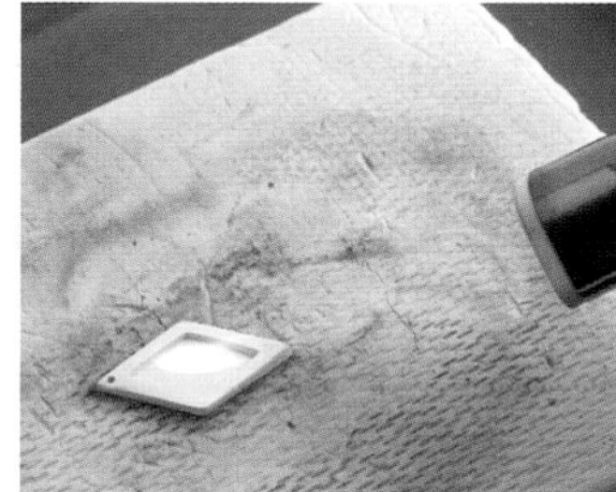

STEP 7
Fire the piece according to the manufacturer's instructions—normally about 1–2 minutes with a blowtorch (or five minutes on a gas hob for Art Clay Silver)—and allow to cool.

STEP 8
Brush the piece with a stainless steel brush to smooth away the frosty layer on the surface. Sand with the sanding pads, working from coarse- to fine-grit, to produce a mirror finish. Polish with silver polish.

ENAMELED SILVER PENDANT
Make a pendant from silver clay and decorate it with polymer clay faux enamel. Roll out a sheet of silver clay and stamp with a small oiled stamp. Cut out a pendant from the stamped sheet using a shaped cutter. Make a hole, then dry and fire the piece. When cool, press colored polymer clay into the depressions made by the stamp. Trim across the surface with a craft knife to remove excess clay. Bake the polymer clay in the silver. Finally, polish the piece.

Try these...

Rectangular mount Use different shaped cutters, such as rectangles or ovals. Instead of drilling a hole for attaching the pendant, add a loop made from a strip of silver clay.

Twisted mount Instead of adding a plain top frame, this oval pendant has a surround made from a twisted strip of silver clay.

25 BOXES

Polymer clay boxes can be so varied that you never need make two alike. Once the basic techniques have been learned, you can vary the box decoration in many different ways. The resulting boxes are sturdy and can be used as jewelry boxes, pill boxes, trinket boxes, gift boxes—the list is endless. Two box-making techniques are covered here.

Star-shaped box formed around a cookie cutter, with half a rolled-up sheet bead used as a knob.

TEMPLATES

Use graph paper to make accurate templates of the sides and base of the box.

- Long side: $2\frac{1}{8}$ x $1\frac{3}{16}$in (55 x 30mm)
- Short side: $1\frac{1}{2}$ x $1\frac{3}{16}$in (38 x 30mm)
- Base: $1\frac{15}{16}$ x $1\frac{1}{2}$in (49 x 38mm)

A simple rectangular box decorated with an image transfer on the lid.

USING BAKED SHEETS OF CLAY

This technique is ideal for making boxes that have straight sides, such as squares, rectangles, and triangles. They look remarkably precise and it is hard to tell that they are made from polymer clay.

MATERIALS AND TOOLS

- Polymer clay: 1 block in the color of your choice
- Pasta machine or roller and rolling strips
- Two ceramic tiles
- Templates, traced and cut out, for sides and base
- Tissue blade
- Paper or baking parchment
- Superglue and needle
- Set square or piece of cardstock

STEP 1

Sides and base Roll out a $\frac{1}{12}$in (2mm) thick sheet of polymer clay and lay on a ceramic tile. Place the template pieces on the clay and use a tissue blade to cut out the box shapes. You will need two long sides, two short sides, and one base. Remove the waste clay from around the pieces. Bake covered with paper or parchment and another tile to keep the pieces flat.

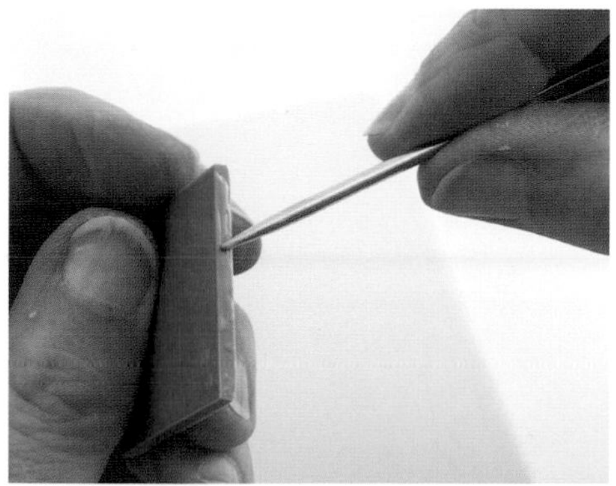

STEP 2
Test that the pieces are a good fit. Slight differences in the thickness of the clay sheet may mean that you will have to trim some pieces so that the box parts fit together exactly. Trim with the tissue blade to ensure a straight cut. Applying glue to the edges, stick the first side to the base.

STEP 3
Glue the next side of the box to the base, using the set square to ensure that the sides are vertical. Repeat for the remaining two sides.

STEP 4
Lid Upend the box onto a clay sheet and cut out around the box for the lid. Allow about 1/16in (1.5mm) extra all around for clay shrinkage when baking. Make a box lid insert in the same way as for a box made using a former (see page 65). Bake the pieces and glue the box lid insert inside the box lid.

Try these...

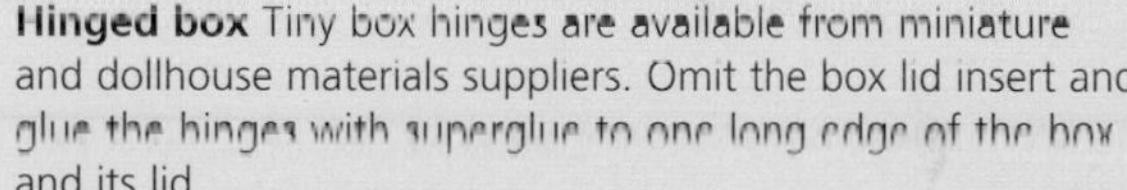

Hinged box Tiny box hinges are available from miniature and dollhouse materials suppliers. Omit the box lid insert and glue the hinges with superglue to one long edge of the box and its lid.

Lined box Make a box out of two sheets of clay pressed lightly together before cutting out. A contrast color looks very effective. The lid is stamped with a dragonfly design and then brushed with metallic powder.

Miniature dollhouse This is made in the same way as a standard rectangular box, but with the sides extended and pointed to accommodate the roof. A small hinge is glued on one side of the front so that the house front opens. More sheets of clay are glued inside to make up the rooms.

Triangular box Use graph paper to make your own templates for different shaped boxes. Remember to allow for the thickness of the box walls when drawing the template. The sides of this box are decorated with pietre dure mosaic.

USING A FORMER

This is the best way to make round or irregular shaped boxes. Avoid using wood or papier mâché formers because these may distort when baked. Always choose a former with straight sides and no lip around the base, so that the box sides can be slid off after baking. As baked polymer clay is flexible, do not make the walls of the box thinner than about 1/16in (1.5mm) or they will flex too much. The following formers are suitable:

- Glass jelly or jam jars with straight sides.
- Ceramic or glass vases with straight sides.
- Short lengths of copper or metal pipe or a test tube for thin boxes.
- Cookie cutters of various shapes.

A sculpted fir tree knob complements the landscape painting on the sides of the box.

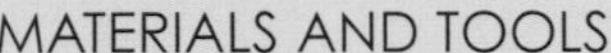

MATERIALS AND TOOLS

- Polymer clay: 1 block in the color of your choice
- Pasta machine or roller and rolling strips
- Ceramic tile
- Tissue blade and craft knife
- Former: 1½in (4cm) diameter round glass jar
- Smoothing tool
- Sandpaper
- Paper, pencil, and scissors
- Superglue and needle

STEP 1

Sides Roll out a 1/12in (2mm) thick sheet of clay and lay on a ceramic tile. Use a tissue blade to cut a strip long enough to go right around the former and about 1¼in (32mm) wide.

STEP 2

Carefully wrap the strip around the jar, keeping the bottom edge level and trimming the ends so that they butt together smoothly.

STEP 3

Smooth the join. Bake the clay on the jar and allow to cool to just warm.

STEP 4

Ease the edge of the clay away from the jar all around on the top and bottom edges and you should then be able to push it gently off the jar. It is easier to do this with the clay still warm, but take care because it is more fragile. Smooth the top and bottom edges if necessary by rubbing the clay cylinder on sandpaper.

STEP 5

Base Roll out more clay to the same thickness and lay the sheet on the tile. Press the box onto the clay sheet and cut around it with a knife for the base. Remove the waste clay. Do not move the clay box; bake it on the tile again to attach the bottom of the box to the sides.

STEP 6

Lid Press the top of the box onto another clay sheet of the original thickness and cut around the inside of the impression to make an insert for the box lid.

STEP 7

Upend the box on some paper and draw around it to get a template for the box lid. Cut out around the outside of the line to allow for the slight shrinkage of the clay during baking. Lay the template on the clay sheet and cut out the box lid. Bake both lid and insert on the tile.

STEP 8

Assembly Sand over the box sides and edges to smooth if necessary. Glue the lid insert to the center of the inside of the lid. The box lid should fit snugly, but you can sand the insert edges before gluing if it is too tight.

Try these...

Silver box Make a round box in black clay and impress the clay with a rubber stamp. Brush with silver powder and then bake. Use a clay teardrop as a knob for the lid, brushed with silver and glued on top.

Cookie cutter box Metal cookie cutters have a slight flex that makes it easy to remove the baked box sides.

Needle case This is formed around a test tube. The lid is a shorter version of the same box. Instead of a lid insert, glue a thin strip of baked clay (bending it to fit) around the inside top of the box.

26 VESSELS

There are several different ways of making vessels from polymer clay. The techniques shown here demonstrate how to make vessels entirely from polymer clay, but you can also make vessels by covering existing forms (see pages 72–73).

Miniature vessels, such as this granite flowerpot, Tudor drinking mug, and china teacup and saucer, are easy to make in polymer clay and extremely realistic.

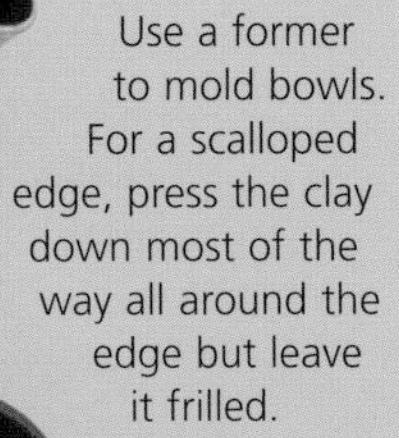

Use a former to mold bowls. For a scalloped edge, press the clay down most of the way all around the edge but leave it frilled.

BALLOON BOTTLES

This technique is fun to do and results in delightful tiny bottles made using an air bubble trapped inside the clay to provide the shape. The little bottles can be used for ornaments or jewelry—they make charming pendants. Use plain clay or a marbled mixture for exotic swirls.

Use a teardrop-shaped ball as a stopper for a balloon bottle, or shape the leftover clay from trimming the top of the bottle into an alternative cork.

MATERIALS AND TOOLS

- Polymer clay: total of about ¼ block in a mixture of colors
- Blunt end of a rolling pin or knife, about ½in (13mm) diameter
- Craft knife
- Needle
- Sandpaper
- Drill bit
- PVA glue for attaching a handle

STEP 1
Marble the clay and then form it into a ball. Push the knife handle into the center of the ball and press the clay up the sides around the handle to form a cup shape.

STEP 2
Twist the knife to remove its handle from the clay. Pinch with your fingers around the inside of the clay cup to thin the sides and make them an even thickness.

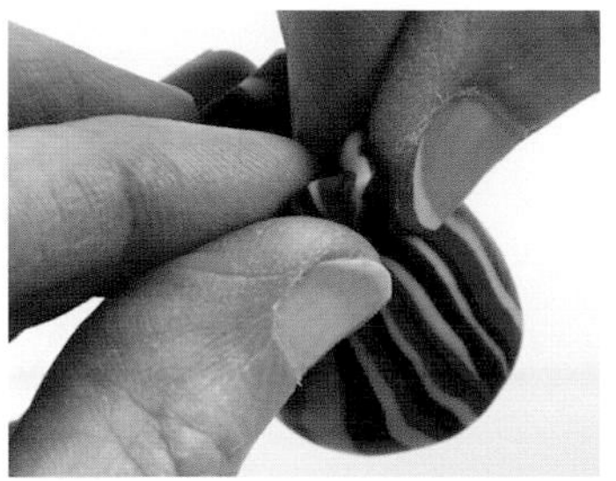

STEP 3
Work around the top of the cup, pushing the clay inward to narrow the neck. Finish by pinching the neck to seal it up and trap the air inside; the excess clay will be trimmed later.

STEP 5
Trim off the excess clay at the top of the bottle shape and make a small indentation in the top for drilling out the hole after baking. Stand upright on a tile and bake. The air bubble will expand slightly inside during baking and puff out the bottle further.

HANDLES
To add a handle to a baked bottle, form a thin strip of clay about 1½ times the height of the bottle. Apply some PVA glue to the rim and press on one end of the strip, with the rest of the strip lying upward. Curve the strip downward and press the other end onto the body of the bottle, again using glue to help the fresh clay stick. Trim the excess and bake.

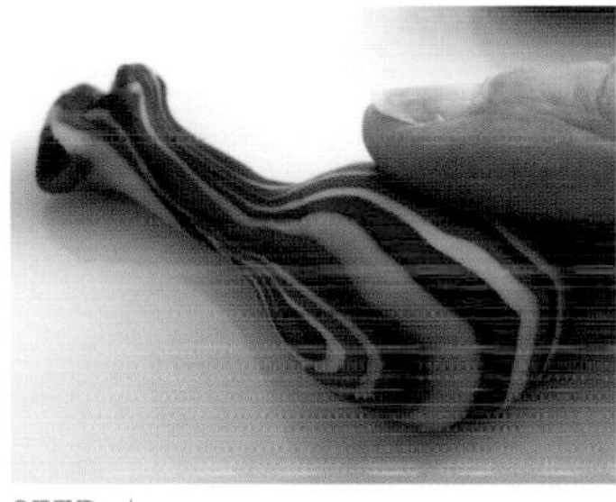

STEP 4
Press the bottle down onto your work surface and start shaping and smoothing it. The trapped air inside will prevent it from collapsing.

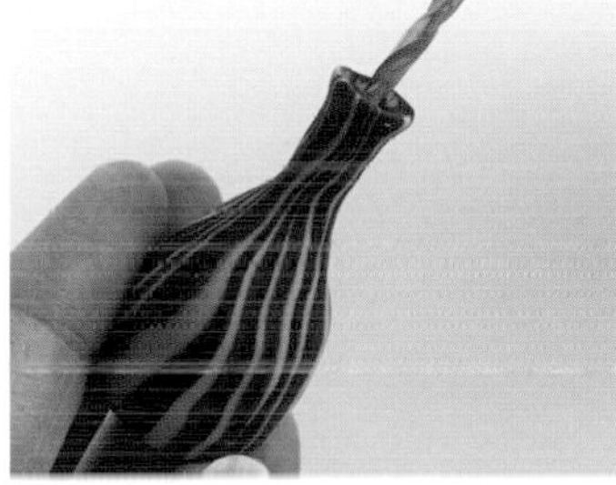

STEP 6
When cool, sand the bottle to smooth any irregularities. Drill out the hole in the neck with a drill bit.

Try these...

Jugs Pull out a small spout in the trimmed top of the bottle before baking. After baking, add a handle on the opposite side.

Variations You can vary the bottles in many ways by adding different styles of corks, applied rims, or a double handle for a flagon.

STEP 7
Make a cork of soft clay by pressing a teardrop shape into the top of the bottle. Remove the cork and bake.

BOWLS

Bowls are quick and easy to make over a suitable former. The best formers to choose are china, metal, or glass bowls with a smooth base and no foot.

A simple round bowl made from marbled clay requires no additional decoration.

MATERIALS AND TOOLS

- Polymer clay: 1 block for a 4in (10cm) diameter bowl
- Pasta machine or roller and rolling strips
- Ceramic tile
- 6in (15cm) diameter round cutter, or template and craft knife
- Former: ceramic or glass bowl
- Tissue blade
- Sandpaper

STEP 1

Roll out an ⅛in (3mm) thick sheet of clay and lay on a ceramic tile. Use the cutter to cut out a circle of clay (or use a template and cut around with a knife).

STEP 2

Place the bowl former in the center of the cutout circle of clay; a glass former is easiest to use because you can see through it. Hold the clay on the former and turn both upside down.

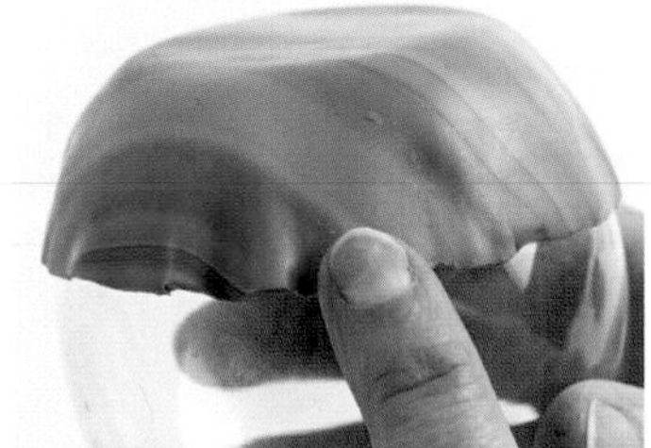

STEP 3

Work your way around the bowl, pushing the clay circle down onto the former. Always work from opposite sides until the frilled areas become smaller and smaller and you can press them down and eliminate them.

STEP 4

Trim around the edge of the clay with a tissue blade to straighten the edge. Remove the waste clay.

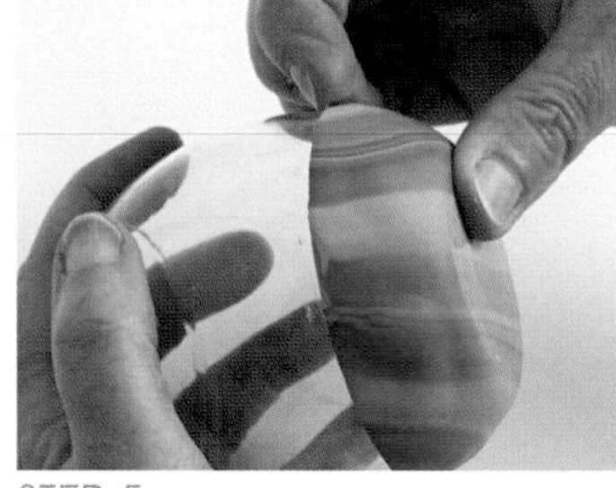

STEP 5

Bake the clay on the former and allow to cool slowly. Ease the clay bowl off its former by working around, slipping a fingernail under the edges of the clay. Sand away any rough areas. You can invert the bowl on a sandpaper sheet to sand the rim straight.

MINIATURE BOWLS

Make the bowls using a large marble as a former. Before baking, press on a disk of clay for a foot.

MINIATURE PLATES

Tiny plates for dollhouses are easy to make using a round cutter. Roll out a thin sheet of clay and cut circles with a ½in (13mm) cutter. Flip over each circle. Use the flat end of a pen or knife dusted with talc to indent the center of each plate. The sides will rise slightly. Bake as usual.

Use miniature bowls and plates as they are, or paint them with tiny designs as decoration.

POTTING

This is a useful technique for making miniature vessels. It takes a little practice but the results are charming. The instructions here are for making small pots about ½in (13mm) diameter and the same height. The pots can be used in many ways for dollhouses or as charms for jewelry.

MATERIALS AND TOOLS

- Polymer clay: use a firm clay in the color required; only small quantities are needed
- Ceramic tile
- Craft knife
- ⅛in (3mm) thick blunt tapestry needle or knitting needle
- 3/16in (5mm) thick blunt tool; the handle of an artist's paintbrush is ideal
- Talcum powder or cornstarch

STEP 1

Roll the clay into a ⅜in (10mm) thick log. Cut several ½in (13mm) lengths from it.

STEP 2

Place one length on its end and pierce with a needle, pushing the needle in about two-thirds of the way. Do not pierce right through.

STEP 3

Lay the log, with the needle still in place, on the edge of a tile. With a slight downward pressure, push the needle from side to side so that the log rotates on the end like a wheel and the hole enlarges.

STEP 4

Dip a paintbrush handle in talc and replace the needle with this. Repeat the rolling and the pot will enlarge further. If the rim of the pot becomes uneven, upend it and press down on the work surface.

STEP 5

Repeat with a thicker paintbrush handle as necessary. Continue rolling until the sides of the pot are thinned and the pot is a pleasing shape. The finished pot can now have a handle applied if required.

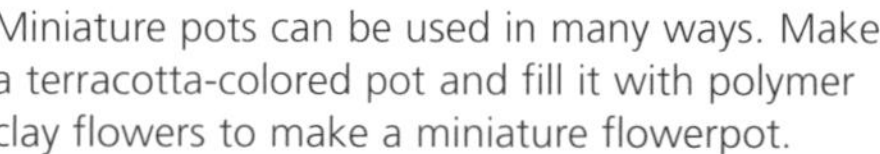

Miniature pots can be used in many ways. Make a terracotta-colored pot and fill it with polymer clay flowers to make a miniature flowerpot.

Try these...

Freeform bowl Cut the clay sheet into a random shape with a tissue blade and apply to the former to create the desired shape. Here, cane slices were rolled into the sheet before applying it to the former.

Two-tone bowl Press together two contrasting colored sheets of clay and roll them out together. Scallop the edge by pressing the side of a needle into the rim all around before baking.

Miniature mugs Make a small pot, about ¼in (6mm) high, and add a handle to make mugs.

27 FRAMES

Easy to make, even for beginners, polymer clay frames add a personal touch to family photographs. Once you have mastered the basic techniques for making frames, you can decorate them in a huge variety of ways, but always remember that the frame should enhance the picture it contains, not be the star of the show. These instructions are for relatively small frames; larger frames are best made by covering a wooden frame with sheets of polymer clay (see pages 72–73).

SIMPLE ROUND FRAME

This is the easiest kind of frame to make using large round cookie cutters. If you do not have cookie cutters in the appropriate sizes, make your own templates from suitably sized round objects, such as a saucer or jar.

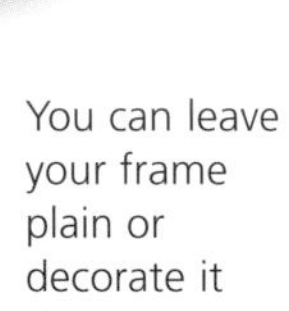

You can leave your frame plain or decorate it if you wish.

MATERIALS AND TOOLS

- Polymer clay: 1 block of clay will make a 3in (7.5cm) diameter round frame
- Pasta machine or roller and rolling strips
- Two ceramic tiles
- Round cookie cutters: 3in (7.5cm) and 1½in (4cm) diameter
- Craft knife
- Wire for the hanging loop
- Pliers and wire cutters
- Sandpaper
- Picture for framing
- Sticky tape and PVA glue

A simple round frame decorated with millefiori flowers and leaves.

Bake strips of stamped polymer clay and then cut and assemble them into frames with mitered corners to make miniature picture frames.

STEP 1

Roll out an 1/8in (3mm) thick sheet of clay and lay on a tile. Use the large cookie cutter to cut out a circle. Remove the waste clay from around the circle (you will leave the frame on the tile without moving it until it is baked).

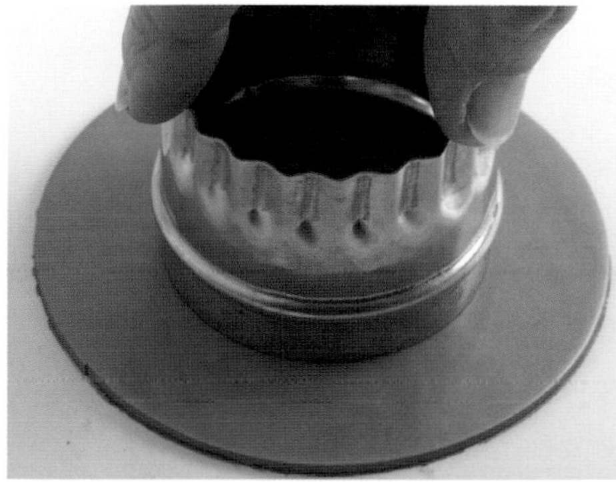

STEP 2
Carefully position the smaller cutter in the center of the circle and cut out the center of the frame, removing the waste clay as before.

STEP 4
Bake the frame pieces on their tiles; when cool, remove from the tiles and sand any rough edges. Cut the picture to size so that it will fit inside the boundaries of the frame and be positioned correctly for the frame front.

STEP 3
Roll out another sheet of clay and lay this on another tile. Cut out a circle using the large cutter for the frame back. To make the hanging loop, cut a length of wire and bend it into a triangular shape. Press this onto the edge of the frame back. Cut a small square from a sheet of clay and press this over the bottom of the triangle to trap it in place.

STEP 5
Tape the picture to the back of the frame front. Apply PVA glue all around the edge of the top surface of the frame back and press the frame front onto it, trapping the picture between the two frame pieces.

Try these...

Metal-effect frame
Frames decorated with stamping and silver or gold powder look like beaten silver or brass.

Octagonal frame Made from clay marbled for a faux wood effect, this frame was cut out around an octagonal tin lid.

Butterfly frame with mat Make a contrasting mat for the frame opening by cutting another layer to place between the frame front and back, about ⅛in (3mm) smaller all around than the frame front. The frame front is decorated with cane slices in the shape of butterfly wings before baking.

28 COVERING FORMS

Smooth a covering of canes over a glass bottle with a roller, as here, or leave them as distinct slices with the glass showing through any spaces.

Polymer clay can be used to cover all kinds of artifacts, provided that the piece is made of materials that can withstand the normal baking temperature of polymer clay. The clay can be applied in many different ways, but rolled-out sheets and cane slices are the methods most frequently used. The covering can be partial, as a decoration, or complete so that the object appears to be made entirely of polymer clay. Do not use very soft clay to cover forms; leach the clay first if necessary (see page 20).

A spoon handle covered with mica shift clay.

The eggshell remains inside the polymer clay covering permanently and the baked clay egg is remarkably strong.

COVERING WITH CANE SLICES

This technique works beautifully for covering eggs, but can also be applied to jars and bottles. Always work from the widest part of the object that is being covered.

MATERIALS AND TOOLS

- Polymer clay flower and leaf canes (equivalent of about 1 block of clay)
- Hen's egg
- Sharp needle
- Bowl
- Tissue blade
- PVA glue may be needed
- Small roller
- Paper or baking parchment
- Fine-grit sanding pad and buffing materials

STEP 1

Puncture a small hole in each end of the egg by tapping firmly with the needle. Stir with the needle inside the egg to break up the yolk. Hold the egg over a bowl and blow hard into the upper hole to expel the contents of the egg. Rinse the egg with water and dry it in the oven at 265°F (130°C) for 30 minutes.

STEP 2

Cut lots of 1⁄32in (1mm) thick slices from the canes. Starting at the widest point of the egg, press the cane slices onto the egg, butting them closely together. The slices should stick to the egg's surface; if they do not, apply a thin coat of PVA glue and allow to dry.

STEP 3
Work your way toward the ends of the egg. Leave part of a hole uncovered at one end or the egg may crack when baking. Use slices from a reduced cane to fill spaces as necessary.

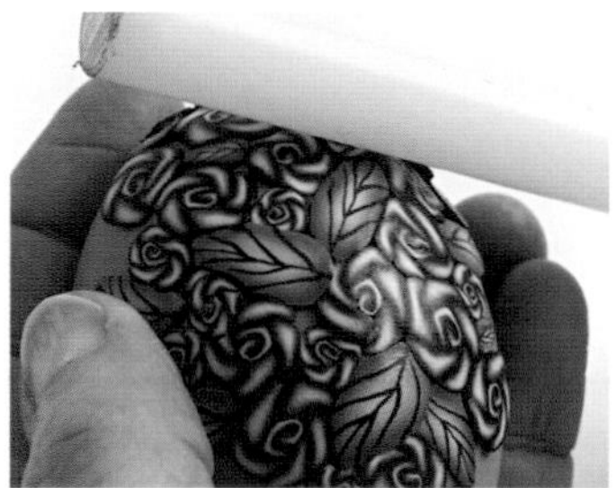

STEP 4
When a large area of egg is covered with slices, roll over the surface with a small roller, smoothing the canes flat and pushing them outward to fill any gaps. Continue until the egg is entirely covered. Bake for 30 minutes; when cool, sand and buff to a shine.

COVERING WITH SHEETS

Covering a form with decorative sheets of clay provides a quick way of transforming an ordinary object, such as this knife handle. Sheets of faux wood and stone make beautiful coverings. Also try using textured or stamped clay, or clay that has transfers or foil effects.

OBJECTS TO COVER

- **Glass and ceramics** Bottles, jars, vases, pots, candlesticks, dishes, bowls, frames, doorknobs, switch plates, door plaques, decorative holiday tree baubles, and other objects made from glass and ceramics all withstand the low baking temperatures without problems. Bake for the usual time but cool slowly to avoid any cracking.
- **Metal** All kinds of metal artifacts work well, including metal tins, vessels, candlesticks, cutlery (cover the handles only), and cruet sets.
- **Eggs** Blown hen's eggs work beautifully when covered with polymer clay and make gorgeous objets d'art. Try using eggs of different sizes, such as quail eggs or even goose eggs, if you can find them.
- **Wooden objects** These can be more difficult to cover than the other materials listed. If the wood is not completely dry, it may warp in the heat of the oven. It is safest to do a trial bake before covering the object.
- **Cardboard and papier mâché** These can warp in the heat so are not recommended.
- **Plastics** Some plastics withstand the baking heat but others will deform or melt, and it is difficult to know which is safe to bake. Only use after careful testing.

MATERIALS AND TOOLS

- Polymer clay: about ¼ block marbled in faux wood effect or similar
- Pasta machine or roller and rolling strips
- Craft knife
- Paper or baking parchment

STEP 1
Roll out a 1/16in (2mm) thick sheet of clay big enough to fit around the handle. Wrap the clay over the handle, pressing the edges of the clay together, then trim to fit.

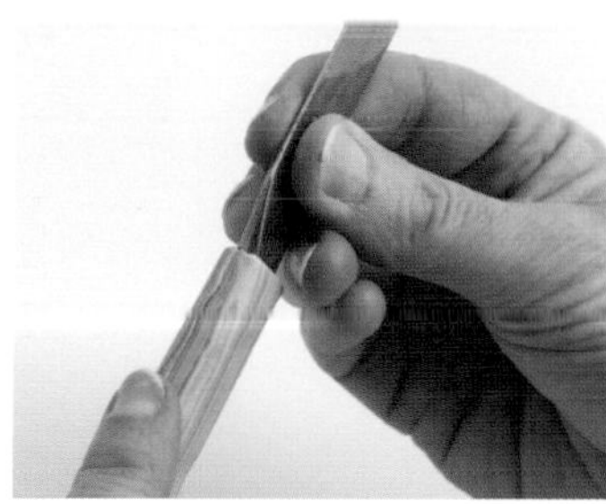

STEP 2
Press your finger along the join to smooth and neaten it.

STEP 3
Roll a small log of clay to fit around the base of the blade, trimming and smoothing it as before. Bake on baking parchment or paper for 30 minutes.

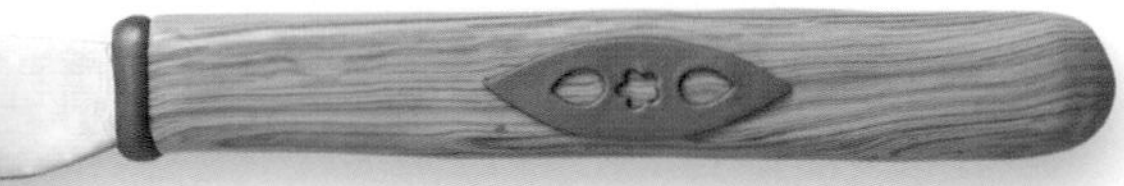

Decorate the handle with a cutout design if desired.

CHAPTER 3:
SURFACE EMBELLISHMENT

The surface of polymer clay can be embellished with a remarkable variety of materials, both before and after baking. Some techniques, such as millefiori and mica shift, use the patterned polymer clay itself as embellishment, while other techniques use an exciting array of art and craft materials that can be brushed, painted, stamped, or rolled onto the clay.

29 MILLEFIORI TECHNIQUES

A bracelet made from bull's-eye canes that have been indented around the outside.

Millefiori is one of the most spectacular uses of polymer clay. The name "millefiori" means "one thousand flowers" in Italian and is a term borrowed from Italian glass makers who make rods of glass with intricate patterns running through their length. Slices from these "canes" are applied to glass beads, paperweights, and other glass artifacts to make glorious colored patterns. Polymer clay canes are created in the same way as a stick of holiday candy, and slices from the soft cane are used to decorate all kinds of jewelry, vessels, and other items.

Try forming the inside log of a bull's-eye cane from a sheet of blended clay.

ARTIST'S TIPS

- Make small canes first. The materials given here are for trial-size canes about 2½in (65mm) long and ½in (13mm) thick. This will give you up to 30 thin slices, or much more if you reduce the cane.
- Contrasting colors work best in all millefiori techniques. The act of reducing a cane will dull the colors, so use colors that are strong and vibrant and provide good contrast.
- Translucent colors can be used to great effect, but need opaque contrasting colors between them for good definition after reduction.
- Use clay that is approximately the same softness for all the colors in a cane. Very soft clay combined with a firmer clay will reduce irregularly.

MAKING A BASIC BULL'S-EYE CANE

This simple cane demonstrates the basics of cane-making, using a round bull's-eye cane as an example. Once you have mastered the basic technique, the following pages have many more cane designs for you to experiment with.

MATERIALS AND TOOLS

- Polymer clay: ½ block each of blue and yellow
- Pasta machine or roller and rolling strips
- Tissue blade

STEP 1

Form the yellow clay into a log, ½in (13mm) thick and about 2½in (65mm) long. Roll the blue clay into a 1/16in (1.5mm) thick sheet that is large enough to wrap around the yellow log. Lay the log on one edge of the sheet and trim the sheet sides with a tissue blade.

STEP 2
Roll up the log in the sheet until the first edge of the sheet meets the sheet again, where it will make a slight mark on the clay surface. Unroll a little and use your blade to cut across the sheet along the mark.

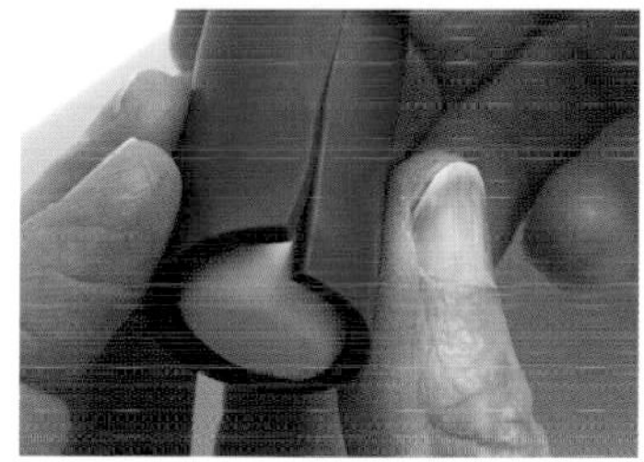

STEP 3
The edges of the sheet should now meet in a butt joint. Smooth the joint with a thumb or finger. You can now reduce the cane (roll it to make it smaller in diameter and much longer) and slice it as necessary, or use it to make more complex canes.

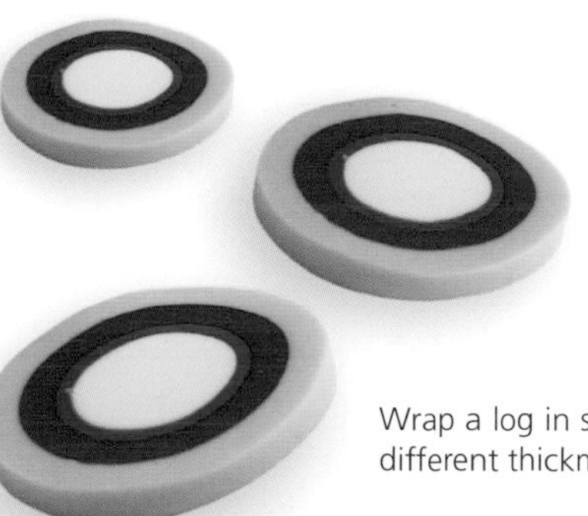

REDUCING THE CANE

The best part of millefiori caning is that you make the cane large, and then reduce it to produce fine and detailed patterns that would be extremely hard to achieve without the reduction process. Reduction also minimizes any irregularities in the cane. There are several techniques for reducing canes, depending on the type of cane.

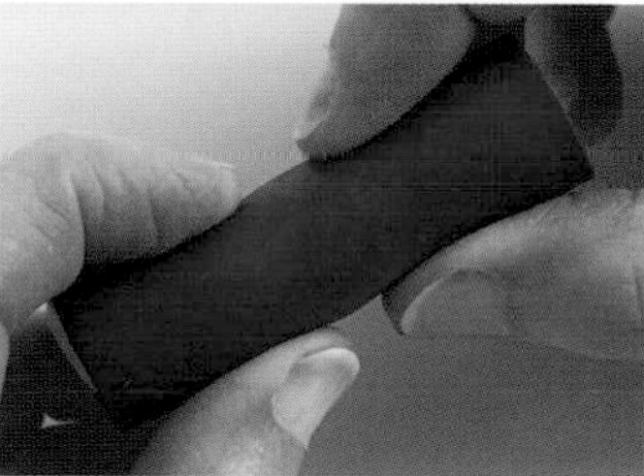

STEP 1
Round cane Squeeze the cane along its length, starting in the center and working outward. Rotate the cane as you work and it will begin to thin and lengthen. If the cane was made some time ago, let the warmth from your hands heat the clay to make it more malleable.

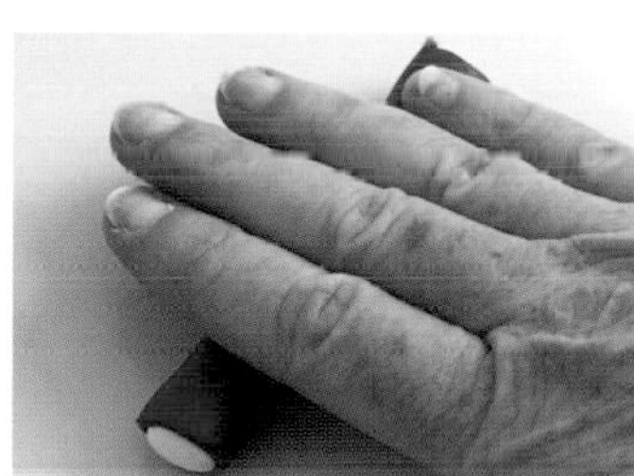

STEP 2
When the cane begins to lengthen easily, roll it on your work surface as though rolling a log. As the cane thins, the ends will become distorted. Squeeze them to tidy them if possible. Do not cut them off until you have finished the cane, because they will help prevent the distortion from moving farther into the cane.

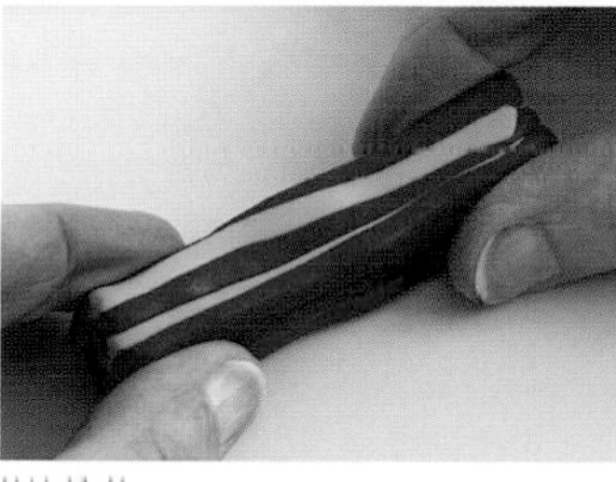

STEP 3
Square cane This type of cane should be pulled to reduce it instead of rolling in order to prevent the square cross-section from being lost. Begin by squeezing the cane along its length in the same way as for a round cane, but taking care to maintain the square cross-section.

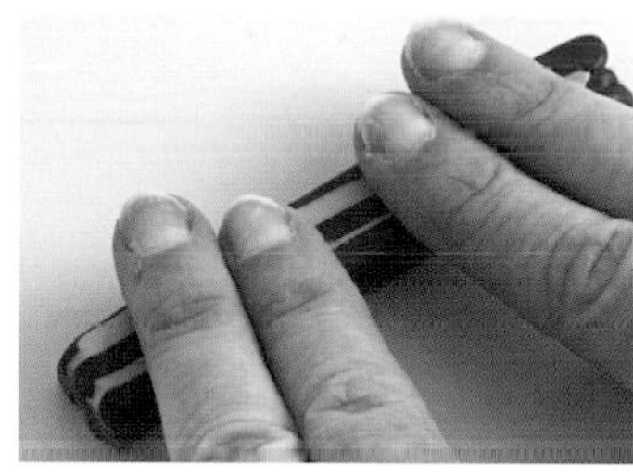

STEP 4
With the cane lying on the work surface, press down along its length. Turn the cane a quarter turn so that the second side is upward and repeat, continuing around the four sides.

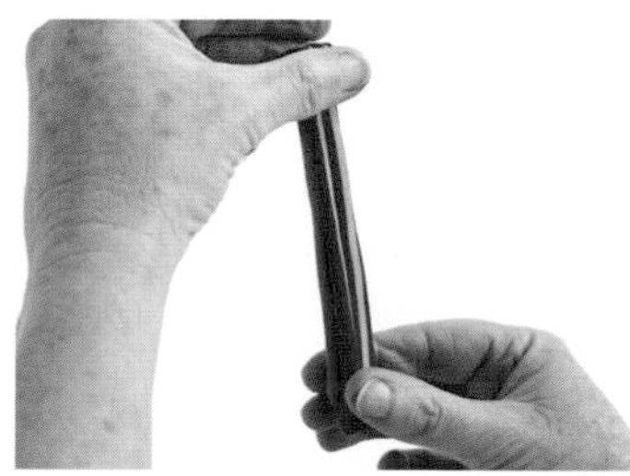

STEP 5
Hold the cane vertically and stroke firmly downward with the fingers of your other hand, pressing two opposing sides simultaneously as you pull and alternating between sides. This will thin and lengthen the cane.

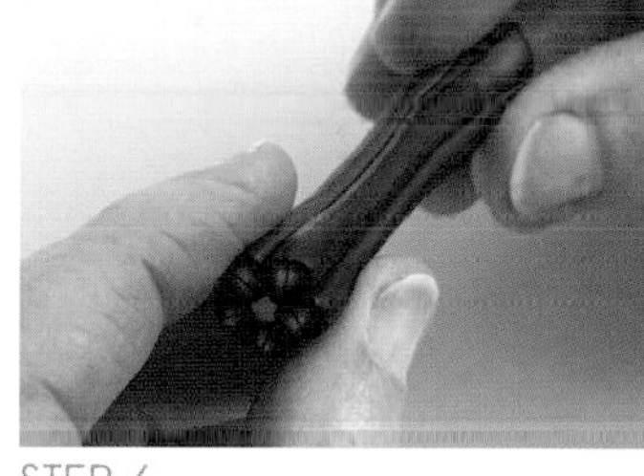

STEP 6
Irregular shaped cane Use this method for flower canes when you want to retain indentations between the petals, and other canes that have a shaped cross-section, such as leaves. Do not squeeze the cane but carefully pull the ends to make it stretch and elongate. Take care not to pull too hard or it may break.

Wrap a log in several sheets of clay in contrasting colors and of different thicknesses to make a more complex bull's-eye cane.

USING CANE SLICES

This technique is a traditional way of using millefiori canes and means that you can apply repeating motifs or patterns to beads or other polymer clay items. Always leave canes to rest for an hour or so before slicing. Alternatively, place the cane in a freezer for 10 minutes so that it becomes cold and firm.

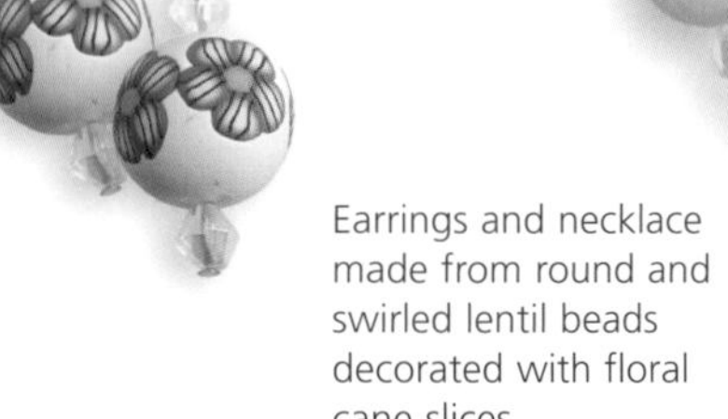

Earrings and necklace made from round and swirled lentil beads decorated with floral cane slices.

MATERIALS AND TOOLS

- Polymer clay cane
- Polymer clay for the beads, in a color to match or contrast with the cane
- Tissue blade
- Needle

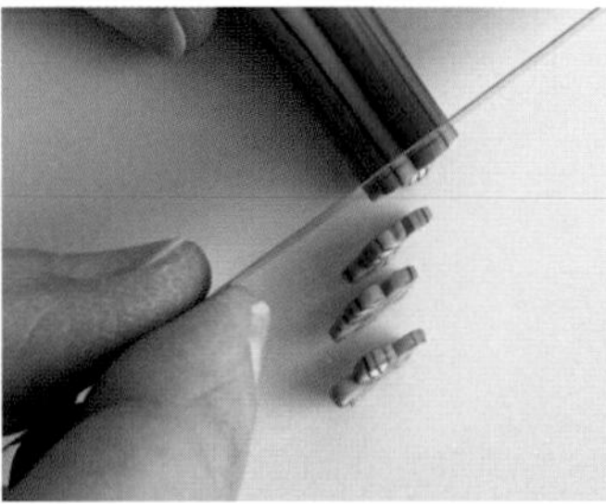

STEP 1

Slicing the cane Use a sharp tissue blade and cut onto a surface that will not blunt the blade, such as a piece of cardstock. Lay the cane on your work surface and look down onto it. Cut down with the blade, rotate the cane a quarter turn, and then slice again. This prevents the cane from becoming flattened by repeated cutting.

STEP 2

Applying the slices Form the polymer clay into beads of the sizes you require, but do not pierce. Apply the cane slices in either a regular pattern or randomly over the bead surface.

STEP 3

Work around the bead, applying the slices. Here, they are being placed slightly apart so that they will not overlap when rolled in.

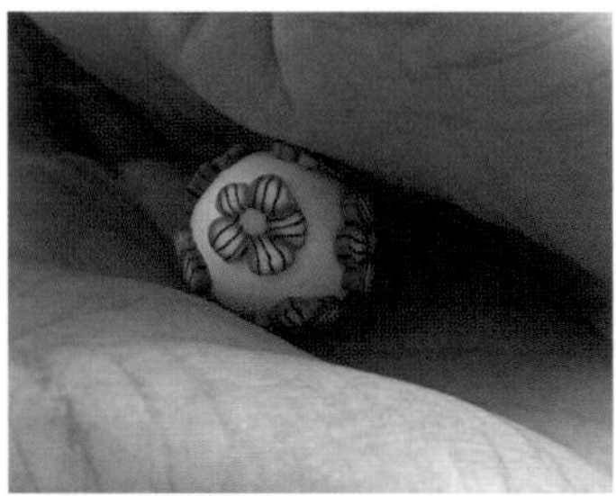

STEP 4

Roll the bead in your hands as if you were forming a ball. The cane slices will sink into the soft clay. You can leave them slightly raised or continue rolling until they are level with the clay surface.

STEP 5

Pierce the bead with a needle as usual and bake.

ARTIST'S TIPS

- Cut the cane as thinly as you can—1/32in (1mm) or less—for slices that you are going to apply to soft polymer clay beads or other soft clay pieces where you will roll the slices so that they are level with the clay surface.
- Slices that are to be made into buttons or disks for earrings should be 1/8in (3mm) to 3/16in (5mm) thick.
- There are various proprietary cane slicers on the market, but with a little practice you should be able to slice canes evenly and accurately by hand.

The accent beads on this necklace are decorated with millefiori cane slices in two different butterfly designs.

30 GEOMETRIC MILLEFIORI CANES

Canes can be made with all kinds of geometric motifs. The bold, clear shapes work well on their own, combined with each other, or used with floral and other pictorial canes. Patchwork, quilting, marquetry, and tile techniques are a great source of pattern ideas for geometric canes.

A striking pendant made from slices of tile-patterned millefiori canes applied to a sheet of black clay.

Geometric caning techniques can be used to create many designs, from chevron stripes to tile patterns.

SPIRAL CANES

Spiral canes are one of the staples of millefiori techniques and can be used in a huge variety of ways.

MATERIALS AND TOOLS

- Polymer clay: ½ block each of black and white
- Pasta machine or roller and rolling strips
- Tissue blade

STEP 1

Roll out 1/16in (1.5mm) thick sheets of black and white clay. Trim the black sheet into a 4 x 2½in (10 x 6.5cm) rectangle and lay it on top of the white sheet. Use a tissue blade to trim the white sheet to match the black sheet. Remove the waste clay. Press along one of the shorter ends to chamfer it.

STEP 2

Begin to roll up the two sheets together, pressing the first roll down well to expel any air that is trapped.

STEP 3

Roll up the two sheets completely and use a finger to smooth the end of the white sheet over to cover the end of the black sheet. The result is a black spiral on a white ground.

Try using black as the lower sheet to produce a white spiral on a black ground.

Use blended sheets to vary the colors within the spiral.

STRIPED CANES

Striped canes provide bold accents and are the starting point for many other cane types.

MATERIALS AND TOOLS

- Polymer clay: 1 block each of blue and yellow
- Pasta machine or roller and rolling strips
- Tissue blade

STEP 2

Chevron stripes Stand the striped log on end, and cut across it diagonally using a tissue blade.

STEP 1

Straight stripes Roll out a sheet of blue clay and a sheet of yellow clay, both about 1⁄16in (1.5mm) thick. Cut them into strips and then stack them on top of one another in alternating colors. Trim into a square log and reduce by pulling.

STEP 3

Flip one of the cut pieces and reassemble to form a square cane. Reduce by pulling in the usual way, then slice as required.

TILE PATTERNS

Simple geometric canes can be combined to make more complex canes with a repeating symmetrical pattern. The easiest way is to base them on a square made of four sections.

The cane shown below has been cut and stacked once more to make the slices for these earrings.

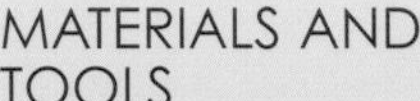

MATERIALS AND TOOLS

- Polymer clay canes: three different spiral and blended log canes
- Tissue blade

STEP 1

Press the three canes together, matching them so that they are aligned in the same way all along their length. Roll together to reduce and cut the cane in half with a tissue blade.

STEP 2

Reassemble the two pieces, matching them so that they make a pleasing symmetrical pattern. Pull to reduce and cut in half again.

STEP 3

Again, press the two halves together. The pattern becomes more intricate with each cut and pairing. Continue until you are satisfied with the result, or add more elements.

NATASHA BEADS

This is not strictly a caning technique, but it uses the symmetrical pairing concept of the tile pattern cane. The resulting beads are all one-offs, but are always fun to make and are a great way of using up scrap clay.

MATERIALS AND TOOLS

- Polymer clay in several contrasting colors, or scraps and cane ends (about a walnut-size quantity)
- Tissue blade
- Darning needle

STEP 1
Press the clay scraps together and shape into an oblong. Use a tissue blade to cut down the center of the oblong.

STEP 2
Open out the two pieces to reveal a perfectly matched pattern in the center. The two halves can be pressed together and made into a pendant, or you can continue on to make a bead.

STEP 3
Cut again on either side of the center cut. Use the matching pattern as a guide as to where to cut.

A single Natasha bead makes a beautiful necklace.

STEP 4
Flip out each outer piece to reveal another matching pattern on each side. Press these pieces together at the back of the other pair to make a bead with four symmetrically patterned sides.

STEP 5
Pierce through the center and bake.

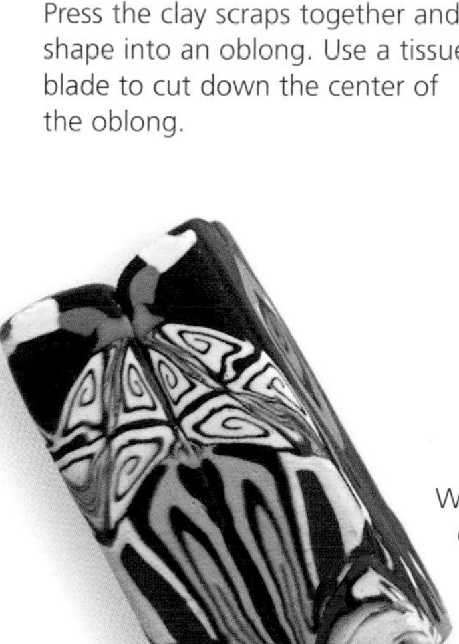

When making Natasha beads, you are in effect turning the original oblong bead inside out.

Try these...

Wedged spiral Use a wedge-shaped sheet for the top layer.

Checked pattern Make a striped log with fairly thick stripes and cut into even slices that are the same thickness as the stripes. Reverse alternate slices to make the check.

Tile pattern variations
This technique can be used to make all kinds of symmetrical cane patterns. It is also useful for using up canes that did not turn out well. Try combining triangular elements into a kaleidoscope cane in the same way.

31 FLORAL MILLEFIORI CANES

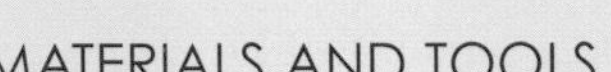

A necklace made from slices of three different flower canes, mixed with slices of leaf canes and glass pearl beads.

There are hundreds of different ways of making flower and leaf canes. The basic techniques shown here can be varied to make a wonderful garden of flowers by altering the colors, blends, wraps, and shapes.

Combine flower and leaf cane slices on a circle of clay to make a posy pin.

MATERIALS AND TOOLS

- Polymer clay for pink flower: ½ block each of pink and white, ¼ block black, ⅛ block yellow
- Polymer clay for rose: ½ block each of gold, golden yellow, and white
- Polymer clay for leaf: ½ block each of light and dark green, ⅛ block black
- Tissue blade
- Pasta machine or roller and rolling strips

PINK FLOWER CANE

This is a basic six-petaled flower with radiating veins on each petal.

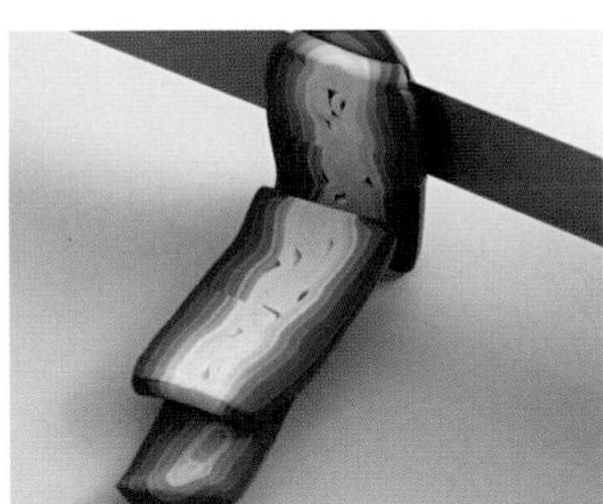

STEP 1
Make a Skinner blend of pink and white (see pages 26–27) and roll up into a round cane with the white in the center. Shape into a cane ¾in (20mm) thick and 2in (5cm) long. Stand the log on end and make three evenly spaced cuts lengthwise.

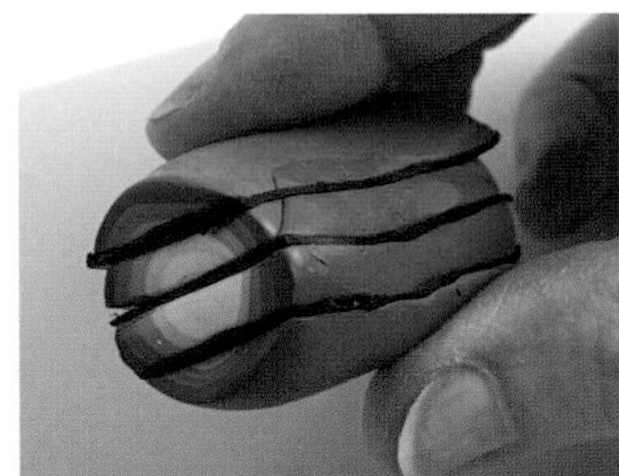

STEP 2
Roll out a $^{1}/_{32}$in (1mm) thick sheet of black clay. Insert a piece of the sheet between each slice and trim the edges.

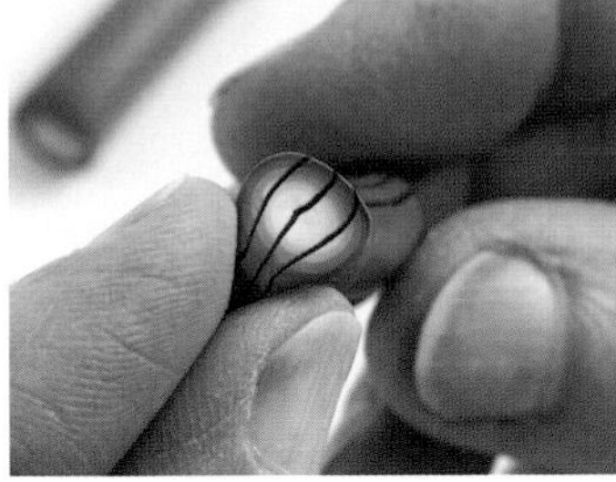

STEP 3
Reduce the cane until it is 7½in (20cm) long, then cut into six 1½in (40mm) lengths. Pinch each one into a petal-shaped cross-section, taking care to align the black streaks in the same way for each.

STEP 4
Roll a log of yellow clay, ¼in (6mm) thick and 1½in (40mm) long. Press each petal cane onto the yellow log with the pointed side inward. Make sure that it touches the yellow log all along its length. Reduce the cane by pulling to maintain the shape.

ROSE CANE

Roses look gorgeous in jewelry and covering artifacts.

STEP 1
Cut a triangle each of gold, yellow, and white clay, then roll together to make a three-color blended sheet graduating from gold to yellow to white (see page 27). Roll into a round log, with white in the center and gold on the outside.

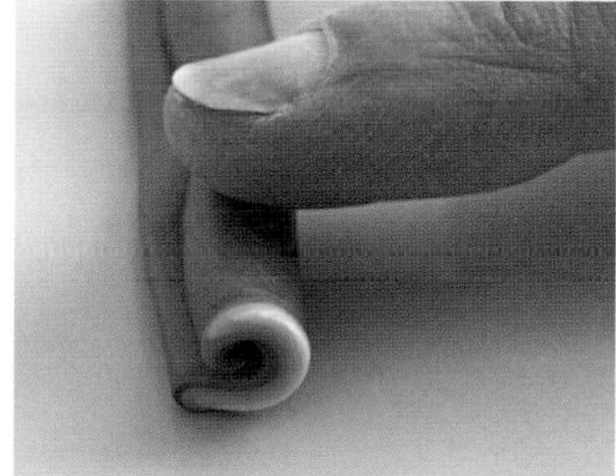

STEP 2
Reduce the log until it is 9in (20cm) long and cut into six equal pieces. Press one piece down on your work surface to flatten it until it is about 1/8in (3mm) thick. Roll this piece up into a spiral; this is the center of the rose.

STEP 3
Flatten the remaining five pieces so that they have a petal-shaped cross-section and apply around the rose center, overlapping them. Tuck the final petal under the first petal. Compress the logs into a cane and reduce by pulling.

LEAF CANE

You can make lots of different leaf canes by altering the leaf colors and the color of the vein slices.

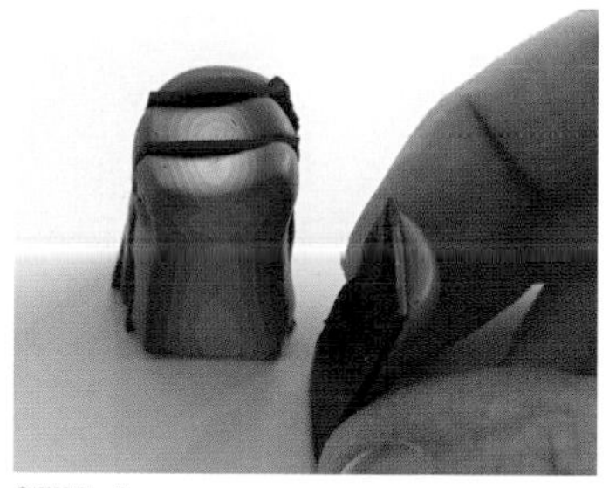

STEP 1
Make a blended log of light and dark green clays, 3/4in (20mm) thick and 2in (5cm) long. Slice into four pieces and insert sheets of black (as for the pink flower cane).

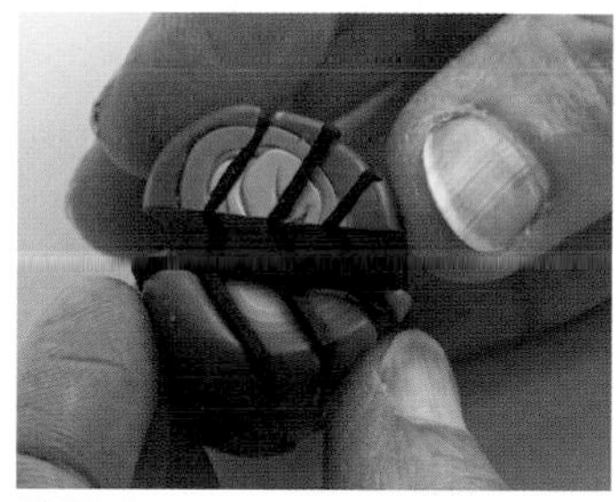

STEP 2
Cut the cane in half lengthwise at an angle to the inserted black sheets. Flip one half lengthwise and press a thin black sheet between the two to make the midrib.

STEP 3
Pinch the cane into a point at the tip of the leaf and reduce the cane by pulling. Slice as required.

Try these...

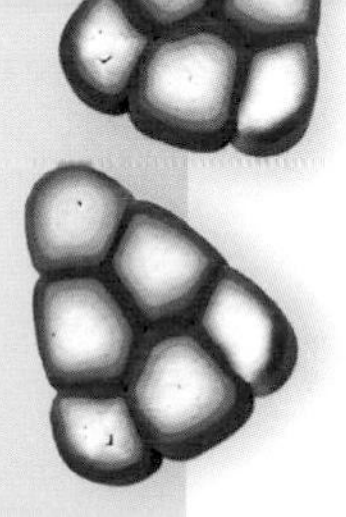

Hyacinth Make a blended log grading from white to blue. Reduce and cut into six sections. Press these together into a triangle, then reduce and slice.

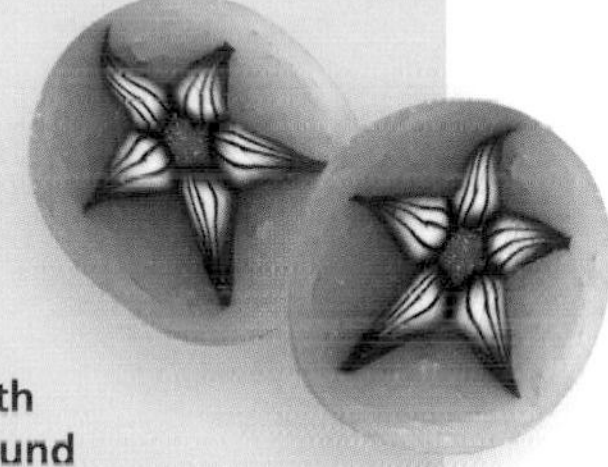

Flower cane with background Fill the space between the petals with thin triangular-shaped canes in a suitable background color.

Chevron leaf Use a green and black chevron-striped geometric cane to make this leaf.

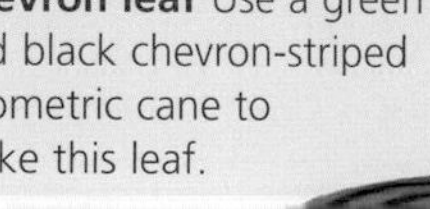

Two-lobed leaf Make a simple variegated leaf from two blended logs pressed together with a sheet of black between and shaped into a leaf cross-section.

32 PICTORIAL MILLEFIORI CANES

All sorts of pictures can be created using millefiori techniques. Face canes can be anything from cartoonlike to beautiful. Simple landscape canes make delightful jewelry items.

Use spiral canes in brown and gold for hair. Frame a slice of face cane with floral cane slices on a roundel of polymer clay to make a pin.

FACE CANE

The following steps show an intermediate technique for a face cane that uses a little shading to give the face dimension. You will find that a different face appears every time you make it. All logs should be 2 1/2in (65mm) long and the thickness specified in each step.

STEP 1

Eyes Form an 1/8in (3mm) log of black and press a 1/32in (1mm) log of white along its length. Wrap both in a 1/16in (1.5mm) thick sheet of blue. Press two triangular logs of white on either side. Roll a thin sheet of burnt umber and curve over the top of the eye. Reduce to double the length and cut in two.

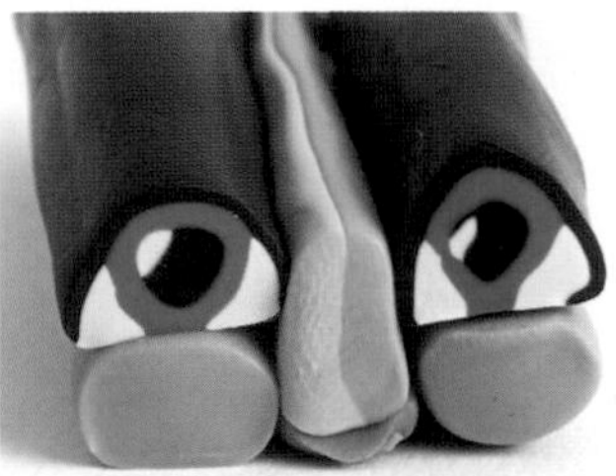

STEP 2

Nose and cheeks Form a 1/4in (6mm) log of basic flesh into a nose shape. Apply a thin strip of light flesh down the left side and a thin strip of dark flesh below. Assemble between the two eye canes and add two 1/4in (6mm) logs of basic flesh for cheeks.

MATERIALS AND TOOLS

- Polymer clay for face: 1 block flesh (Premo beige), 1/2 block white, 1/8 block alizarin crimson; small quantities of cobalt blue, black, burnt umber
- Polymer clay for landscape: 1/2 block each of light blue and leaf green, 1/4 block each of yellow and dark brown
- Tissue blade
- Pasta machine or roller and rolling strips
- Round tool, such as the end of a paintbrush

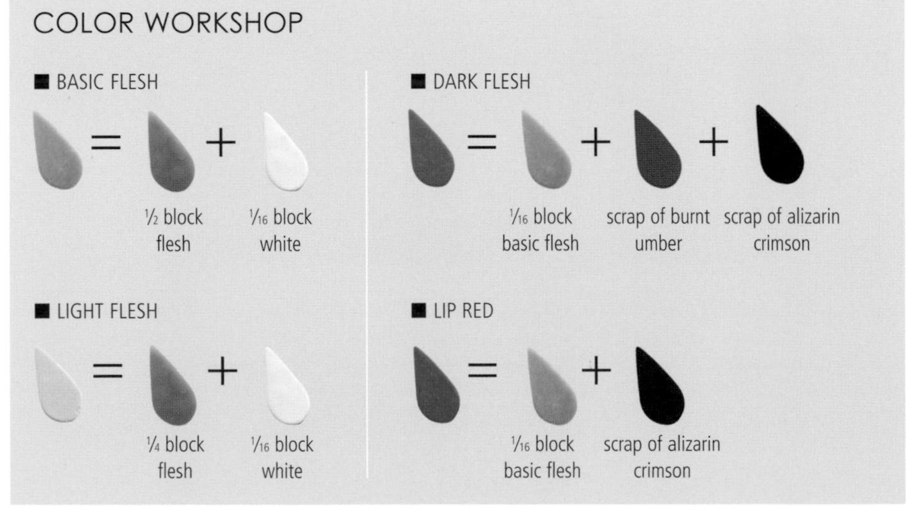

STEP 3
Mouth Roll two 1/16in (1.5mm) logs of lip red, and press onto a thin strip of alizarin crimson. Apply a semicircle of lip red under the strip. Apply a thin triangular log of basic flesh to the top of the mouth.

STEP 4
Assembly Press a log of basic flesh above the nose and cover with a sheet of the same. Apply two thin sheets of burnt umber for eyebrows. Apply a flattened log under the nose and press on the mouth.

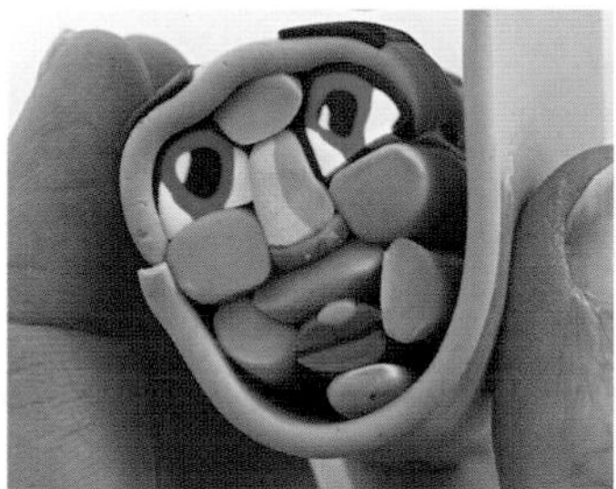

STEP 5
Apply wedges of basic flesh on either side of the mouth and a flattened log for the chin. Wrap the whole face in a sheet of basic flesh and press all together to consolidate and squeeze out any trapped air.

STEP 6
Reduce the cane by pulling and then cut in half to reveal the face. You can adjust the shape of the face by pinching the cane into a different cross-section if required.

LANDSCAPE CANE

This cane can be varied to make a whole sequence of landscape canes in different colors to represent the four seasons.

STEP 1
Roll out a sheet of light blue: 1/4in (6mm) thick, 2 1/2in (65mm) long, and 1in (25mm) wide. Make three longitudinal cuts and sandwich in three strips of dark brown for tree trunks. Indent the top of the brown clay with a round tool for the treetops.

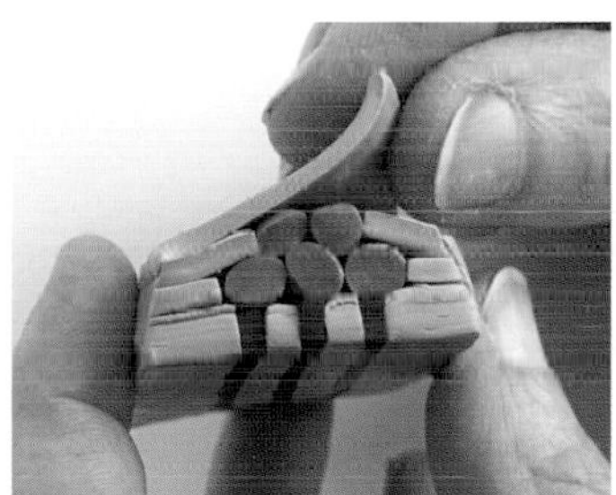

STEP 2
Roll five 2 1/2in (65mm) long logs of leaf green, about 3/8in (10mm) to 1/8in (3mm) thick. Lay these on top of the trunks. Pack the area around the treetops with light blue clay to make a semicircular cross-section. Cover with a sheet of light blue.

STEP 3
Make a blended log of leaf green and yellow, with the leaf green in the center. Stand the log on end and cut into three parts lengthwise.

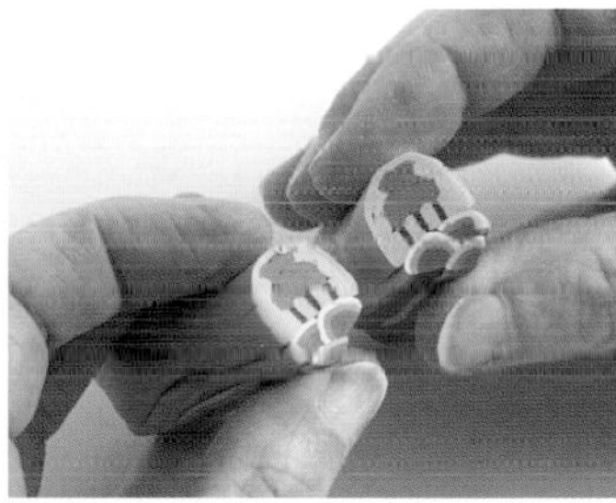

STEP 4
Press the three sections of blended log under the trees for the hills and squeeze to consolidate the whole cane into a round log. Reduce by rolling or pulling and cut the cane in half to reveal the picture.

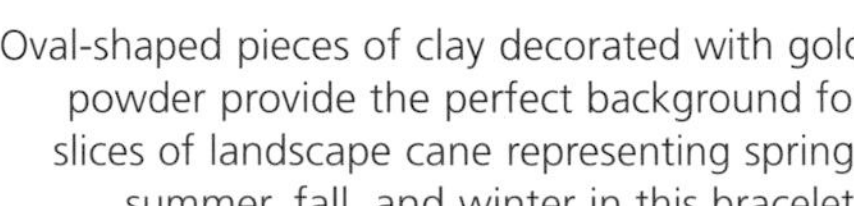

Oval-shaped pieces of clay decorated with gold powder provide the perfect background for slices of landscape cane representing spring, summer, fall, and winter in this bracelet.

Mica shift ghost images make beautiful and unusual jewelry.

33 MICA SHIFT EFFECTS

Some brands of polymer clay metallic and pearl colors contain mica particles. Mica particles are saucer-shaped; the flat top and bottom surfaces reflect light, while the edges do not. If a sheet of mica clay is rolled and folded repeatedly, all the mica particles are flattened so that their reflective surfaces are parallel to the surface of the clay. If these sheets are stacked, the sides of the stack will have dull edges, while the top and bottom surfaces will be shiny. The technique has been given various names, such as mica shift, ghost images, and chatoyant.

Strips cut from a sheet of mica clay will have two shiny and two dull sides. These strips can be twisted and applied like filigree.

Cut strips from a sheet of mica clay. Twist the strips and apply them to another sheet of mica clay in a spiral design, then roll flat.

ARTIST'S TIPS

- The effect is usually most pronounced with gold clay.
- Sanding and buffing the clay surface after baking increases the effect and adds to the shine.
- Do not attempt to reduce canes with mica shift effects or the effects will be lost.

MATERIALS AND TOOLS

- Polymer clay: 1 block gold containing mica
- Pasta machine or roller and rolling strips
- Ceramic tile
- Tissue blade
- Rubber or wooden stamp with a strong image

CANE PATTERN

Slices taken from the different surfaces of a mica sheet can be assembled into a cane to make patterns. This example produces a spiral pattern.

STEP 1

Roll out the clay repeatedly, folding and rolling until all streakiness has vanished and the surface looks like shiny satin. Roll to 1⁄16in (1.5mm) thick. Cut and stack the sheet into a block. The sides of the stack will be much duller than the top and bottom.

STEP 2

Roll and fold another 1/16in (1.5mm) thick sheet of shiny clay. Cut a 1 x 2in (25 x 50mm) rectangle. Cut slices from the side of the stack and lay these along the shiny rectangle, butting the edges of the slices together.

STEP 3

Trim the two sheets, then roll them together into a spiral cane. Press lightly to consolidate, but do not reduce.

STEP 4

Cut 1/32in (1mm) thick slices from the cane, and apply these to another shiny sheet of clay.

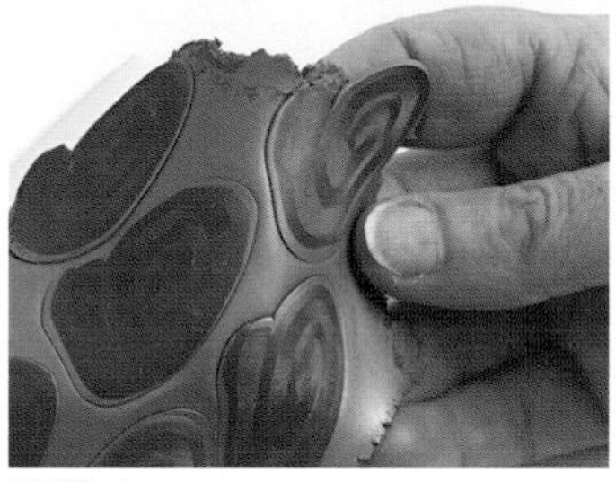

STEP 5

Pass the sheet through the pasta machine on the same setting as the original sheet. This will smooth the added slices into the sheet. Roll again at thinner settings until the added slices have sunk into the sheet and the sheet has a smooth surface. Alternatively, roll with a roller and rolling strips. Do not over-thin or the effect will disappear.

STEP 6

The resulting sheet can be used as a veneer to cover objects, create jewelry, or make mosaics.

GHOST IMAGES

Stamping the surface of a shiny sheet of mica clay with a rubber stamp impresses the pattern into the lower layers as well. When the top surface of the clay is sliced away, a smooth surface results, but the image is still visible and looks three-dimensional.

STEP 1

Roll out a 1/16in (1.5mm) thick sheet of shiny gold clay. Make a stack three sheets high and press onto a tile to anchor it. Impress the clay firmly with a moistened stamp and pare away the embossed surface with a tissue blade.

STEP 2

Roll the sheet flatter with a roller to enhance the effect. The surface will now be completely smooth, but the image still visible and catching the light as though it were in relief.

Try these...

Stripes, checks, and chevrons Stack alternating dull and shiny sheets for stripes. Cut and assemble to make chevrons and checks.

Ripple blade Stack together two shiny sheets to make a sheet about 1/8in (3mm) thick. Use a ripple blade to cut across the sheet at a low angle to make grooves across the surface. A cross-cut will give a trellis effect.

34 STAMPING AND TEXTURING

A texture sheet made using fern leaves was impressed onto clay to make these earrings. The design is highlighted with metallic powder.

Polymer clay takes rubber stamp impressions beautifully, and all kinds of variations are possible using inks and powders. There are also many proprietary texturing sheets available for polymer clay. Some are made like sheet rubber stamps, while others are simply formed plastic. Alternatively, you can texture clay with found objects, embossed paper, lace, or fabric, or even make your own texture sheets.

The stamped design on this mounted pendant has been emphasized with pastel powders.

ARTIST'S TIPS

- Stamps do not have to be commercial rubber stamps. Wooden fabric printing blocks and printer's blocks work well.
- Use permanent or crafter's heat-set stamping inks. Small individual stamp pads are easiest to use.
- Try stamping or texturing into scrap sheets of clay first to gauge how much pressure is required for that particular stamp or texture sheet.
- Suitable materials for making texture sheets include fabric, lace, embossed paper, woven mats, metal mesh, natural leaves and grasses, dried leaves, and sequins.

STAMPING

For stamping into soft clay, choose deeply cut rubber stamps with well-defined images. Shallow-cut stamps and those with photographic images work less successfully. Rubber stamps can also be used on baked clay.

MATERIALS AND TOOLS

- Polymer clay
- Pasta machine or roller and rolling strips
- Ceramic tile
- Rubber stamps
- Folded paper towel placed in a shallow dish and wetted
- Stamping inks and powders

Position a heart-shaped cutter around the stamped design to cut out shapes for earrings.

STEP 1

Roll out a 1⁄16in (1.5mm) thick sheet of clay and lay on the tile. Press the stamp onto the damp paper towel; wetting it will prevent it from sticking in the clay.

When impressing patterns onto foiled sheets of clay, or clay brushed with powders, the foil or powder will prevent the texture sheet or stamp from sticking.

STEP 2
Press the stamp firmly into the clay, but do not let it sink in as far as the edge of the stamp or it will leave a mark.

STEP 3
Remove the stamp and repeat as necessary with the same stamp, or another according to your design.

STEP 4
Embellish the stamped clay with powders, inks, or paints if you wish. Here, gold powder is being brushed over the clay surface to highlight the raised areas and accentuate the stamped design.

USING A TEXTURE SHEET

The main concern when using a texture sheet is to avoid it sticking firmly into the clay. Water, talc, and cornstarch all act as resists for polymer clay. Water is usually preferable, because the powders can leave a white residue and make it difficult to apply decorative powders to the clay after texturing.

STEP 1
Roll out the clay slightly thicker than the thickness required for the project. Sponge or spray water onto the clay surface. Lay the clay, damp surface down, over the texture sheet and either roll firmly over it with a roller, or pass it through the pasta machine on a thicker setting to allow for the thickness of the texture sheet.

STEP 2
Peel the clay off the texture sheet and use as required.

MATERIALS AND TOOLS

- Polymer clay
- Pasta machine or roller and rolling strips
- Ceramic tile
- Damp sponge or fine mister spray bottle with water
- Texture sheet

MAKING A TEXTURE SHEET
These are easy to make in polymer clay and, provided you use a strong clay, will last indefinitely. Talcum powder or cornstarch combined with hand rolling works best for dried materials, while fabrics should be wetted first. Roll the material firmly into the clay surface, remove it, and then bake the clay on the tile.

Try these...

Stamping pad Press the stamp onto a stamping pad instead of the damp sponge. The ink will prevent the stamp from sticking and the design is accentuated with the colors.

Powder color Stroke powder color over the surface of the stamp and then press it into black clay for a brocade effect.

Blended clay with powder A three-color blend stamped and then brushed with gold powder.

Wood-effect clay Use a marbled sheet or a wood-effect mixture as the background for stamped clay.

35 POWDERS

Artist's pastels are perfect for coloring floral designs.

Total coverage with metallic powder gives a solid metallic look, while highlights accentuate the relief design.

Raw polymer clay has a naturally tacky surface and this quality means that all kinds of decorative powders can be applied to the clay surface before baking. Pearlescent and metallic powders are particularly effective. These are widely available for craft and art applications, and are applied directly to the polymer clay surface. The results are glorious, turning polymer clay into gold, silver, pearl, or a rainbow of shining colors. The effects of the powders vary according to the background color of the clay used, so it is fun to experiment.

Seahorse pendant colored with pastel powders and framed with a twisted rope of clay.

ARTIST'S TIP

Mica powder is available as "Pearl" or "Pearl White" in several brands. This color makes an excellent bright silver on black clay, and a simulated pearl on white clay.

METALLIC AND PEARLESCENT POWDERS

Metallic powders are made of tiny particles of metal (often aluminum) and are normally only available in gold, silver, and copper colors. Mica powders are very fine-grained and make the clay look almost like real metal. There are several brands and the powders come in a large range of colors: gold, silver, copper, pearl, and many other bright colors with a pearlescent or metallic sheen. They can be applied directly to polymer clay by brush for total coverage, or by fingertip for highlighting.

MATERIALS AND TOOLS

- Unbaked molded or sculpted item in black polymer clay
- Pearlescent or metallic powders
- Ceramic tile
- Soft paintbrushes
- Gloss varnish

STEP 1

For total coverage, place the piece to be coated on a tile. Dip a paintbrush into the powder and brush over the clay surface. Excess powder that falls onto the tile can be scooped up on the brush and applied again.

STEP 2
Continue until the clay surface is covered in a sheen of color. Covering the clay totally will create a piece that looks like solid metal. Bake the piece on the tile for the usual time.

STEP 3
When the piece is cool, varnish all over the surface. This will prevent the powder from rubbing off during wear or handling.

ARTIST'S PASTELS

White or pale-colored clays work best with pastel powders, because the colors are not as strong as metallic and pearlescent powders. Artist's soft pastels are the best to use with polymer clay because the colors are so durable. They come in a wide range of colors in stick form. Colored chalks and eye makeup powders can also be used, but are not as durable and can fade.

STEP 1
To release the powder from the pastel stick, rub each color firmly onto paper to create your palette.

STEP 3
Instead of using a paintbrush, rub a rubber stamp over the powder to coat the surface.

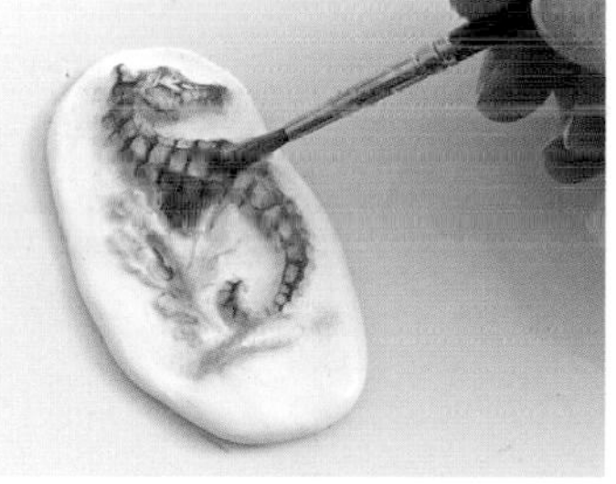

STEP 2
Use a paintbrush to sweep up the powder from the paper and apply it to the raw polymer clay surface. You will get lovely graded effects and soft edges to the areas of color.

STEP 4
Press the stamp into the clay to make an inlaid colored image. Bake the pieces on the tile for the usual time. When cool, varnish all over the surfaces.

HIGHLIGHTING WITH POWDERS
Use a fingertip to stroke powder over the raised areas of a molded or stamped piece. Here, a rainbow of pearlescent colors has been applied to a molded panel. Bake and varnish as usual.

MATERIALS AND TOOLS

- Unbaked polymer clay item with a relief design
- Small piece of polymer clay
- Artist's pastels
- Sheet of coarse white paper (artist's watercolor paper is ideal)
- Ceramic tile
- Soft paintbrush or rubber stamp
- Matte or gloss varnish

Try these...

Powdered mold Brush the raised surfaces of the mold with blue pearlescent powder, then press white clay into the mold.

Copper highlights Copper powder highlights on black clay.

Miniature hydrangeas The hydrangeas have pastel blue brushed onto the translucent white flowers.

36 INK AND PAINT

Water-based ink and paint of all kinds can be used on polymer clay, either before or after baking. This gives an exciting repertoire of techniques that you will add to constantly. Try making swatches to experiment; different brands of ink and paint behave differently, so you can create infinite variations. The most exciting techniques with ink and paint are those where you decorate the clay surface before baking. This means that you can work on a flat surface and, when the clay is decorated and the ink or paint has dried, the clay can be shaped into all kinds of projects.

This sculpted jewelry pin of a blue tit was made with translucent clay and covered completely with semi-translucent washes of paint to give a porcelain effect.

ARTIST'S TIP

Artist's inks are widely available in a wonderful range of colors and effects, and water-based acrylic inks are the best to use with polymer clay. They are waterproof and permanent, and both the transparent and pearlescent colors give beautiful effects.

CRACKLE EFFECTS

This is an opulent effect that is ideal for making beads. The results are similar to using metal leaf, but inks have a wider color range and the patterns are finer.

Wind a strip of crackle-effect clay around a knitting needle and bake on the needle to make a great pair of spiral earrings.

MATERIALS AND TOOLS

- Polymer clay: ½ block black, rolled into a ⅛in (3mm) thick sheet
- Paintbrush and water pot
- Alcohol
- Acrylic ink in pearlescent colors
- Pasta machine or roller

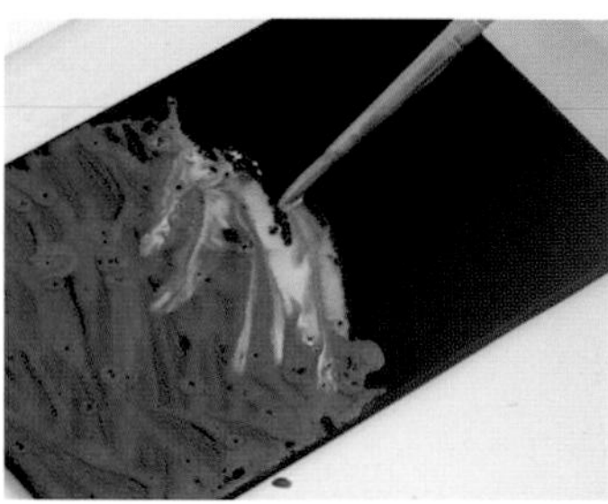

STEP 1

Lay the sheet of clay onto a tile and brush over with alcohol to degrease. Allow to dry thoroughly. Paint the surface liberally with pearlescent ink, blending several colors if you wish. Allow the ink to dry. If the clay is visible, apply a second coat, then allow to dry thoroughly.

STEP 2

Pass the clay through a pasta machine at one thinner setting than originally, or use a roller. This crackles the surface.

STEP 3

If you roll over the surface again in another direction, the crackles will become squares rather than lines. The sheet can now be cut into pieces to apply to beads or other forms, or shaped with cutters.

PAINTING

The baked surface of polymer clay makes an excellent painting canvas, and all kinds of polymer clay artifacts can be painted. Water-based artist's acrylic paints are the best to use. Do not use oil paints of any kind because these may never dry on polymer clay. Mistakes can easily be removed by scraping the paint away with a blade.

MATERIALS AND TOOLS

- Baked polymer clay piece
- Alcohol
- Pencil and fine sanding pad
- Acrylic paints
- Paintbrush and water pot
- Matte or gloss varnish

STEP 1
Brush over the surface of the baked clay with the alcohol to degrease it and allow to dry thoroughly.

STEP 2
You can draw an outline design with a pencil if you wish. If you make a mistake, sand away the pencil marks with a fine sanding pad.

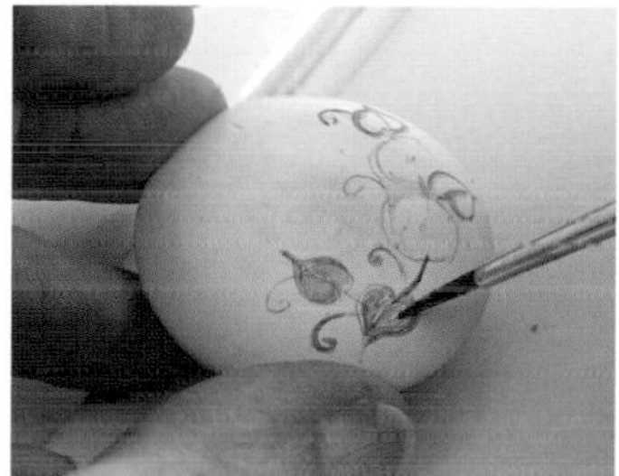

STEP 3
Paint your design onto the surface. You can dilute the paint to make subtle washes as well as apply it more thickly.

STEP 4
Allow the paint to dry overnight to make sure that it is completely dry before varnishing. Varnish to protect the painted surface using matte or gloss varnish.

Try these...

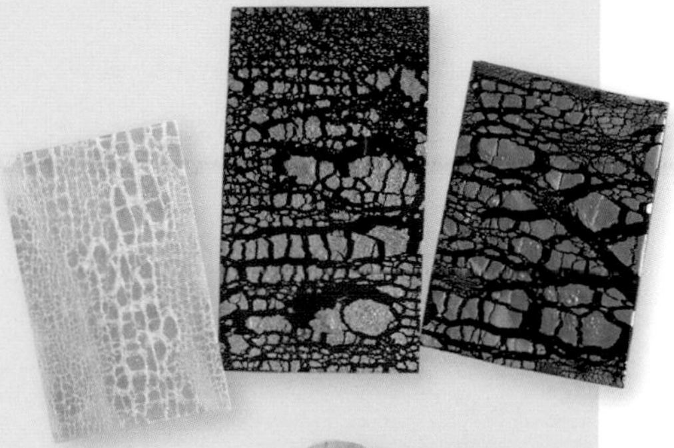

Color experiments Experiment with different colored inks and clays to make a wonderful variety of effects.

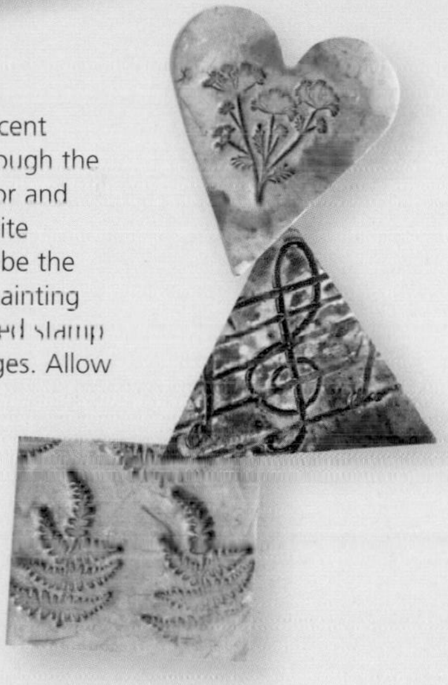

Watercolor effects Nonpearlescent acrylic inks are transparent, although the transparency varies with the color and thickness of application. Use white polymer clay and stamp or inscribe the surface before degreasing and painting with washes of ink. The impressed stamp or lines will show as darker images. Allow to dry and use as required.

Background blends Use polymer clay blends as a background to add depth to the painted image.

Swirled lentil bead The wave pattern in the clay of a swirled lentil bead is used as the background for a painting of a tiny boat in this necklace.

37 METAL FOIL AND LEAF

Foil beads

The foils that can be used on polymer clay come in many metallic and holographic colors. They have a Mylar (or plastic) backing sheet; when applied to polymer clay and the backing sheet removed, they leave wonderful metallic effects on the clay's surface. Metal leaf also works beautifully applied to the surface of polymer clay and gives a truly opulent result. Sheets of foil- and leaf-covered clay can be cut up and used in many ways, such as for decorating jewelry, beads, and mosaics; covering vessels; and making frames.

Try applying metal leaf to different colored background clays.

Metal foil comes in a huge range of colors and patterns.

APPLYING FOIL

Not all colors of foil work with polymer clay—some simply refuse to release onto the clay—so it can be a matter of trial and error.

MATERIALS AND TOOLS

- Black polymer clay
- Foil
- Baking parchment
- Tissue blade

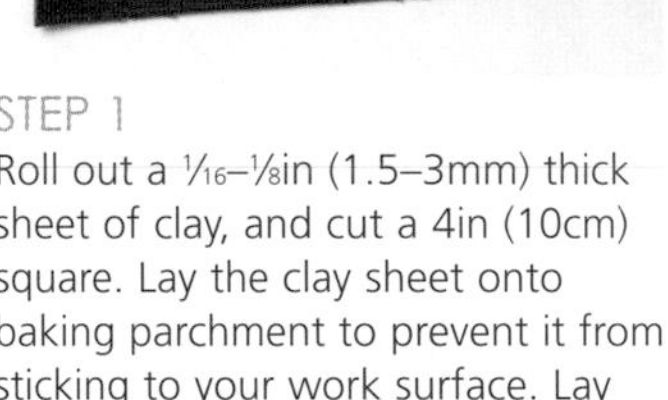

STEP 1

Roll out a 1⁄16–1⁄8in (1.5–3mm) thick sheet of clay, and cut a 4in (10cm) square. Lay the clay sheet onto baking parchment to prevent it from sticking to your work surface. Lay the foil, color-side upward, on top.

STEP 2

Press down all over the sheet of foil, smoothing outward with your fingers to eliminate any air bubbles.

STEP 3

Scrape firmly over the surface of the foil sheet with a tissue blade, applying pressure, but not so hard as to distort the clay below. Take care to scrape away any air bubbles. After scraping several times in one direction, scrape again at right angles to the first direction.

STEP 4

Take hold of one end of the foil sheet and pull it off the clay surface in one rapid movement. The backing will come away from the foil, leaving it attached in a shiny layer to the surface of the clay. If there are any gaps in the foil layer, reapply it as before.

APPLYING METAL LEAF

Real gold leaf costs a small fortune, so use artificial leaf. It comes in a range of colors, such as gold, silver, copper, and even variegated colors. After baking, you will need to varnish the leaf-covered clay to prevent the leaf from tarnishing.

MATERIALS AND TOOLS

- Polymer clay
- Artificial metal leaf
- Baking parchment
- Paintbrush
- Pasta machine or roller
- Varnish

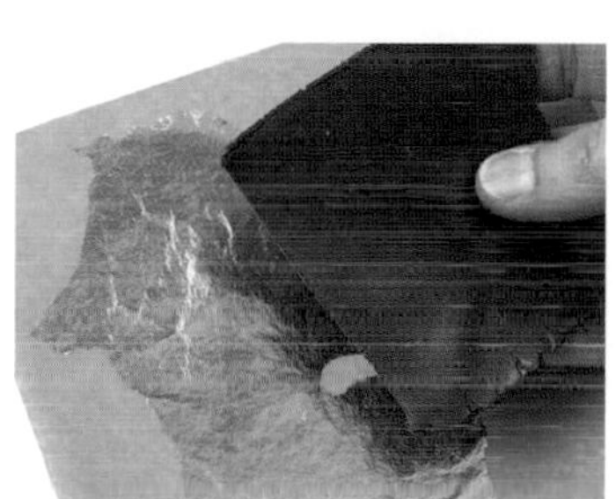

STEP 1
Roll out a sheet of clay about 1⁄16in (1.5mm) thick and 6in (15cm) square or the size of one sheet of leaf. Open the packet of leaf and remove the top protective tissue paper covering the leaf. Lay the clay on top of the leaf.

STEP 2
Press the clay down gently onto the leaf, smoothing outward with your fingers to eliminate any air bubbles. Lift the clay sheet and flip it over. The leaf will have stuck to the clay in an even sheet.

STEP 3
Lay the clay sheet on the baking parchment and use a paintbrush to brush over the surface to ensure that it is smoothly pressed down. Avoid touching the leaf as much as possible because your fingerprints will encourage tarnishing.

STEP 4
Crackle effects You can now use the sheet as it is or crackle the leaf by rolling over the surface with a roller. The leaf will crackle all over the clay, allowing the clay color to show through.

STEP 5
You can roll over the clay surface again, at 90 degrees to the first rolling. This will cause the crackling to become fractured into small rectangles. Alternatively, pass the clay through a pasta machine on one setting thinner than the clay was rolled out. Then set it one thinner again and pass through a second time at right angles to the first.

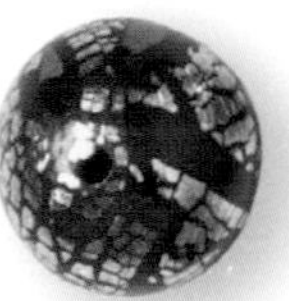

Metal leaf beads

Try these...

Foil shapes Foil shapes can be textured with texture sheets to make fabulous jewelry motifs.

Foil strips Cut strips of foiled clay and apply in layers to a backing sheet of plain black clay. Cut shapes from this to obtain pieces that simulate dichroic glass jewelry.

Leaf veneers Leaf-covered clay is a wonderful veneer for making frames or cutting out shapes for jewelry.

38 IMAGE TRANSFERS

Teardrop polymer clay pendant with a water slide transfer.

Image transfers open up exciting possibilities for the polymer clay artist, whether using commercial images or hand drawings. Lettering can be transferred using the same techniques, but remember to reverse the writing on your computer first.

Clay decorated with a black and white toner transfer.

Black and white toner photocopy colored with coloring pencils and then transferred onto clay.

TONER TRANSFERS

Polymer clay has the ability to pick up images from photocopiers or laser printers that use toner. The results are sharp, clear, and permanent. The success of this technique can be variable and depends on several things, such as the type of copier used and the brand of polymer clay. The answer is to experiment to find what works for you. White or light-colored clay gives the best result with black and white toner transfers.

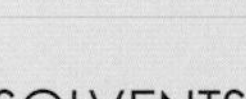

WHAT TO USE

Prints that work:

- Black and white photocopies from a copier of the kind that uses powder toner. These are the most widely available in copy shops and public libraries. Use fairly recent prints; they seem to be less successful after time.
- Black and white prints from a laser printer that uses toner. Beware—not all laser prints work. Make a test print first.
- Some color laser prints will transfer, but give a pale image.

Prints that don't work:

- Prints from ink jet printers.
- Prints from magazines and catalogs.
- Photographs.

Toner transfer colored with coloring pencils.

SOLVENTS

A solvent of some kind is used to soak the back of the print to help the image release onto the clay. Rubbing alcohol and acetone or nail polish remover work well. Experiment to find the one that suits the prints you are using.

MATERIALS AND TOOLS

- White polymer clay
- Black and white toner photocopy
- Roller and rolling strips
- Solvent
- Ceramic tile
- Coloring pencils if wished

STEP 1
Roll out a ¹⁄₁₆in (1.5mm) thick sheet of clay on the tile. Cut out the photocopied image and lay it face down onto the clay surface.

STEP 2
Burnish the back of the paper firmly with your finger. The aim is to make sure that all parts of the image are in contact with the clay surface.

STEP 3
Dip your finger into the solvent (or use a brush) and apply over the back of the paper. The solvent will soak the paper, so you will see a trace of the image through it. Cover all areas of the image and allow to soak in. When this first application is dry, repeat and allow to soak for at least 15 minutes.

STEP 4
Peel away the paper to reveal the transferred image. The piece can now be used as required.

COLORING PENCIL TRANSFERS

Drawings made with good-quality artist's coloring pencils and HB pencils make successful transfers. Use the pencils to create images or to color areas on a toner transfer. When using coloring pencils, it is usually necessary to bake the clay with the paper in place so that the heat of the oven helps to lift the color from the paper.

WATER SLIDE TRANSFERS

There is a bewildering variety of printer papers available today for using with your computer to apply images to fabric, T-shirts, ceramic, and so on. One of the most successful to use with polymer clay is Lazertran Silk, a proprietary brand that produces intense color images on the clay.

MATERIALS AND TOOLS

- 1 sheet of Lazertran Silk
- White polymer clay
- Roller and rolling strips
- Ceramic tile
- Bowl of cold water

STEP 1
Use a color photocopier to copy your chosen color image onto the Lazertran sheet. It is best to copy a sheet that you have crammed with color images so that you make good use of the entire sheet. Alternatively, use a color laser printer to print the image onto the Lazertran.

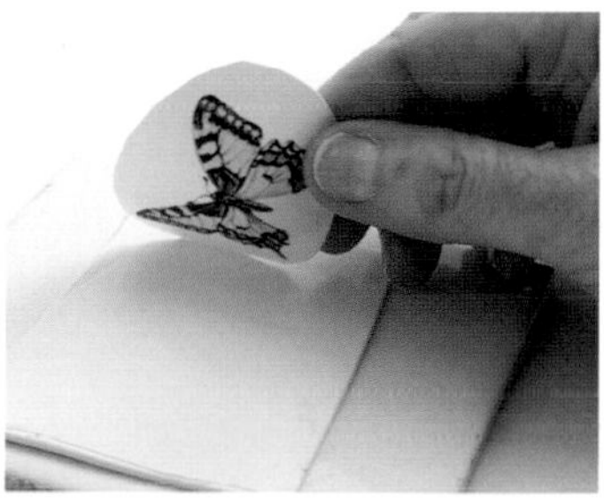

STEP 2
Cut out an image. Roll out the clay as for toner transfers and lay on the tile. Press the image face down onto the clay and burnish the back firmly. Leave for about 30 minutes.

STEP 3
Immerse the whole tile in a bowl of water and leave for about 5 minutes. After this time, the paper backing will have floated loose and you can remove it. The image will have transferred onto the clay surface. Mop the clay dry carefully and bake as normal.

39 LIQUID CLAY

Several of the main brands of polymer clay include a liquid form of clay in their range. This usually comes as a syrupy translucent liquid that can be used as it is or tinted with oil paints to give a range of translucent colors. There are many wonderful techniques for using liquid polymer clay; the main ones are given here, with brief descriptions of further techniques to try.

Decorate clay with liquid clay feathering effects to make an attractive trinket box.

Liquid clay transfer

ARTIST'S TIPS

- Use artist's oil paints to tint the liquid clay. Acrylic or water paints will bubble in the clay when baked.
- Use alcohol to wash brushes and clean up liquid polymer clay.
- Use the glass from a clip picture frame because the edges will have been ground smooth. Alternatively, use a cut piece of glass and sand the edges for safety.

STAINED GLASS EFFECTS

Liquid polymer clay can be tinted and painted onto glass or ceramic tile in thin sheets. The liquid is baked on the glass and then peeled off to give a remarkably strong sheet of transparent clay that is shiny on the surface that was in contact with the glass. This quality is put to great effect to make window clings and decorations in the style of stained glass windows.

MATERIALS AND TOOLS

- Polymer clay
- Liquid polymer clay
- Sheet of glass
- Drawn design on a piece of paper
- Masking tape
- Alcohol and cloth
- Roller
- Tissue blade
- Thick tapestry needle
- Oil colors
- Mixing palette
- Darning needle

STEP 1
Tape the design to the back of the sheet of glass so that the image shows through. Wipe over the glass with alcohol to degrease it.

STEP 2
Roll out a 1/16in (1.5mm) thick sheet of polymer clay and cut several strips of the same thickness.

STEP 3
Use the clay strips to outline the design as though it were the leading in a stained glass window. As you curve the strips around the design, press them down onto the glass to ensure a good contact.

This leaf pendant can be hung as a window ornament or glued with superglue to a glass window.

STEP 4
Make a hanging loop if you want to hang the finished piece.

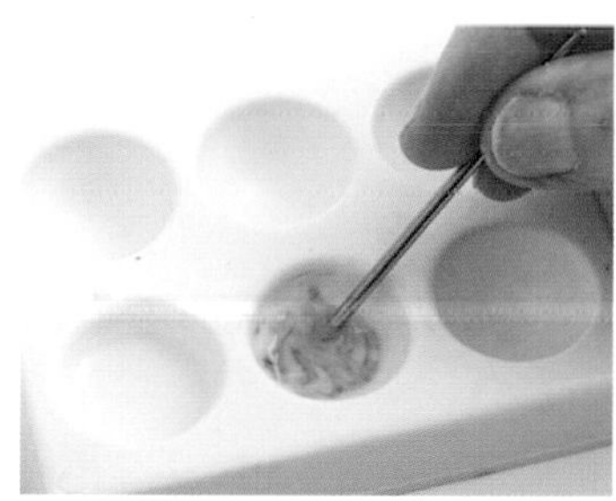

STEP 5
Pour some liquid clay into a mixing palette and add a small quantity of oil paint in the color required. Mix in the paint well. Use the color sparingly because too much will affect transparency. The colors will be darker after baking, so aim for a pastel color.

STEP 6
Use the tapestry needle to scoop up some tinted liquid clay and apply it to one of the sections. Push the color into all the corners, adding more if necessary. The coating should be continuous and as even as possible. The minimum thickness should be about 1/32in (1mm).

STEP 7
To make some of the cavities multicolored, apply contrasting colors to different areas of the cavity. Use the darning needle to draw streaks of one color into another for a feathering effect. After feathering, place the glass in the oven immediately to avoid the colors merging and bring the temperature up from cold. Bake for about 20 minutes, taking care that the full baking temperature is reached or the piece will not be strong. Allow the piece to cool on the glass and then peel it off gently.

Try these...

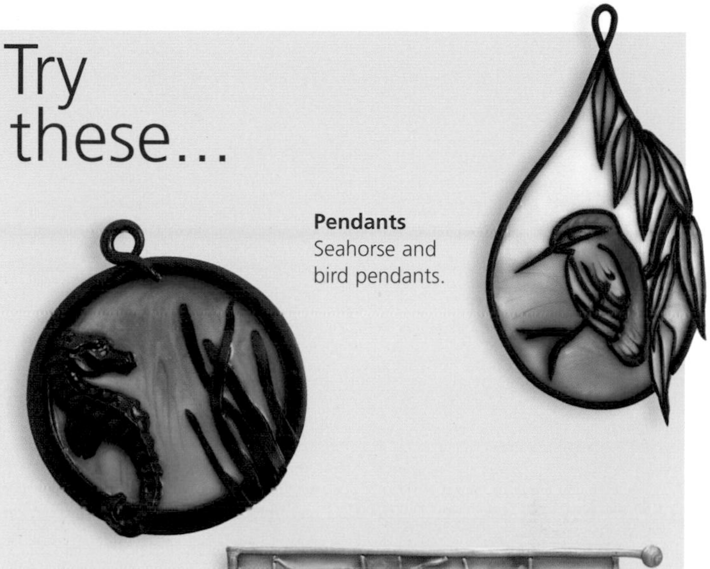

Pendants Seahorse and bird pendants.

Panel Combine motifs, such as sycamore leaves and seeds, to make larger stained glass panels.

Glass motifs Apply swirled colors of liquid clay in thin sheets to glass and bake. When cool, peel off the transparent sheets and either cut out shapes or use a paper punch to cut out motifs. Press shiny side down onto glass bottles or drinking glasses for an instant decorative effect. For a more permanent result, use superglue to fix the motifs onto the glass.

FEATHERING EFFECTS

This technique is great fun to do and gives some beautiful jewelry effects.

OTHER USES

- **Enamel effects** Liquid clay can also be used for cloisonné effects (see pages 104–105).
- **Mosaic grout** Use liquid clay for grouting polymer clay mosaics. The clay can be left translucent or tinted. The mosaic will need to be baked after grouting if you use liquid clay, so make the mosaic on a support that can withstand the baking temperature.

MATERIALS AND TOOLS

- Baked white polymer clay blank, such as a star
- Liquid polymer clay
- Paintbrush
- Mixing palette
- Oil paints, including white
- Tapestry needle
- Darning needle

STEP 1
Spread a thin coat of untinted liquid clay over the surface of the star. Mix up several colors, including an opaque white.

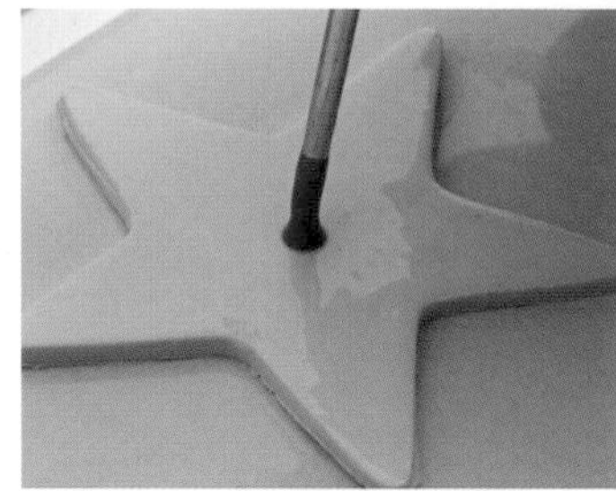

STEP 2
Dip the tapestry needle into the first color and hold it vertically over the painted star. A small drip should form at the point of the needle. Lower the needle and touch the point onto the clay surface. The small drip will become a circle of color in the translucent clay coating.

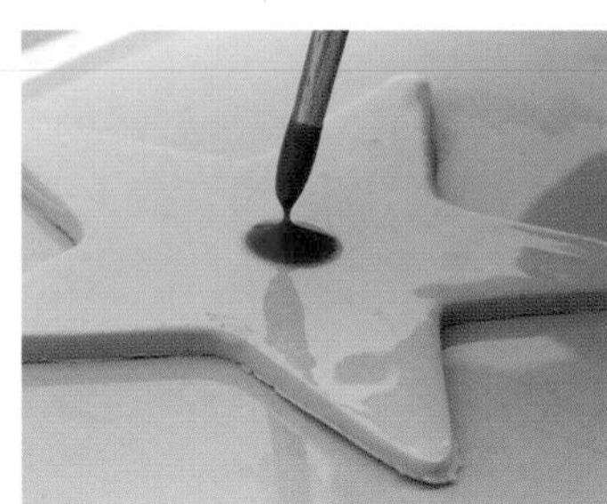

STEP 3
Lift the needle straight upward until the thread of liquid breaks.

STEP 4
Now load the needle with a contrasting color and repeat, touching the needle point into the center of the first spot. This will create a bull's-eye of color. Repeat with a third color.

STEP 5
Using the darning needle, touch the point into the center of the bull's-eye and drag the needle tip outward to make the point of a star. Repeat from the center outward all around the bull's-eye and a full star will develop.

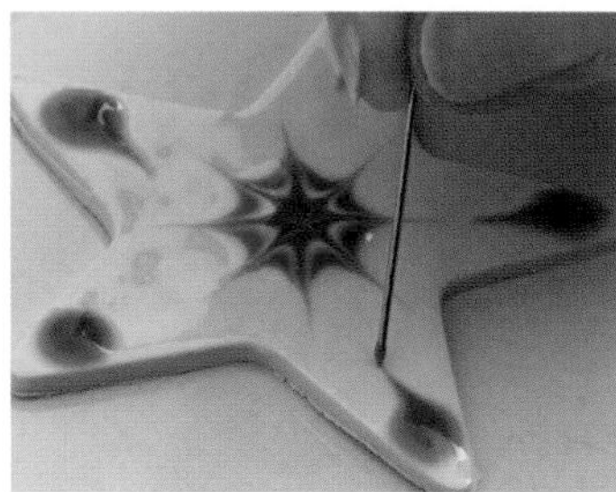

STEP 6
Now apply two-color bull's-eyes to the points of the clay star. Drag the point of the darning needle inward through each bull's-eye to make a heart. Bake the piece on the tile immediately to prevent the colors from spreading.

LIQUID CLAY TRANSFERS

Liquid clay has the happy ability to take transfers from color catalogs or magazines. These publications use the offset-litho type of printing, and the printer's ink is picked up by the liquid clay and becomes embedded in the baked clay sheet. The resulting transfers are robust, color, transparent, and paper thin. They can be incorporated into jewelry and other decorative artifacts, or used as embellishments for embroidery, glassware, window decorations, and votive candleholders.

MATERIALS AND TOOLS

- Liquid polymer clay
- Color picture from a magazine or catalog
- Ceramic tile
- Paintbrush
- Bowl of water
- Nailbrush

STEP 1

Use the paintbrush to paint a thin layer of liquid clay all over the surface of the image. When the paper is held up to the light, you should see a continuous shine of liquid covering the paper with no drier areas.

STEP 2

Check that there are no completely opaque areas—a slight milkiness is all you want. Let the liquid settle on the paper for 5 minutes to smooth out and allow any air bubbles to disperse. Lay the piece on a ceramic tile and bake at the highest temperature recommended by the manufacturer. This will make the piece more translucent and strong.

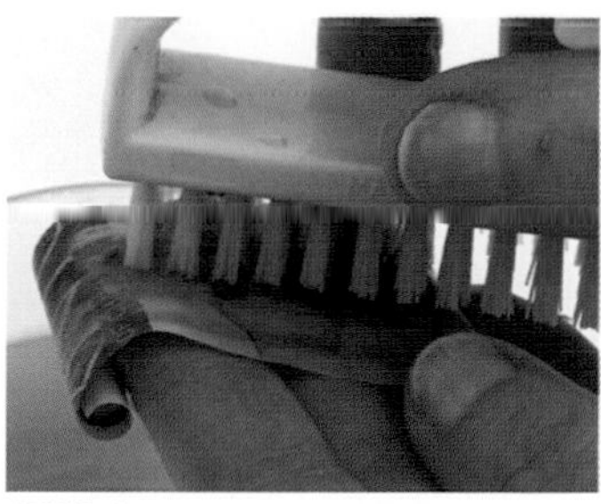

STEP 3

Drop the piece into a bowl of cold water and allow to soak for about 15 minutes. Hold the piece in your hand and brush firmly over the paper on the back of the piece with a nailbrush to disturb the surface.

STEP 4

You will now be able to rub the paper with your fingers to roll it off the clay surface. You may need to brush again with the nailbrush to remove all traces of the paper, which will appear as a white bloom.

STEP 5

The finished piece can now be trimmed and mounted into jewelry or glued to glass for transparent decorations. These images are waterproof and permanent and can also be incorporated into embroidery or collage. If they are not being used for transparent effects, it is best to back them with a sheet of white clay and bake again.

Try these...

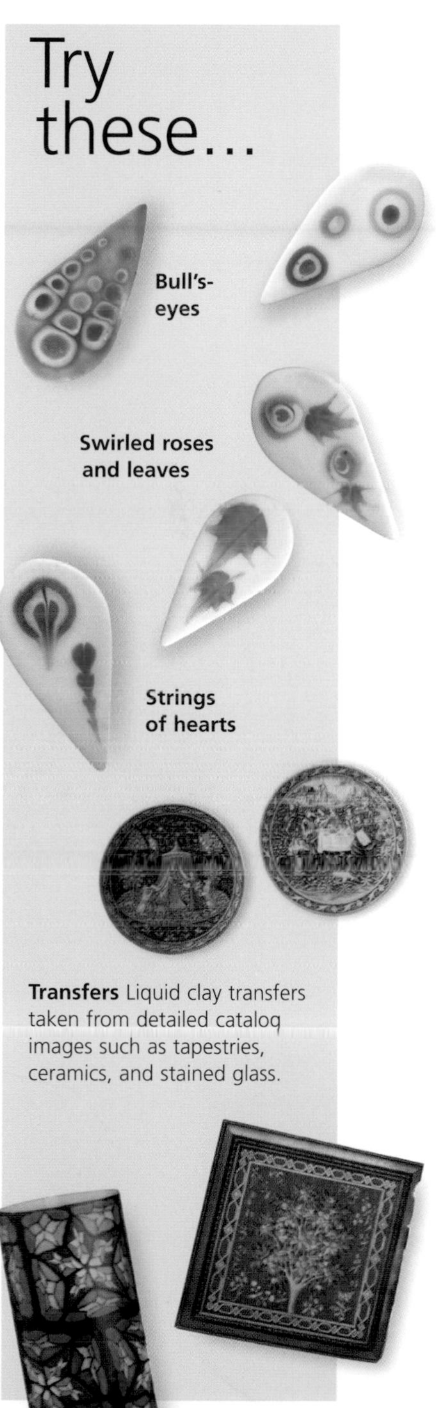

Bull's-eyes

Swirled roses and leaves

Strings of hearts

Transfers Liquid clay transfers taken from detailed catalog images such as tapestries, ceramics, and stained glass.

CHAPTER 4: SIMULATIONS AND INCLUSIONS

Polymer clay is a great imitator and this chapter demonstrates some wonderful techniques for simulating all kinds of materials, from ceramics and semiprecious stones to wood and ivory. The clay can also be mixed with various materials to transform its appearance so that it is virtually impossible to tell it is polymer clay.

40

ENAMEL AND CLOISONNÉ

There are various ways to simulate enamel effects with polymer clay, but the following technique is the one that looks the most realistic. Polymer clay coated with mica powder simulates the underlying precious metal, while clear resin is virtually identical to the wonderful pools of color found in true transparent enamel. Liquid polymer clay can also be used, but it is not shiny or transparent enough to simulate the melted glass of true clear enamel.

Enameled dove pendant and seascape pin. The resin dries very hard and looks like shiny glass.

SEASCAPE

This sequence also shows how to use an inscribed blank of baked polymer clay as a press mold for creating lines to separate the cloisons (or enclosures) of cloisonné enamel. The alternative is to apply thin threads of clay by hand to outline the design, but that is more time-consuming.

MATERIALS AND TOOLS

- Baked disk of polymer clay, about 2in (5cm) diameter and ⅛in (3mm) thick, for the mold
- ¼ block of white polymer clay
- Tracing of the design
- Ceramic tile
- Needle or engraving tool
- Talcum powder
- Silver or gold pearlescent powder
- Gloss varnish
- Clear resin and hardener
- Mixing cups for resin
- Oil paints
- Brushes
- Tapestry needle

STEP 1

Draw or trace your design onto the polymer clay blank and use a needle or engraving tool to scribe over the lines. Work over each line several times to make them well incised. Use a soft paintbrush to brush away the excess clay.

STEP 2
Brush over the engraved image with talcum powder to prevent sticking. Roll out the white polymer clay into an ⅛in (3mm) thick sheet. Press the clay onto the engraved image, pushing it down firmly so that the clay fills all the engraved lines.

STEP 3
Peel off the clay to reveal the image as a series of raised lines over the clay surface. If the lines are not clear and raised, engrave the mold more deeply and impress the clay again.

STEP 4
Lay the white clay on a tile and cut around with a knife or cutter to neaten the edges. You can now embellish areas of the design with more lines and add texture or details.

STEP 5
Brush over the clay surface with the silver or gold powder to cover it completely. Bake the piece on the tile for 30 minutes; when cool, varnish to prevent the powder from lifting when the resin is applied.

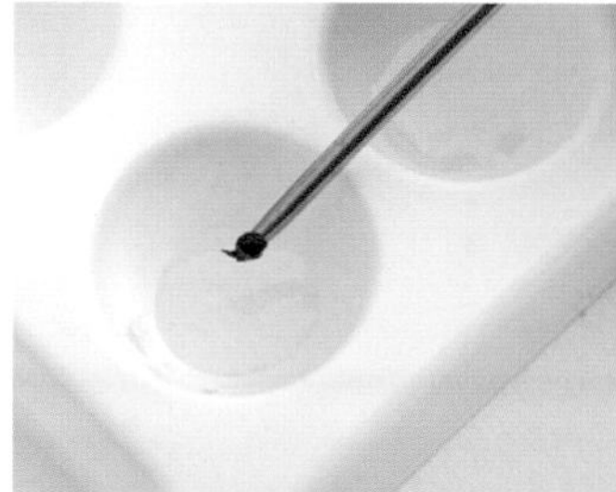

STEP 6
Mix the resin with hardener according to the instructions on the pack. Divide into several mixing cups for the different colors. Add a tiny dab of oil paint to a cup and stir in thoroughly to tint the resin.

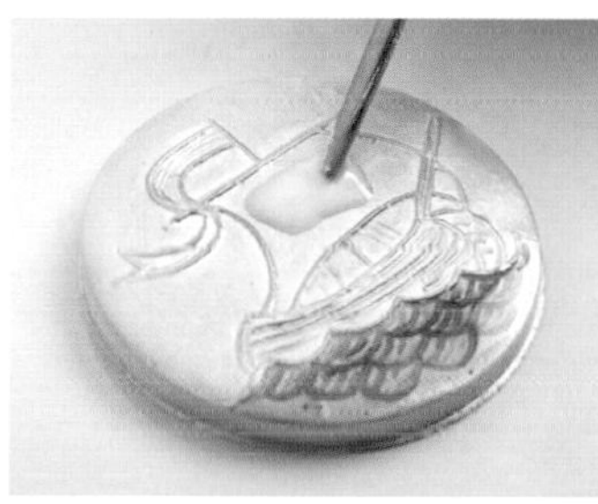

STEP 7
Use the needle to scoop up some color and apply to the first area of the design, pushing the resin into the corners and adding enough to coat the area in a continuous layer. The raised lines will prevent the color from flowing into other areas Apply colors to the different areas as required. Leave the resin to set overnight with a box covering it so that no dust lands on the surface. Some resins may take at least 24 hours.

This seascape has two different blues applied to the sea, and the sail is resin mixed with white oil paint for an opaque effect.

Try these...

Seahorse pendant and earrings This jewelry set uses stamped and textured clay with swirled areas of resin for color.

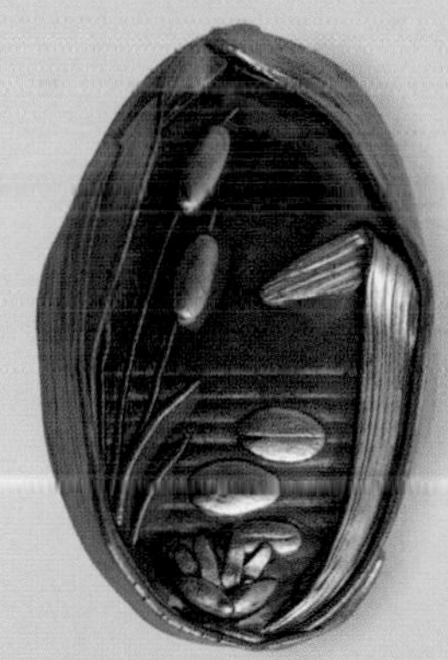

Bullrush pool A background of resin has been applied to sculpted details of polymer clay. Two colors were applied and then feathered together by drawing a needle through the resin while still wet.

41

AGGREGATE STONES

Aggregate stones are stones made up from lots of small pieces. Many semiprecious stones fall into this category: turquoise, jade, amber, lapis lazuli, and the various quartz stones. The basic technique of simulating all these stones in polymer clay is remarkably similar, and the use of a grater makes the task quick and easy. Once you have learned the basic technique, you can simply alter the recipe and the fine details in order to create a wide variety of simulated stones.

A pendant featuring, from top to bottom, faux turquoise, amber, and lapis lazuli beads.

A faux jade pendant on a leather thong embellished with copper wire.
A faux jade scarab can be used to make all sorts of jewelry, from bracelets to pins.

BASIC GRATING TECHNIQUE

You will need a grater with large and small holes. Always chill any clay mixtures before grating, because it will make grating much easier. Grate unmixed clay directly from the block—there is no need to condition the clay before you begin.

COLOR WORKSHOP

JADE = 16 parts translucent + 1 part dark green

AMETHYST = 16 parts translucent + 1 part purple

TURQUOISE BASE = 2 parts turquoise + 1 part ultramarine + 1 part white

PALE TURQUOISE = 3 parts white + 1 part turquoise + 1 part cobalt blue

ORANGE AMBER = 16 parts translucent + 16 parts zinc yellow + scrap of alizarin crimson

YELLOW AMBER = 16 parts translucent + 3 parts orange amber + 1 part zinc yellow

MATERIALS AND TOOLS

- Polymer clay: ½ block turquoise base; ¼ block pale turquoise; small piece of gold
- Grater
- Aluminum foil
- Acrylic paint: burnt umber, black
- Paintbrush

TURQUOISE

This recipe simulates Middle Eastern turquoise, with its vibrant color and distinctive network of lines.

STEP 1
Grate the turquoise base mixture using the coarse holes of the grater. Place the gratings onto a piece of foil.

STEP 2
Squeeze a generous blob each of burnt umber and black acrylic paint onto the foil and mix them roughly with a brush. Add a little water if necessary and stir the grated clay into the paint until all surfaces are covered. Allow to dry thoroughly for several hours in a warm place.

STEP 3
Coarsely grate the pale turquoise onto the dried mixture, using short strokes so that the gratings form short lengths. Grate the gold through the fine grater holes. Mix together until the new gratings are evenly distributed throughout the paint-covered clay.

Mount a mosaic of turquoise stones in a twisted rope of metal clay to make a piece of jewelry.

STEP 4
Press the mixture together into a log-shaped mass. Do not roll the log to lengthen it or the mottled effect will turn into streaks.

STEP 5
Now you can cut slices from the log to use. The paint will have made a lovely network of lines among the turquoise pieces. These slices can be used to cover polymer clay beads or cabochons.

STEP 6
You can also press the slices into a sheet and use a cutter to cut out mosaic tiles. After baking, sand and buff to a shine.

Try these...

Jade

Use jade for Eastern-inspired pendants and charms.

Jade mixture

Jade grated

Black clay grated

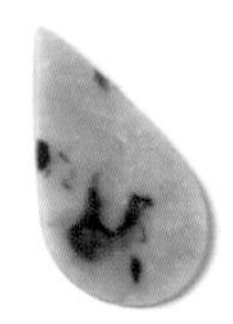
Jade and black gratings pressed together

MATERIALS AND TOOLS

- Polymer clay: ½ block jade; small piece of black
- Grater
- Sandpaper and batting

METHOD

Grate the jade mixture coarsely; grate black clay finely to make speckles. Press together and use for beads or press into a push mold to simulate carved stone. Bake the pieces. Quench in ice-cold water to make the clay more translucent. Sand and buff to a glassy shine.

Amber

Use amber to make pretty charms and large feature beads.

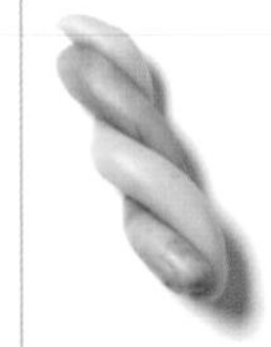
Twist clays together

Roll them until streaky

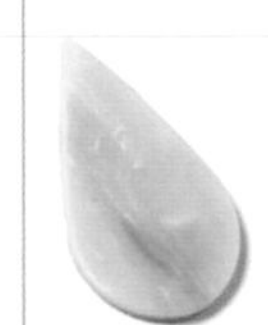
Press-molded

MATERIALS AND TOOLS

- Polymer clay: ¼ block orange amber; ¼ block yellow amber
- Sandpaper and batting

METHOD

This is a simulation of the milky amber called butter amber. Mix the two colors together until streaky. Cut pieces from the log to make beads, or press into molds for a carved amber effect. You can also use each of the color mixtures on its own to make several different colors of amber. Bake, quench in ice-cold water, then sand and buff.

Amethyst

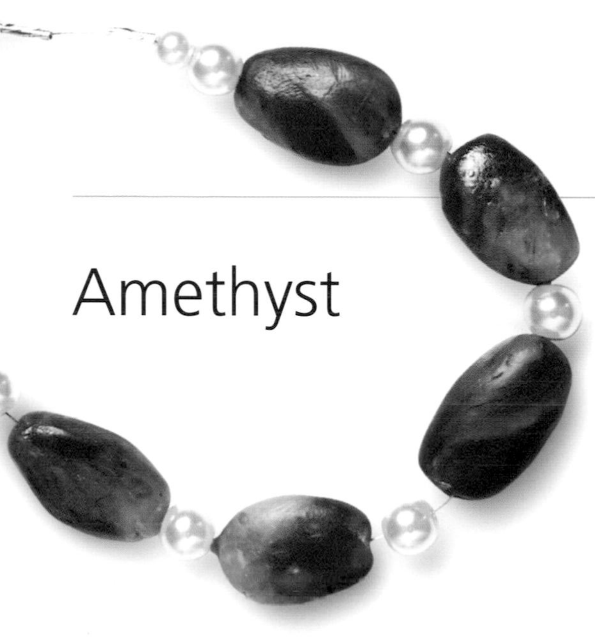

The luster on amethyst beads combines well with pearls.

Amethyst mixture

Amethyst grated

Translucent clay

Translucent grated

Clay gratings pressed into a log shape

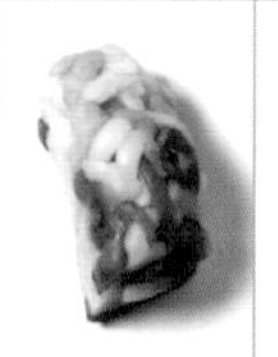

Rolled and pressed

MATERIALS AND TOOLS

- Polymer clay: ¼ block amethyst; ¼ block translucent
- Grater
- Sandpaper and batting

METHOD

Amethyst varies in opacity, from crystal clear to quartz-like mottling. Grate the amethyst mixture coarsely and press together with grated translucent clay to form a log-shaped mass. Cut pieces to make cabochons and beads. Bake, quench, then sand and buff.

Lapis Lazuli

Lapis lazuli makes wonderful jewelry. True lapis from Italy has flecks of pyrites, or fool's gold, in the stone.

Ultramarine blue clay

Ultramarine blue grated

Translucent clay

Translucent grated

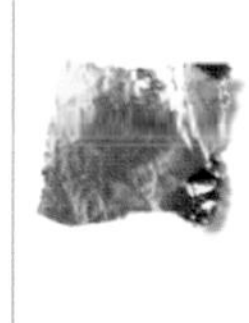

Artificial gold leaf

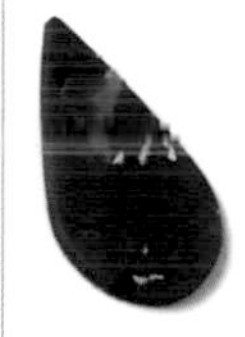

Clays and leaf rolled and pressed

MATERIALS AND TOOLS

- Polymer clay: ¼ block ultramarine blue; ¼ block translucent
- Small piece of artificial gold leaf
- Grater
- Sandpaper and batting

METHOD

This wonderful blue stone makes beautiful jewelry. Grate the ultramarine and translucent clays coarsely. Apply the leaf to the blue clay and grate through the fine holes to make specks of gold. Press the gratings all together and apply the gold flecks to the surface. Shape into beads and cabochons. Bake, then sand and buff.

42 BANDED MATERIALS

Faux onyx earrings

Many kinds of natural materials and semiprecious stones consist of layers or bands of colors. Onyx, malachite, agate, wood, and bone are all examples. Polymer clay can be used to simulate these materials extremely realistically, either by layering sheets of clay or by marbling several colors together to give a banded or finely striped surface. The marbling technique is faster and easier, and gives a realistic random quality.

Faux agate cabochon in a heart-shaped mount of metal clay embellished with a floral design.

MARBLING METHOD—ONYX AND MALACHITE

The basic technique is the same for many different semiprecious stones and other natural materials; the examples given here are for making onyx and malachite. Onyx has distinctive straight bands of brown, white, and black and makes beautiful jewelry. Malachite is a lovely deep green stone that looks gorgeous with silver.

ARTIST'S TIP

All the clay used in this section is Premo Sculpey so that exact colors can be obtained. If you use another brand, you will need to match the colors in the photographs as closely as possible.

MATERIALS AND TOOLS

- Polymer clay for onyx: ¼ block each of gold, black, raw sienna, translucent, white
- Polymer clay for malachite: ½ block sea green; ¼ block white; ¼ block black
- Roller
- Tissue blade or craft knife
- Cutter

STEP 1

Onyx Form a ⅜in (10mm) thick log each of gold and black and several 1/16in (1.5mm) thick logs of raw sienna and translucent white. Trim all logs to about 3in (75mm) long.

COLOR WORKSHOP

■ DARK MALACHITE

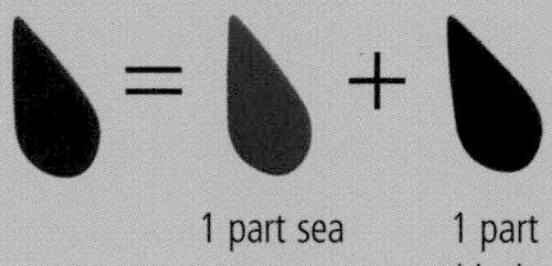

1 part sea green + 1 part black

■ LIGHT MALACHITE

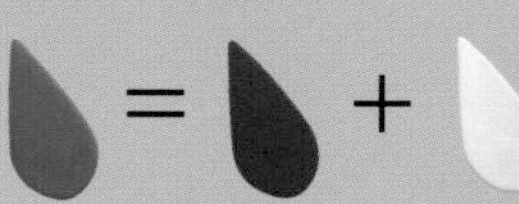

1 part sea green + 1 part white

■ TRANSLUCENT BLUE AGATE

¼ block translucent + pea-sized piece of ultramarine + pea-sized piece of white

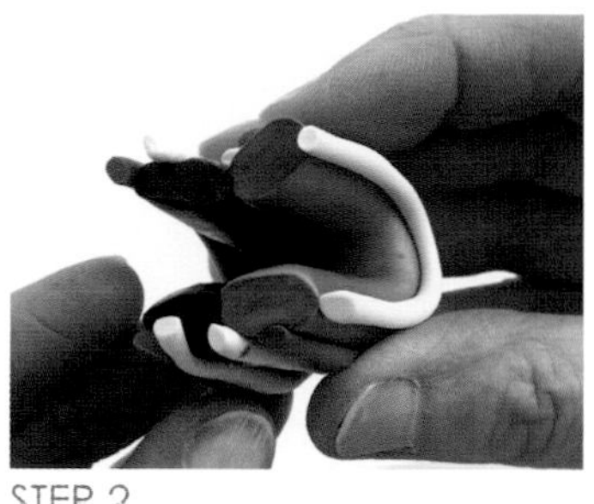

STEP 2
Press the black and gold logs together and press on the thinner logs between. Aim to have all the different colors visible on one side. Fold the log in half so that all colors are visible at least in one stripe on the outside.

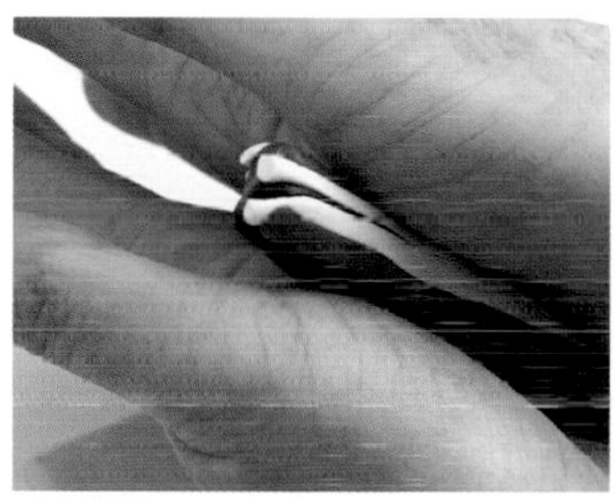

STEP 3
Roll the log in your hands to lengthen and thin it, then fold in half again, keeping all the stripes parallel. Continue to marble the log by folding and rolling until the narrower lines are very fine and the black bands are about ⅛in (3mm) wide.

STEP 4
Cut lengths from the log and flatten these slightly with your finger. Either pass through a pasta machine on a medium setting in the direction of the lines, or roll flat with a roller.

STEP 5
The sheet can now be used to cover cabochons, rolled onto beads, or cut out with cutters. After baking, sand, buff, and polish the stones for maximum depth and shine. Alternatively, varnish with gloss varnish. Stones that contain translucent clay can be plunged into cold water straight from the oven to enhance the translucency.

Malachite Marble together logs of sea green, dark malachite, and light malachite. Marble until the streaks are very fine and then roll flat. This malachite cabochon is framed with a twisted rope mount.

A necklace made from slices of faux agate.

LAYERING METHOD—AGATE

Agate is a semi-translucent stone that occurs in nodules in rocks. It comes in many different colors; this recipe is for blue agate, but you can vary the colors to make brown, cream, flame, or gray agates. This recipe shows how to make agate slices.

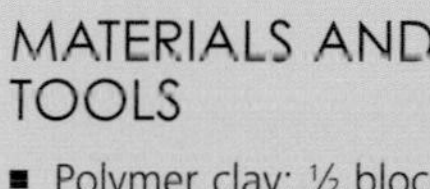

MATERIALS AND TOOLS

- Polymer clay: ½ block white, ½ block translucent, small piece of ultramarine
- Roller
- Table knife

STEP 1
Roll out ¹⁄₁₆in (1.5mm) thick sheets of translucent blue agate, translucent, and white and cut into rough 3in (75mm) squares. Starting with white, make a stack, rolling some of the sheets thinner and stacking some in pairs to vary the thickness of the layers.

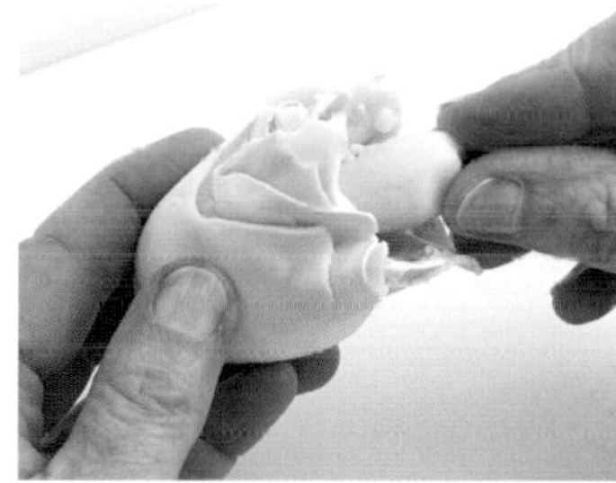

STEP 2
Place the end of a small roller or knife handle into the center of the stack and draw up the sheets around it to make a cup. Remove the roller and insert a ½in (13mm) log of translucent into the hole.

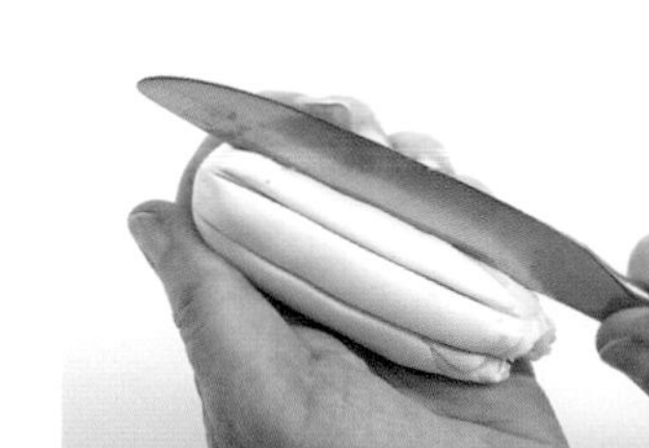

STEP 3
Press the back of the knife around the log to indent the sides deeply. Pull to reduce the log a little (see page 77). Slice and bake, then plunge into cold water to enhance the translucency. Sand and buff.

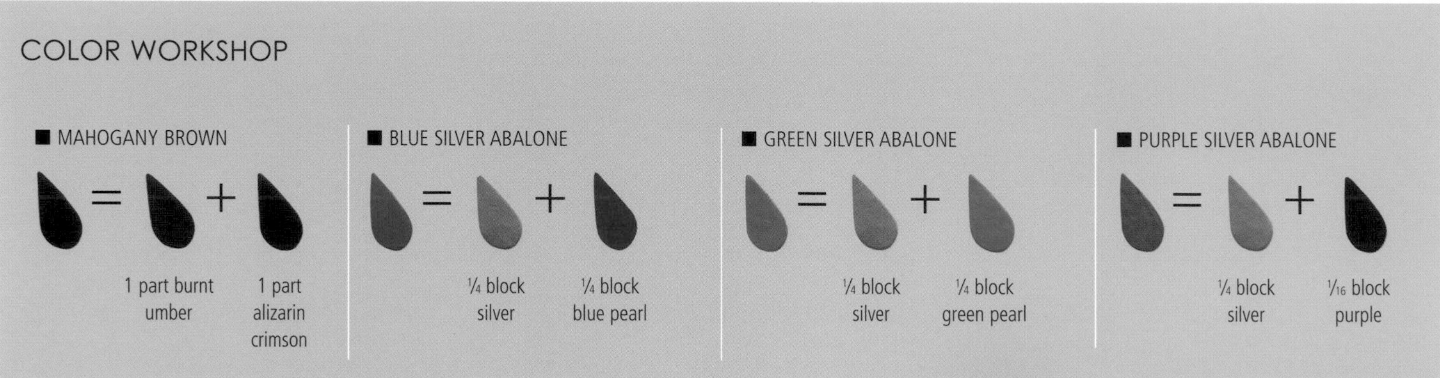

WOOD

Polymer clay makes extremely realistic wood that can be used for simulated wood jewelry and artifacts or for dollhouse miniatures. To make sheets of wood-grain clay, follow the marbling method on pages 110–111, using the colors in the recipes below. Loops in the grain from the last few folds of the log should be rolled into the sheet and not discarded; they add to the realism.

MAHOGANY
¼ block each of burnt umber, mahogany brown, black, and gold.

TEAK
¼ block each of raw sienna, ocher, and gold; 1/16 block burnt umber.

NEW PINE
¼ block ecru; 1/16 block each of gold and translucent.

OAK
¼ block each of raw sienna, ocher, and burnt umber.

OLD PINE
¼ block each of ecru and ocher; 1/16 block each of white and burnt umber.

MATERIALS AND TOOLS

- Polymer clay (see individual recipes)
- Roller
- Tissue blade or craft knife

Miniature cuckoo clock and artist's paintbox and palette in faux wood.

These beads were made in faux new pine clay and then painted as matrioshka dolls. Gloss varnish completes them.

Use diamond-shaped cutters to cut pieces of faux wood and arrange them into marquetry designs.

A pendant made from pale abalone in a silver clay mount. Pale abalone is made by adding 2 parts pearl clay to 1 part of each silver mixture.

ABALONE

Mother-of-pearl is the beautiful iridescent lining of certain types of shell; abalone and paua shell are deeper colored varieties.

MATERIALS AND TOOLS

- Polymer clay: 1 block silver; ¼ block each of blue pearl and green pearl; ¹⁄₁₆ block purple
- Roller
- Black artist's pastel
- Paintbrush
- Ripple blade

STEP 1

Roll out ¹⁄₁₆in (1.5mm) sheets of blue silver, green silver, and purple silver abalone mixtures and trim into 3in (75mm) squares. Brush each square thickly with black pastel powder.

STEP 2

Cut the sheets into quarters and stack randomly into a block. Add a final unpowdered sheet to the top of the stack and squeeze the block all over firmly to compress and thin the layers a little.

STEP 3

Stand the block on one end and curve it slightly, pressing it down onto the tile to secure it. Use a ripple blade to cut slices from the side that was the top. Vary the angle of the slices to make different patterns. Roll the slices flat to make faux abalone sheets. Bake, then sand and buff.

Antiqued faux ivory pendant.

BONE AND IVORY

These two materials can look very similar, although the streaks in ivory are often barely discernible. This mixture looks particularly good pressed into molds to simulate carved bone or ivory. Aging bone and ivory and other simulated materials is simply done with dark brown acrylic paint. This works best on pieces that have been molded or carved and have plenty of crevices or detail in the surface.

MATERIALS AND TOOLS

- Polymer clay: ¼ block translucent white; ⅛ block white; ⅛ block ecru
- Ceramic tile
- Roller
- Tissue blade
- Alcohol
- Brown acrylic paint and paintbrush
- Sandpaper

STEP 1

Follow the marbling method on pages 110–111, marbling the clays together until the streaks are very fine. Roll flat and use as required. Sand, buff, and polish to give a rich patina.

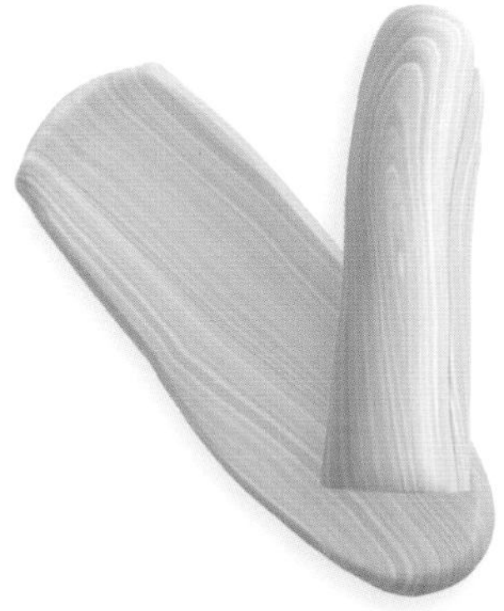

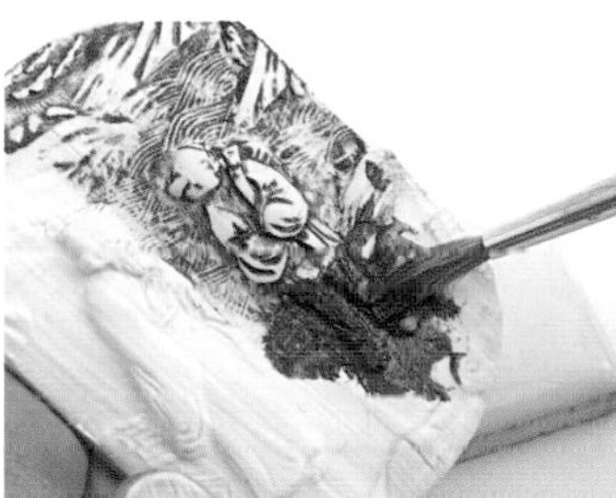

STEP 2

Antiquing Brush the piece with alcohol to degrease and then brush the paint all over the surface, working it into the crevices.

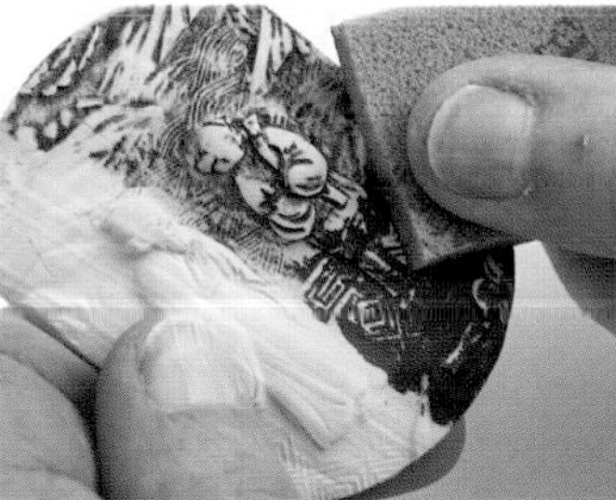

STEP 3

Allow to dry, then sand to remove paint from the raised areas.

Each bead in this necklace has a different inclusion.

43 INCLUSIONS

Polymer clay can be mixed with other materials to make lots of beautiful effects. Translucent clay works best because the inclusions will be visible within the clay body; sanding and buffing or varnishing will add to the translucency. Opaque clays work well with inclusions for simulating miniature ceramics or textured food. Inclusions can also be mixed into liquid clay. The quantity of inclusion material needed will vary, depending on the softness of the clay and the effect required.

Miniature loaf of bread textured with cornmeal and brushed with brown pastel powder.

CHOOSING MATERIALS

- **Inclusions for beads and jewelry:** embossing powders; colored sand; glitter; finely chopped fibers; dried herbs and flowers; ground spices; metallic and pearlescent powders; metal leaf; grated baked polymer clay.
- **Inclusions for miniature food:** cornmeal; ground rice; semolina; poppy seeds for currants; sesame seeds for almonds.
- **Inclusions for miniature ceramics:** ground spices; tea bag dust.
- **Materials to avoid:** anything that might decay, such as fresh flowers and leaves; hygroscopic materials, such as salt and sugar, that will become sticky in time.

Tea bag dust added to a miniature ceramic pot.

ADDING INCLUSIONS

This method is the easiest way to add glitter or other types of inclusions to polymer clay. The amount given is for a sample; you may need to increase quantities, depending on the project.

MATERIALS AND TOOLS

- Polymer clay: ¼ block translucent
- Glitter or other material for inclusion
- Plate
- Pasta machine (much faster) or a roller
- Craft knife

STEP 1
Roll out the clay on a medium setting on the pasta machine (or roll by hand with a roller). Pour about one teaspoon of glitter onto a plate and spread it out. Press one side of the sheet of clay onto the glitter until the clay is well coated.

STEP 2
Fold the sheet in half with the glitter to the inside and pass through the pasta machine again. Fold and roll several times, then press the sheet onto the glitter again. Continue in this way until the glitter within the clay body looks dense and well dispersed.

STEP 3
The sheet can now be used as required. Here, it has been formed into a log and cut into lengths to make beads.

STEP 4
After baking (right-hand swatch), the translucent clay will become more translucent and the inclusions will show up distinctly in the body of the clay. Buffing and polishing will enhance this effect.

MOKUMÉ GANÉ

This method originally simulated a Japanese metalwork technique, but polymer clay has made the results much more exciting by using artificial leaf and translucent clay. Gold leaf is shown here, but you could use silver leaf and tint the translucent clay with color for a more colorful effect.

MATERIALS AND TOOLS

- Polymer clay: 1 block translucent
- 6in (15cm) square sheet of artificial gold leaf
- Ceramic tile
- Pencil
- Tissue blade
- Craft knife

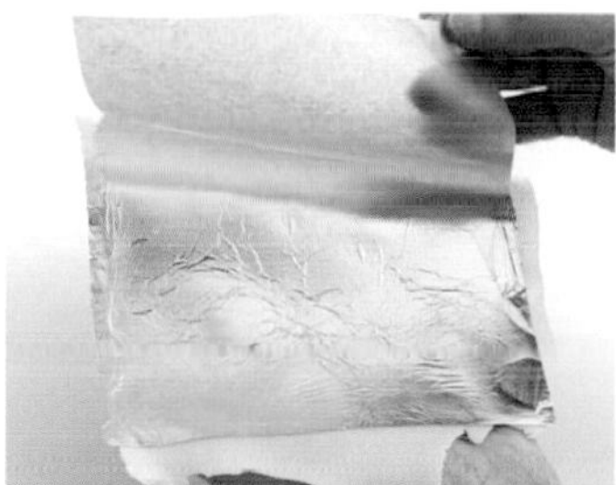

STEP 1

Roll out the translucent clay as thinly as possible—1/32in (1mm) thick or less. Lay the clay sheet on the sheet of leaf. (This is much easier than trying to lay the leaf onto the clay sheet.) Flip over the two sheets together and peel off the backing paper from the leaf. Trim the excess clay.

STEP 2

Cut the sheet in half and stack the two halves, then cut again and repeat until the stack is eight layers deep and makes a 3 x 1½in (75 x 38mm) block. Cover the block with a final thin sheet of translucent clay.

STEP 3

Push deep holes all over the block with a blunt tool, pushing about two-thirds of the way through the block. Fill each hole with a ball of translucent clay. Flip the block over and press it down on a tile so that it sticks firmly. Press down with your fingers between where you can feel the balls of clay below. This will accentuate the hilly surface.

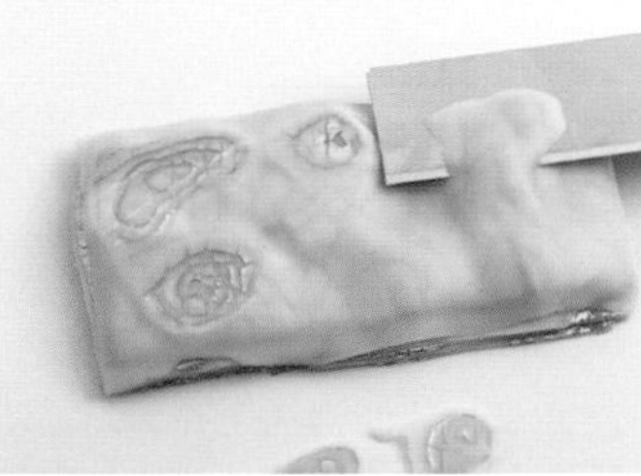

STEP 4

Use a tissue blade to cut thin slices from the hills of the block. Wonderful irregular patterns of gold leaf will be revealed. Cut very thin slices at random from the top surface. Do not attempt to cut right across the block; small pieces are easiest.

STEP 5

Apply slices all over a base layer of clay, filling in gaps between with smaller slices and pressing them all down firmly to make a continuous surface. Cut into shapes as required; bake and quench in cold water for maximum transparency. Sand and buff the surface, then apply a coat of varnish to prevent any exposed leaf from tarnishing.

A bracelet made from squares of mokume gane framed in twisted rope mounts.

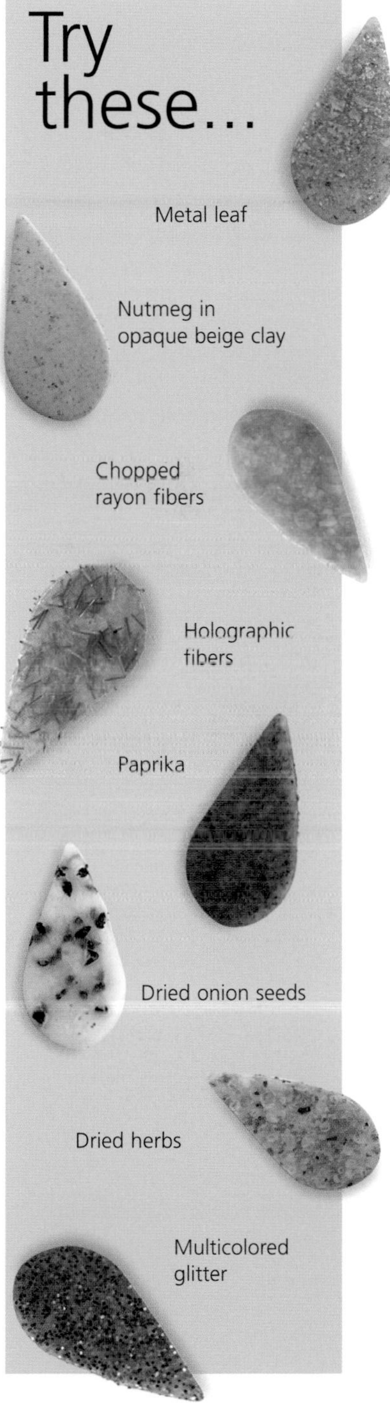

44 TRADITIONAL MOSAIC

Polymer clay is an ideal material for making mosaics of all kinds. Ceramic and tile effects can be effectively simulated, while the huge range of mixable colors gives a wonderful palette. Texture and surface effects can add to the variety. Roman and Byzantine mosaics are some of the most famous and the technique shown here simulates these. Polymer clay is rolled into sheets that are cut into small squares, called tesserae, and baked. These are then glued onto a support to form the mosaic. While polymer clay is very durable, it is not suitable for use outside because it can deteriorate in frost and ultraviolet light over time, so the mosaics shown here are for indoor use only.

MATERIALS AND TOOLS

- Polymer clay in the colors required
- Pasta machine or roller and rolling strips
- Graph paper
- Darning needle
- Ceramic tile
- Tissue blade
- Talcum powder or cornstarch

MAKING TESSERAE

Baked polymer clay is softer to cut than traditional mosaic materials, such as glass, stone, and ceramic tile, so making mosaics from polymer clay is much easier on the hands than the traditional methods. To ensure even mosaics, roll out the different clay colors to the same setting on the pasta machine, or using the same thickness rolling strips.

STEP 1
Roll out a sheet of clay about 1/12in (2mm) thick and place on a tile. Lay a sheet of graph paper over the clay sheet.

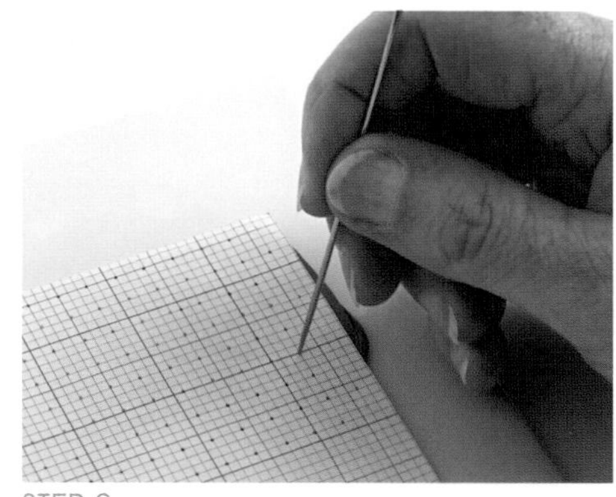

STEP 2
Use a needle to prick a regular pattern of squares through the graph paper into the clay below—1/4in (6mm) squares are an ideal size for traditional mosaic.

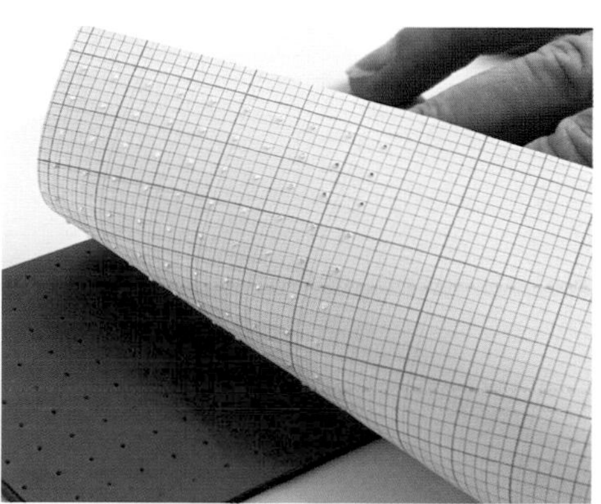

STEP 3
Once you have pricked over a sheet of graph paper, you can simply press the paper onto the next clay sheet and the prickings will mark the grid onto the clay.

STEP 5
Once the cuts are all made in one direction, repeat for the other direction. A little talc or cornstarch on the clay surface or on the blade will prevent sticking. Do not attempt to move the clay sheet. Remove waste clay and incomplete tesserae from around the edges.

STEP 4
Use a tissue blade to cut along the lines of the grid. Press the blade in vertically, then rock it back and forth to widen each cut.

STEP 6
Bake the clay sheet on the tile. When cool, remove it from the tile and snap the sheet along the cut lines to separate the tesserae.

Try these...

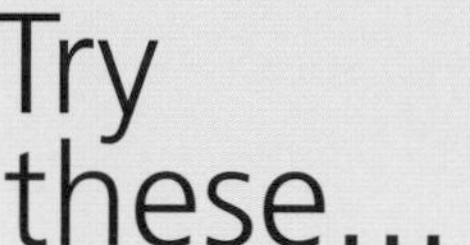

Stone-effect tesserae Use a stone-effect polymer clay.

Pearlescent tesserae Use pearl clay.

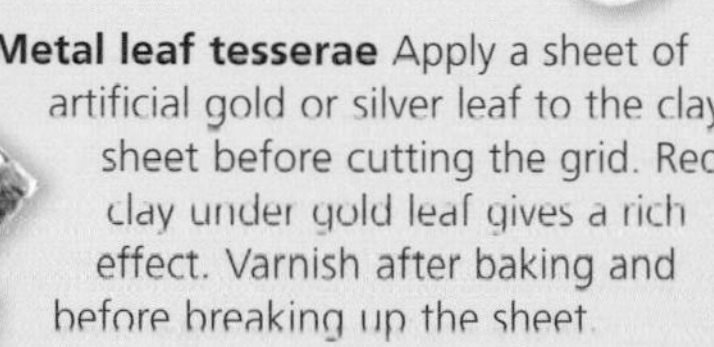

Round tesserae Use a ¼in (6mm) round cutter—good for spot details in a mosaic.

Metal leaf tesserae Apply a sheet of artificial gold or silver leaf to the clay sheet before cutting the grid. Red clay under gold leaf gives a rich effect. Varnish after baking and before breaking up the sheet.

Surface effects Surface treatments give tesserae unusual effects: pearlescent, crackled, inked, and so on.

Cane tesserae Small slices of millefiori cane can be used as accents in a mosaic.

FRUIT TREE COASTER MOSAIC

Mosaic can be applied to all kinds of supports, from flowerpots, picture frames, and wooden boxes to bathroom backsplashes, jewelry, and even furniture. The example given here is for a small coaster using a circle of baked polymer clay as the support. The number of tesserae required is only a rough guide.

MATERIALS AND TOOLS

- Baked circle of polymer clay in a neutral color, about ⅛in (3mm) thick and 3½in (9cm) diameter
- Tesserae: ¼in (6mm) squares in eight different colors—80 navy blue, 15 dark brown, 20 leaf green, 15 light leaf green, 10 brick red, 10 orange, 10 white, 10 golden yellow
- ¼ block of polymer clay in navy blue
- Design traced onto tracing paper and a pencil
- Craft knife
- PVA glue
- Glue spreader
- Tile grout
- Black acrylic paint
- Cloth and silicone polish

STEP 1
Transfer the design onto the coaster of baked polymer clay. Do this by scribbling across the back of the tracing paper design with a pencil. Place the design scribble-side down onto the clay. Firmly draw over the top of the design so that some of the graphite beneath transfers onto the surface of the clay. Draw over the transferred design directly on the clay to make it clearer if necessary.

STEP 2
Spread the area of the fruit with glue and press the brick red tesserae onto the design, following the curve of the fruit. Leave a slight space between the tesserae.

STEP 3
Cut the last few tesserae at each end to fit around the curve.

STEP 4
Cut smaller pieces to fit between the squares as necessary.

TEMPLATE

Enlarge on a photocopier by 180%.

STEP 5

Continue applying glue and adding tesserae. It is best to complete the design first before doing the background. When the fruit and leaves are finished, start on the background. Following the lines of the design, work toward the edge of the coaster. This will give a lively background with curved lines of squares that mirror the design. Cut the tiles to fit at the edge of the coaster.

STEP 7

Add a little black paint to some tile grout to make a neutral gray. Use a glue spreader to press the grout into the spaces between the tesserae.

STEP 8

Wipe off the excess grout with a damp cloth. Allow to dry overnight. Polish with silicone polish for a sheen.

STEP 6

Cut a strip of navy blue clay to wrap around the outside of the coaster; the top edge should be level with the top of the mosaic. This will help to contain the grout. Apply the strip, using PVA glue to help it bond, then bake.

Embellish a wooden key holder with a polymer clay mosaic. The garden of flowers is formed from floral milletiori cane slices, and the background from plain mosaic pieces.

This wooden tray has a traditional bunch of grapes mosaic applied to the central part. The raised rim is gilded with gilding wax to finish it off.

45

MICROMOSAIC

True micromosaic consists of pictures made of minute chips of colored semiprecious stone set into a precious metal surround. First developed to an exquisite level of craftsmanship during the Roman Empire, micromosaics enjoyed a revival in 18th- and 19th-century Rome. The fantastically detailed pictures were made into all kinds of jewelry and used to embellish small boxes. Polymer clay gives us the opportunity to simulate this delightful art form in a fraction of the time that it would take to create the original kind.

A delightful fairytale castle micromosaic in a silver clay mount with a hanging loop to form a pendant.

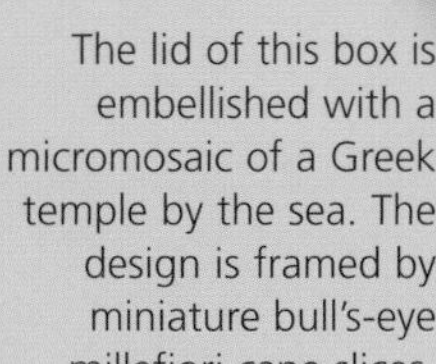

The lid of this box is embellished with a micromosaic of a Greek temple by the sea. The design is framed by miniature bull's-eye millefiori cane slices.

DOVE OF PEACE MOSAIC

Working soft on soft, as in appliqué (see pages 46–47), makes micromosaic quick and easy to do. You can vary the shapes of the tiny tesserae between squares, rectangles, and longer strips, according to the requirements of the design.

MATERIALS AND TOOLS

- Polymer clay: walnut-size pieces in beige (ecru), white, gold; tiny amounts of leaf green, yellow, black
- Pasta machine or roller and rolling strips
- Ceramic tile
- Circle cutter: 1¼in (30mm) diameter
- Traced design
- Darning needle
- Tissue blade
- Craft knife with a curved blade

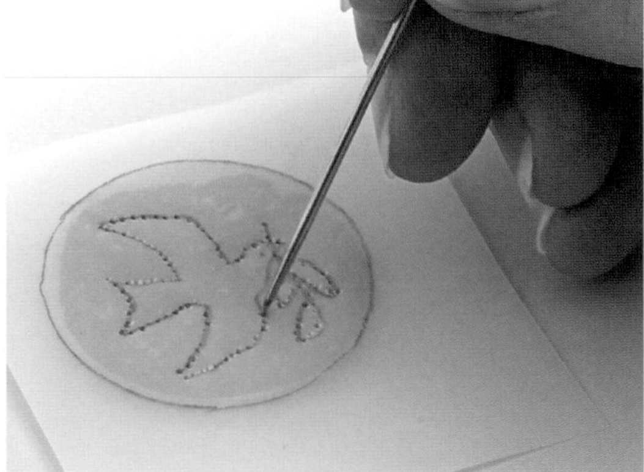

STEP 1

Roll the beige clay into a 1/16in (1.5mm) thick sheet and lay it on a tile. Cut out a circle with the cutter and remove the waste clay. Do not attempt to move the mosaic from the tile until after baking. Lay the tracing onto the clay and use a needle to prick the design onto the clay below.

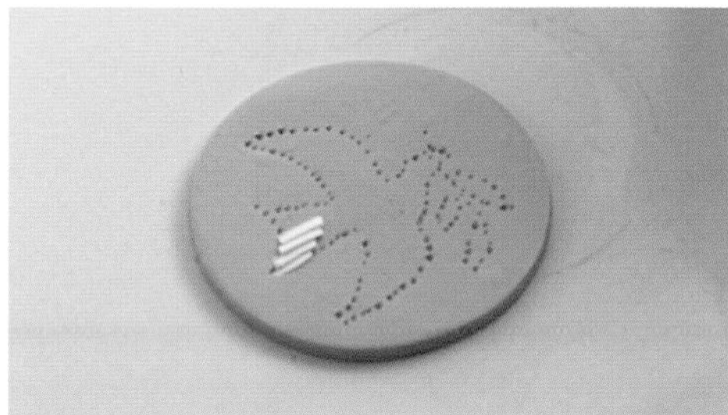

STEP 2

Roll out the colored clays into 1/32in (1mm) thick sheets and lay ready to use. Cut an 1/8in (3mm) wide strip from the white clay sheet and lay it at an angle so that you can cut slices from it easily with a knife. Using the appliqué technique, cut and apply thin slices from the white strip to the bird's tail, following the pricked design to suggest overlapping feathers.

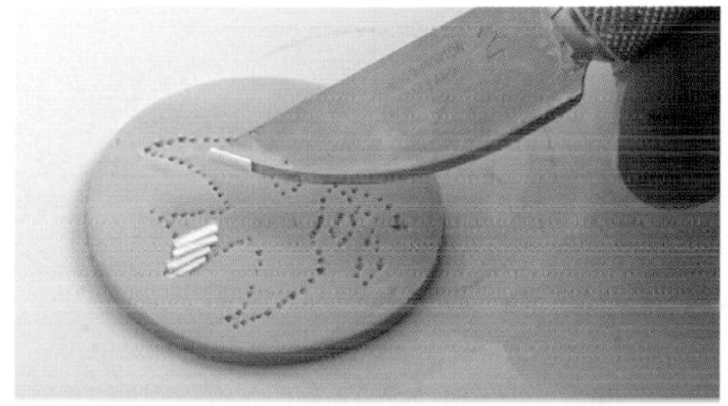

STEP 3

Each slice should be cut so that when you lift it on the knife, the end just protrudes from the tip of the knife. This means that you can tell where to place it when you turn the knife over and apply the slice. Use these longer slices for the tail and wing feathers.

STEP 4

Cut a narrower strip of white to make smaller slices to use for the body and head, angling the feathers along the bird's body.

STEP 5

Cut a 1/32in (1mm) wide strip of black and apply tiny squares for the eye and beak. Cut a 1/32in (1mm) wide strip of green for the olive branch and cut and apply tiny squares, aligning them along the line of the leaves and branch. Highlight the leaves with a few squares of yellow.

TEMPLATE

The template is shown actual size.

STEP 6

Cut a 1/32in (1mm) wide strip of gold and apply squares to the background, working from around the bird outward to the edge of the piece. Finish with a row around the perimeter of the circle.

STEP 7

Pat lightly over the mosaic surface with a fingertip to make sure that all the squares are attached. Bake the mosaic on the tile. The piece can now be mounted in a bezel to make jewelry or used as the top of a box.

The dove was a favorite theme in ancient Rome. The mosaic is framed with a double twisted rope mount to form a miniaure tray.

46 PIETRE DURE MOSAIC

Pietre dure means "hard stones" and is the Italian term for a beautiful type of intarsia mosaic that flourished in Florence from the 16th century onward. Pieces of colored semiprecious stone were cut into shapes and made into elaborate pictures in a similar way to the craft of marquetry in woodworking. The results are very beautiful and can be used for wall panels, tabletops, and jewelry of exquisite quality—the pictures are barely discernible from high-quality oil paintings, but have a magical brilliance and permanence.

This floral design would make an attractive lid for a trinket box. You could use any motif you wish, from cherries to butterflies.

FLORAL MOSAIC

This simplified technique involves fitting together marbled and blended sheets of polymer clay in sections to create a picture. Small cutters are useful, but you can cut out the shapes freehand with a knife if you have a steady hand.

MATERIALS AND TOOLS

- Polymer clay: small quantities in black, white, violet, golden yellow, leaf green
- Pasta machine or roller and rolling strips
- Ceramic tile
- Tissue blade
- Tracing paper and design
- Darning needle and blunt tapestry needle
- Craft knife with a curved blade
- Talcum powder or cornstarch
- 3/8in (10mm) long diamond cutter
- Sandpaper and buffing materials

TEMPLATE

Enlarge on a photocopier by 170%.

STEP 1

Roll out a 1/12in (2mm) thick sheet of black clay. Keep to this thickness throughout the project. Lay the sheet on the tile and cut out a 2¾ x 1¾in (70 x 45mm) rectangle. Remove the waste clay. Do not move the piece until after baking. Lay on the traced design and score along the lines lightly with a darning needle to impress the design into the clay below.

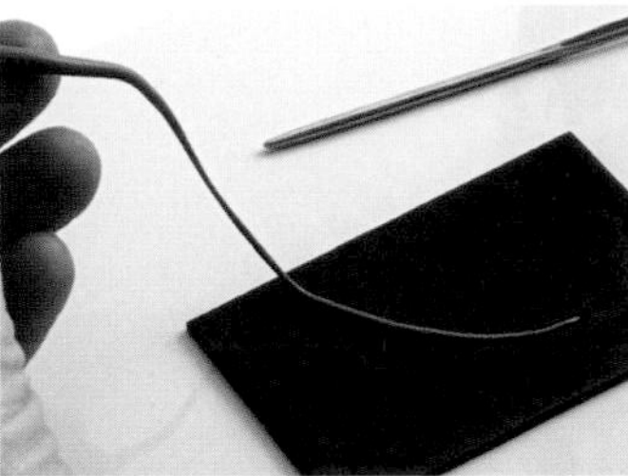

STEP 2

Mark along the line of the stalk with a tapestry needle to indent a line about 1/16in (1.5mm) deep in the clay surface. Roll out or extrude a 1/32in (1mm) thick thread of leaf green clay and lay it into the indented line for the stalk. Smooth over with a finger.

STEP 3

Make a strip blend using leaf green and yellow clays (see page 27) and roll into a sheet the same thickness as before. Cut at an angle across the sheet and reverse one side to make a central rib for the leaves.

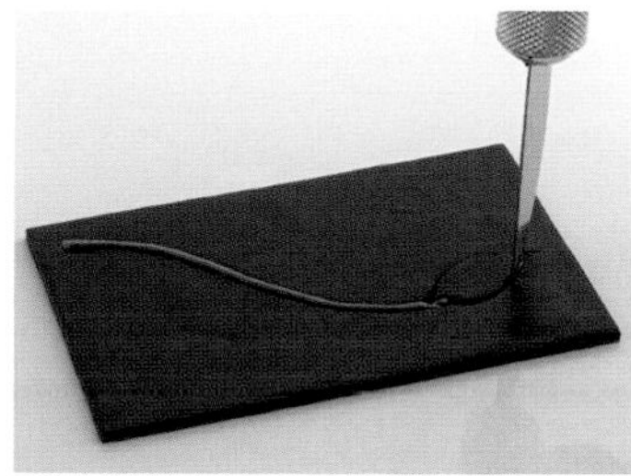

STEP 4
Cut out a leaf shape at the end of the stalk and carefully remove it from the background. You can use a needle to ease it out. Take care not to damage the surrounding clay.

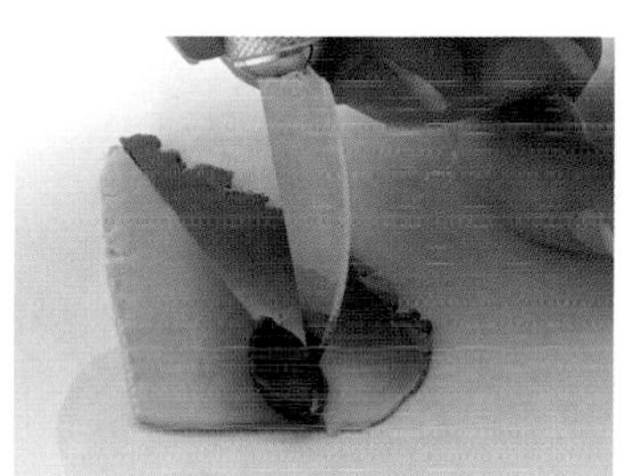

STEP 5
Spread a little talc over the blended sheet and lay the black cutout leaf on top as a pattern to cut out a green leaf shape, centered down the midrib.

STEP 6
Carefully insert the leaf into the cutout shape in the background and press it down lightly to fit. Repeat for the other two leaves.

STEP 7
Make a strip blend of white and violet. Use the diamond cutter to cut out the flower bud, partly cutting through the end leaf. Carefully remove the piece with the point of a needle.

STEP 8
Use the cutter to cut out the bud from the white/violet blend, positioning it across the strip, and insert this piece into the space in the background as before.

STEP 9
Repeat with the diamond cutter to cut out the second bud and the flower petals. Remove each piece from the background and replace with the white/violet cutout before cutting the next piece each time.

STEP 10
Finally, make a hole in the center of the flower and insert a small length of yellow clay.

STEP 11
Lay a piece of tracing paper over the clay surface and rub gently over it with a finger to smooth and consolidate all the clay pieces. Bake on the tile. When cool, sand and buff the surface until it is smooth and shiny.

Try these...

Seaside town Vary the colors of the building to simulate light and shade, and use blends and marbled clay for the setting.

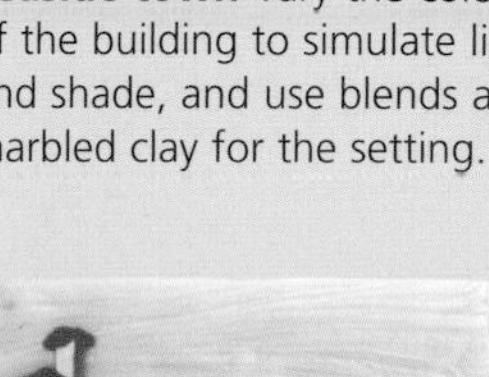

Landscape Use hand-marbled clay to make a wonderful landscape with swirling skies and lakes, mottled trees, and distant misty mountains.

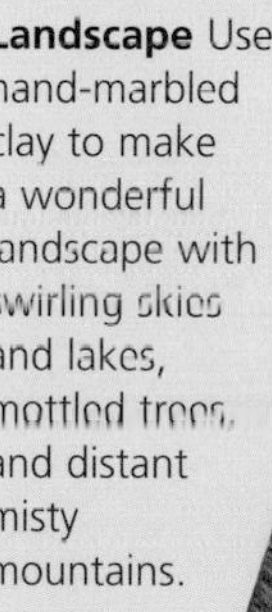

Seascape Vary the types of hand-marbled clay to create a still sea and cloudy sky. Use marbled clay with visible stripes to simulate the wooden planks of the boat.

CHAPTER 5:
SCULPTING

Polymer clay was originally created for a doll maker, and this chapter shows that sculpting techniques are some of the most exciting in the polymer clay repertoire. Simple sculpted animals are easy for beginners to master, while the increasingly advanced techniques that follow include sculpting the human face and using armatures.

47 ANIMALS

Charming small animal models are easy to sculpt with polymer clay, and even children and beginners can adapt the basic techniques to make their own designs. The natural rounded forms of simple clay shapes lend themselves perfectly to making little animals of all kinds. For sculpting more complex animals, see pages 136–137.

Vary the eyes to suit the animal. Oval eyes are ideal for a cat model.

MATERIALS AND TOOLS

- Polymer clay in various colors
- Ceramic tile
- Craft knife
- Sculpting tools, such as a tapestry needle and cone-shaped tool
- Gloss varnish and brush

BASIC FEATURES

When making a pair of anything, such as eyes, ears, paws, and so on, form a log of clay and cut equal lengths so that they are the same size.

STEP 1

Ears Form a log of clay about the same thickness as the ears you need to make. Cut two equal lengths of clay and shape into balls and then teardrops.

STEP 2

Press the teardrops onto the animal's head in the appropriate place. Push a hole in the base of each ear for an ear hole. This also attaches the ear to the head more firmly. You can alter the basic ear shape by starting with a disk or ball of clay instead of a teardrop.

STEP 3

Eyes Make two holes with the cone-shaped tool in the head, deep enough to take the eyeballs. The dried-up refill for a ballpoint pen makes a useful cone-shaped tool for eye sockets. This will automatically indent the clay surrounding it as well and add facial expression.

STEP 4

Make two equal-sized balls of black clay and press them into the eye sockets. After baking, varnish the eyes with gloss varnish to make them twinkle.

STEP 5
Feet and paws Form teardrops of equal size and press down onto the work surface to flatten them, with the pointed end toward the back. Make several cuts with your knife lengthwise into the front of the foot for toes. Remove the feet from the work surface and splay out the toes or curl into a claw as required.

STEP 6
Wings Form two teardrops from equal-sized balls of clay. Flatten each into a wing shape and press onto the side of the bird.

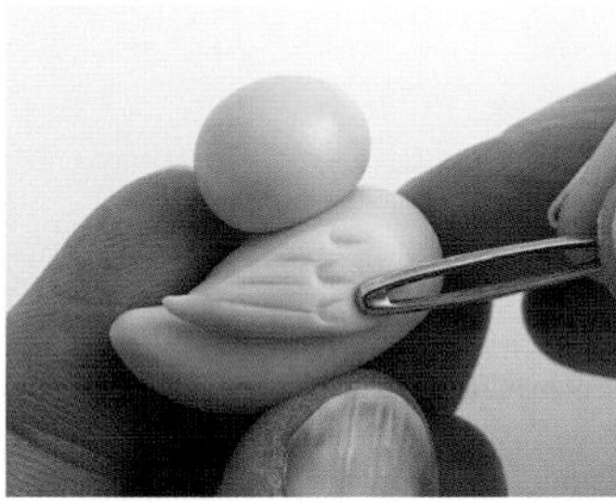

STEP 7
Use the eye of a large needle to mark feathers on the wing. The pressure will help secure the wing to the body.

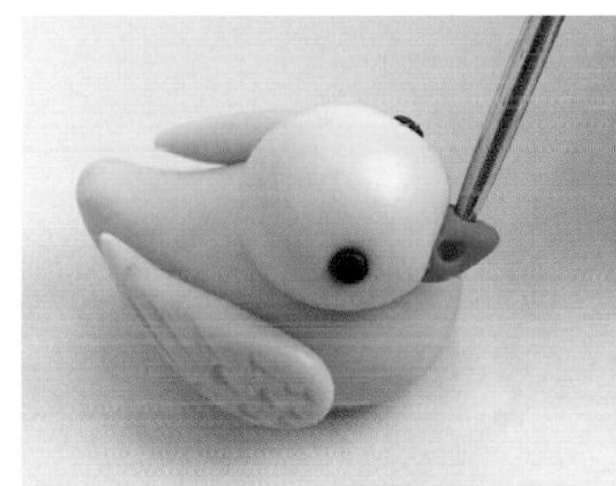

STEP 8
Beak Form a cone of clay and press onto the bird's face. Make two holes with a tapestry needle for nostrils, pushing the beak toward the head to anchor it in place.

BUILDING THE MODEL

Animals that stand or sit on their back legs make attractive models. The secret is to work from the base upward.

STEP 1
Make four feet from ¼in (6mm) balls of brick red clay. Press two onto the tile, a little apart for the squirrel's feet, and set the other two aside for the front paws. Form a ¾in (20mm) ball of brick red and press a flattened disk of white onto it. Roll together into an oval and press onto the feet with the white at the front for the body.

STEP 2
Press a ½in (13mm) ball of brick red on top of the body for the head. Apply ears made from two ⅛in (3mm) balls of brick red shaped into teardrops. Make eye sockets and fill with small balls of black. Add a thin slice of black for the nose.

STEP 3
Marble white and brick red clay together and roll a 1¼in (32mm) long tapered log. Press onto the back of the body and head for the tail, curving it over at the top. Curve the toes of the front paws and press each paw onto the front of the body. Make small holes below each eye to add expression. Bake the squirrel on the tile and varnish the eyes.

48 FACES

Sculpting faces in polymer clay is a relatively challenging technique, but achievable with practice and the results are satisfying and inspiring. The technique shown here is for sculpting a relief face for jewelry or decorative pieces, but is identical to sculpting faces for dolls and figurines. Young and beautiful faces are harder to sculpt than character faces, so do not worry if your first attempts look like wizened goblins—just make goblin jewelry!

This Green Man relief face has been gilded with bronze powder rather than painted.

A pearlescent scarf frames the face and adds movement to the piece.

ARTIST'S TIPS

- Use pictures of faces as reference when sculpting so that you can keep the proportions of the face accurate.
- Once you have sculpted and baked a face you are pleased with, make a mold of it so that you can create more faces with ease.
- Commercial face molds are available from polymer clay suppliers if you find this technique too challenging.

SCULPTING THE FACE

The measurements are for sculpting a face 1¼in (32mm) high. You can adjust the measurements to make faces of all sizes when you become more confident.

MATERIALS AND TOOLS

- Firm polymer clay in a flesh tone
- Ceramic tile
- Sculpting tools, such as a pencil, tapestry needle, darning needle, ball-ended tool, and craft knife

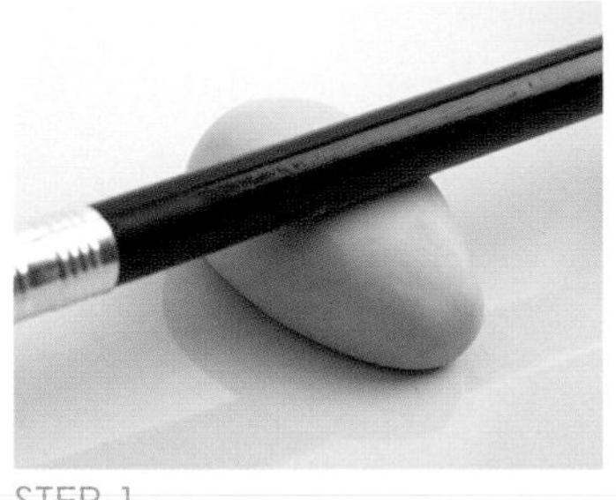

STEP 1

Form a 1in (25mm) ball of clay into an egg shape. Press down onto the tile. Use the side of a round pencil or similar tool to indent the front of the face horizontally across the center of the egg.

STEP 2

Form a 3/16in (5mm) ball of clay into a teardrop and press onto the center of the face for the nose, with the pointed end upward. Smooth the sides of the nose outward with a sculpting tool to eliminate the join. Pinch the nose into a pleasing shape, checking the profile as well.

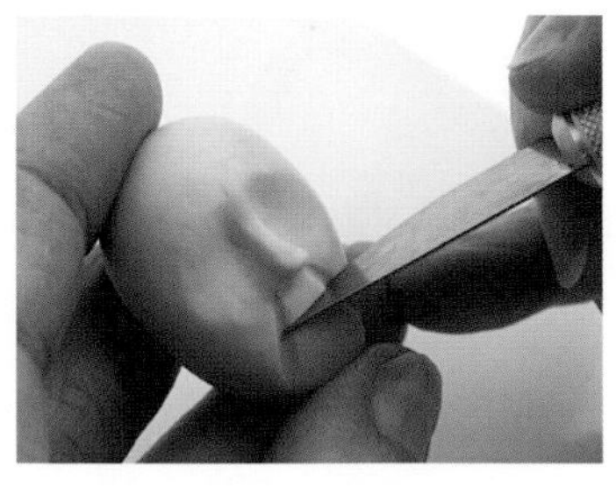

STEP 3

Make grooves with a tapestry needle running from the bottom of the nose down to the chin, angled outward. Make a cut with your knife about ⅛in (3mm) from the bottom of the nose for the mouth.

Little touches, like a stray strand of hair, can bring a sculpted face to life.

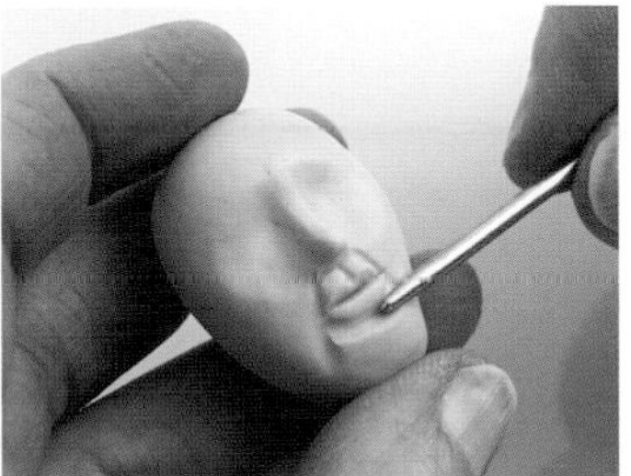

STEP 4

Indent the center of the upper lip with a needle and stroke upward from the mouth cut to make the upper lip. Indent just below the mouth cut to create the lower lip, and smooth around the mouth to make it a pleasing shape.

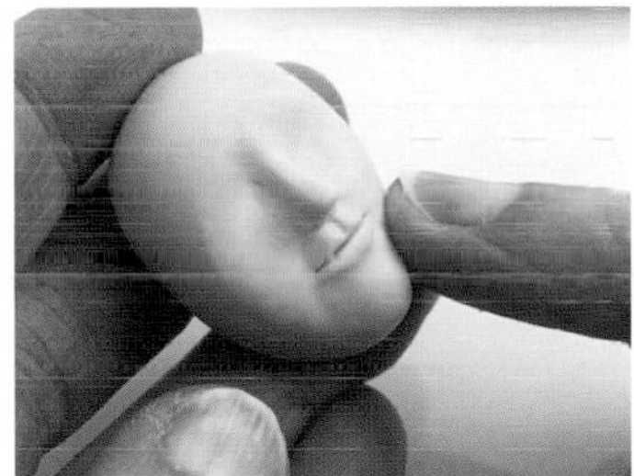

STEP 5

Pinch the chin to accentuate it and squeeze the face to make it fatter or thinner. Use a ball-ended tool to smooth the eye sockets. You can now incorporate the face into a piece of jewelry or decorative piece. Alternatively, bake the face to harden it. You can then apply hair, fabric, hats, and so on without fear of damaging the sculpture.

STEP 6

Hair Roll out clay in a suitable color to make 1/16in (1.5mm) thick sheets (for mohair or viscose hair for dolls, see page 133). Cut pieces that are gently curving and pointed at top and bottom and apply them to the head.

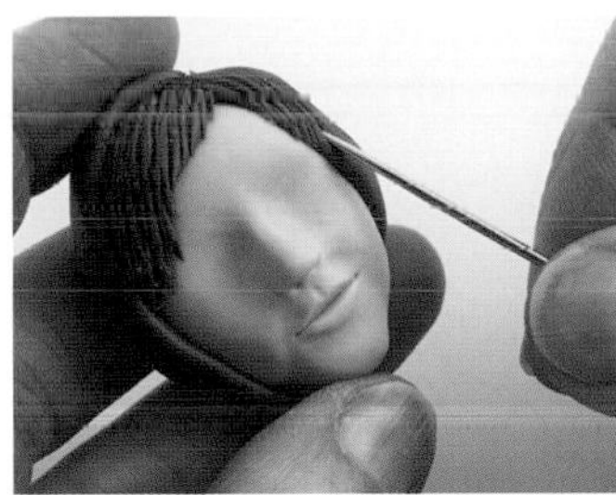

STEP 7

Use a needle to texture the hair and separate the pieces of hair into fronds and locks. Apply a scarf, hat, or other embellishments and bake the head again.

PAINTING THE FACE

Use a quality artist's synthetic brush with a good point, size 0 or 00.

MATERIALS AND TOOLS

- Acrylic paint: brown, black, white, blue, crimson
- Paintbrush
- Alcohol
- Matte varnish

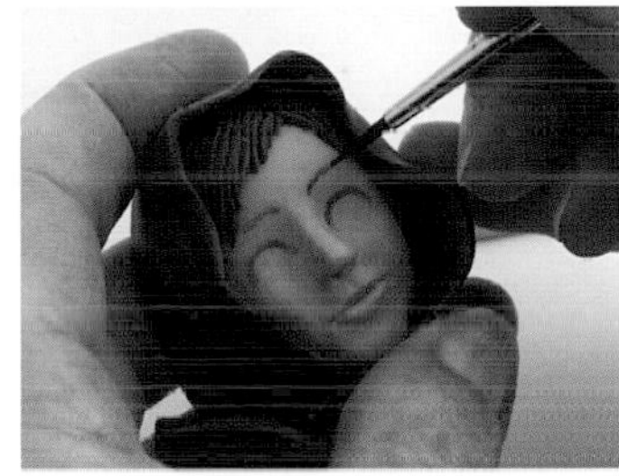

STEP 1

Brush the face with alcohol to degrease and apply a coat of matte varnish to protect the clay from the paint bleeding over time. Allow the varnish to dry, then brush again with alcohol so that the paint will stick well. Draw the upper eye line with a pencil to guide you. Paint the eye line and eyebrows with brown paint.

STEP 2

Paint circles of blue paint for the irises and allow to dry. Paint white triangles on each side of the irises and a black spot for each pupil. A touch of white paint makes each eye sparkle. Paint a thin brown line under each eye and some black streaks on the upper eyelid for lashes.

STEP 3

Paint a thin wash of crimson onto the lips. Allow the face to dry thoroughly overnight, then apply another coat of matte varnish to protect the paint.

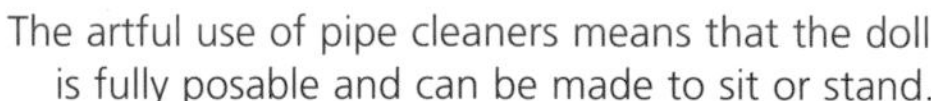

49 FIGURES

Figures are particularly successful in polymer clay, because the excellent doll and flesh clays available give realistic flesh tones, while the rich variety of colored clays can be used with textile techniques to clothe the figure. You can use the same basic sculpting techniques to create a figurine with fixed limbs, using an armature if necessary (see pages 134–135), or a posable doll figure. These instructions are for a miniature girl doll in the scale of 1:12. This is the most popular scale for dollhouses, so the doll can be used in a standard dollhouse, or as a delightful gift on its own.

MATERIALS AND TOOLS

- Firm polymer clay in a flesh tone
- Sculpting tools (see page 14)
- Large ⅛in (3mm) thick tapestry needle
- Ceramic tile
- Craft knife
- 2 pipe cleaners, flesh or white
- Wire cutters
- Superglue
- Acrylic paints and paintbrush
- PVA glue
- Fabrics, ribbon, lace, and sewing equipment for clothes
- Mohair or viscose doll hair
- Fine knitting needle

The artful use of pipe cleaners means that the doll is fully posable and can be made to sit or stand.

SCULPTING A DOLL

Refer to the template on page 132 throughout the sculpting process to ensure that the parts of the doll are made to scale. All holes need to be large enough to take a pipe cleaner, either threaded through in the case of the upper arms and thighs, or glued into as for the lower arms and lower legs. The ⅛in (3mm) tapestry needle should be just right for this.

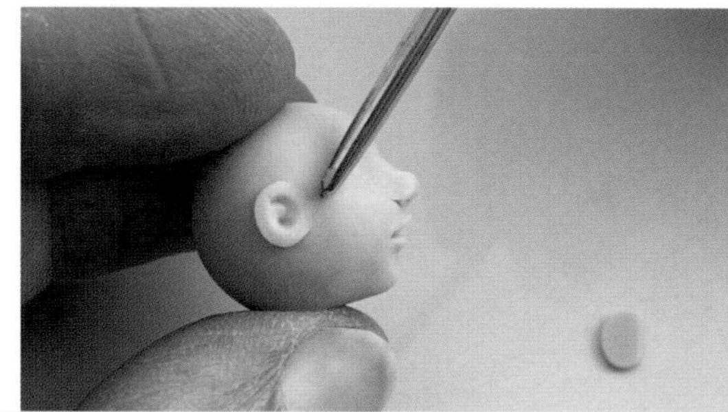

STEP 1

Head Form a ⅝in (15mm) ball of flesh clay and sculpt a face on the front (see pages 128–129). For ears, cut two thin slices from a 3/16in (5mm) log and apply to the sides of the head, with the tops level with the top of the eyes. Smooth each ear toward the face and indent the center with a ball-ended tool. Pierce an ear hole with the tapestry needle.

STEP 2

Pierce a hole, about ¼in (6mm) deep, in the bottom of the head with the needle.

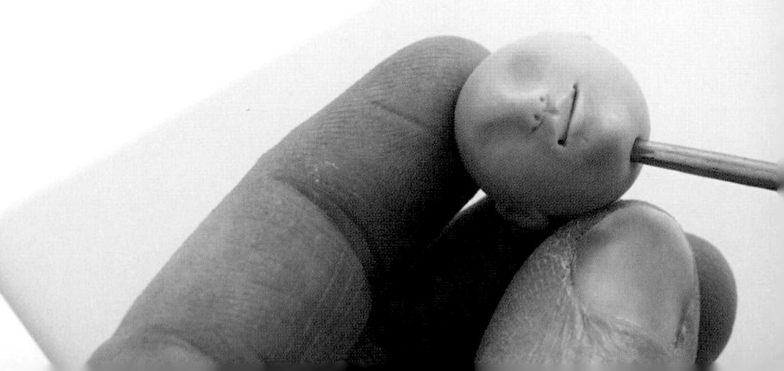

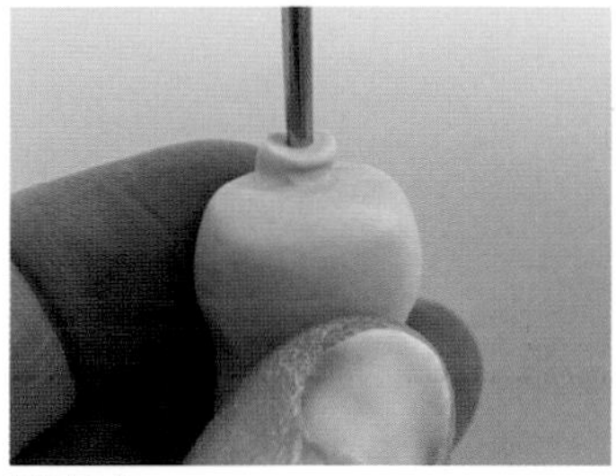

STEP 3

Body Form a 1¹⁄₁₆in (18mm) ball of clay and shape into an oval. Press onto the work surface and shape as shown in the template. Cut a ³⁄₁₆in (5mm) slice from a log of that thickness and apply to the top of the body for the neck, smoothing in the joins. Trim the neck to match the template and press the bottom of the head onto the top of the neck to ensure a good fit. Remove the head and pierce a hole in the neck to align with the one in the bottom of the head.

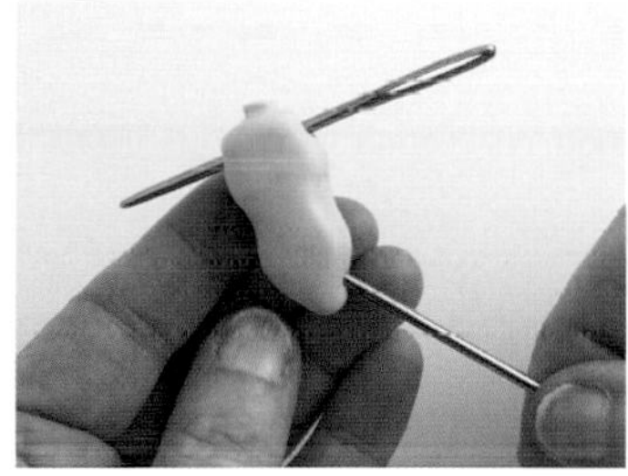

STEP 4

Pierce right across the shoulders with the needle for the armholes and make two holes in the bottom of the body angled upward for the leg holes.

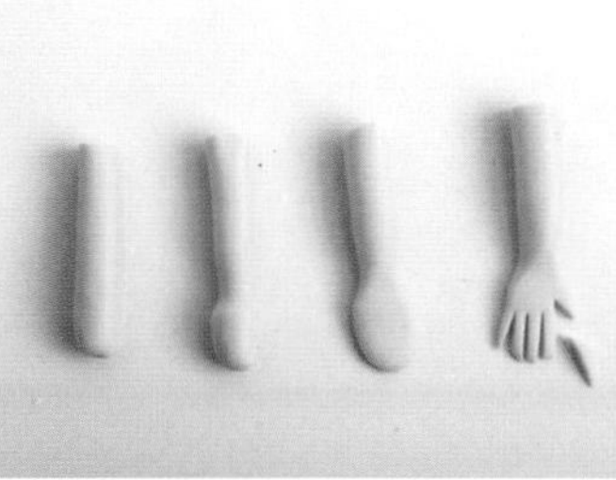

STEP 5

Forearms Form a ³⁄₁₆in (5mm) thick log and cut two ⅝in (15mm) lengths. Round one end of each and roll a wrist between your forefingers. Press the rounded end onto the tile to make a paddle shape. Cut a wedge out of each hand and make cuts to separate the fingers. Remember to reverse the fingers on the second hand.

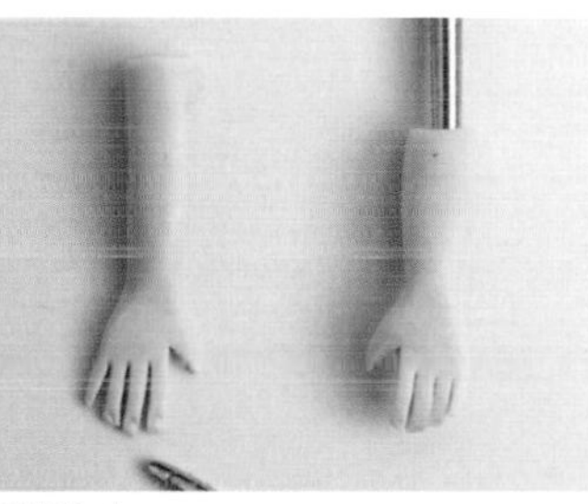

STEP 6

Trim and shape the fingers, then press the eye of the needle onto the end of each to suggest nails. Curve the hand into a realistic shape. Trim each forearm, referring to the template, and make a hole in the end with the needle.

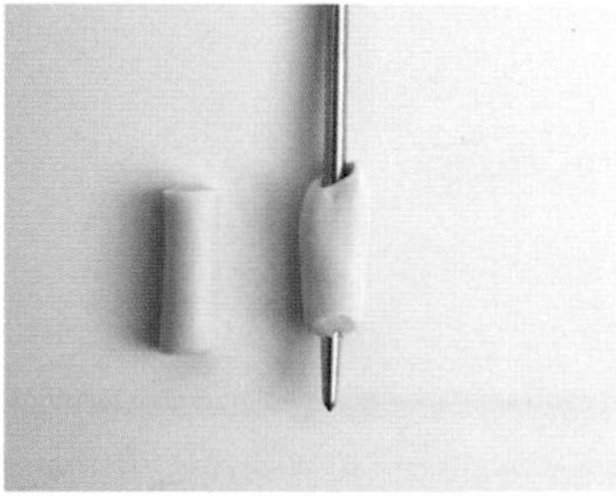

STEP 7

Upper arms Cut two ¾in (20mm) lengths from the same log. Pierce right through each length. Angle the clay at the shoulders where the arms will rest against the body and slope the clay at the front for the inside of the elbows.

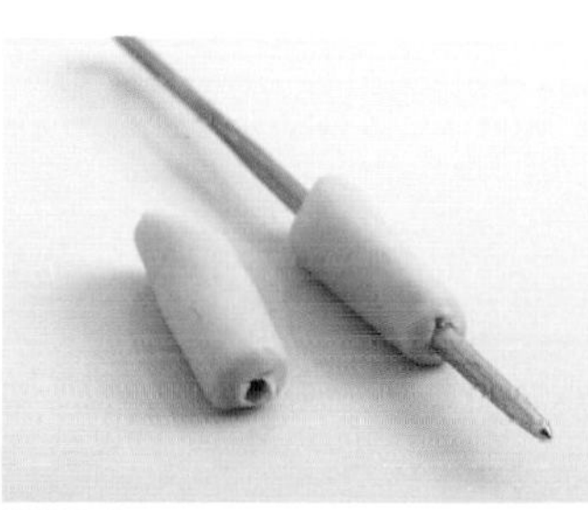

STEP 8

Upper legs Form a ¼in (6mm) thick log and cut two ⅞in (23mm) lengths. Pierce right through each length. Angle the inside of the top of each where it will join the body. Shape the backs of the knees at an angle.

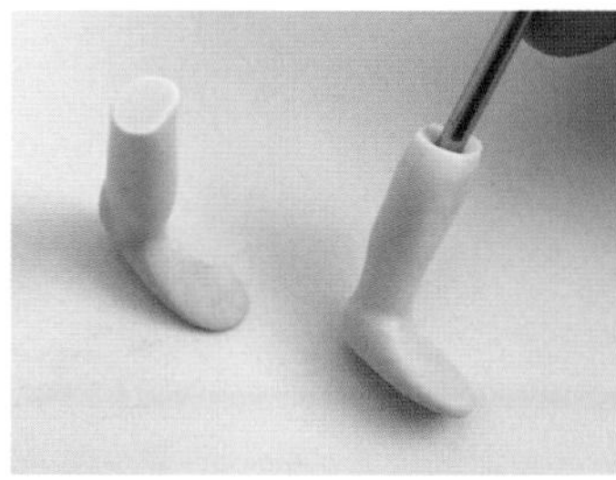

STEP 9

Lower legs Cut two 1¼in (30 mm) lengths from the same log. Round one end of each and pull a heel downward, about ⅜in (10mm) from the rounded end, to make a hockey stick shape. Press the foot onto your work surface and refine the shape. Thin the ankle by rolling it between your forefingers. Make sure that the foot is at right angles to the upright part of the leg or the doll will not stand straight. Trim the lower leg to length and pierce as for the forearms. Bake all the pieces on baking parchment to prevent shiny patches.

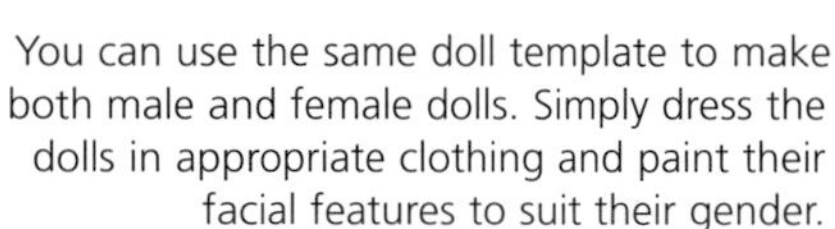

You can use the same doll template to make both male and female dolls. Simply dress the dolls in appropriate clothing and paint their facial features to suit their gender.

ASSEMBLING THE PIECES

Assemble the doll completely before gluing so that you can adjust the pipe cleaner lengths to ensure a good fit.

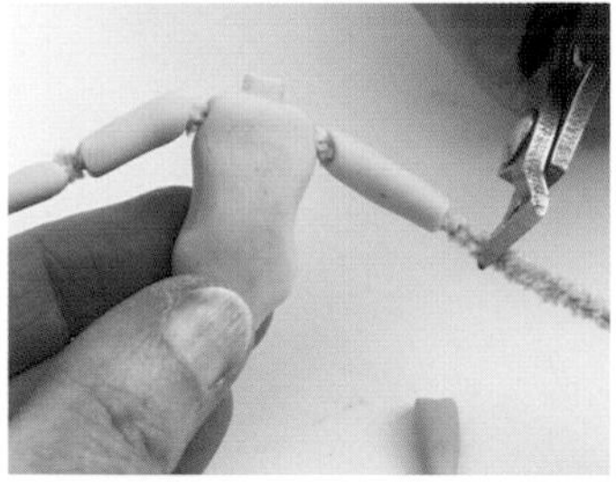

STEP 1

Push the end of a pipe cleaner into the hole in the right forearm. Thread on the right upper arm and then the body and the left upper arm. Cut the pipe cleaner to length and then push the end into the left forearm. Leave a small gap between each limb for easy movement of the joints.

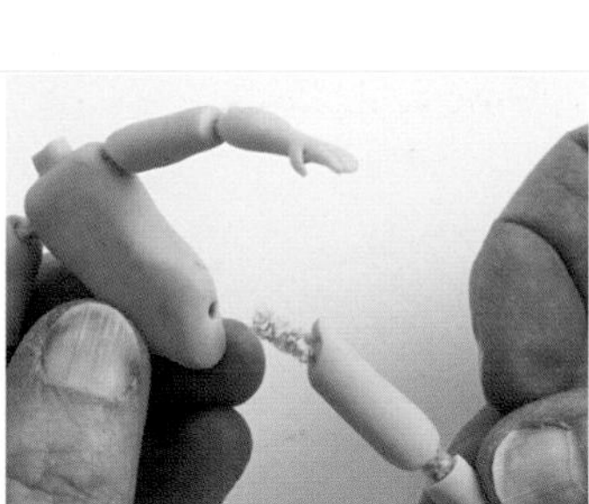

STEP 2

Push the second pipe cleaner into the top of the left lower leg, thread on the left upper leg, and trim the pipe cleaner to about ½in (13mm). Push the end into the left lower leg hole in the body. Repeat for the other leg using the remaining pipe cleaner.

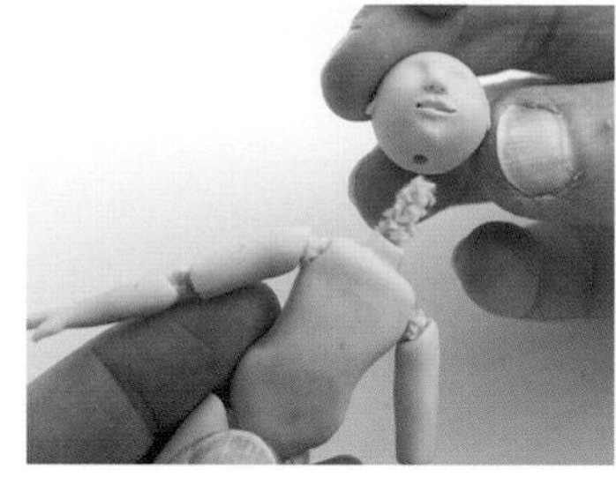

STEP 3

Push a piece of pipe cleaner into the neck hole in the body and trim so that the head can be pushed right down onto the neck.

STEP 4

Adjust all the limbs so that they look natural, then trim any excess clay so that the joints work well. Finally, glue the pipe cleaner ends into their respective holes with superglue.

TEMPLATES

The doll template is actual size. Enlarge the dress templates on a photocopier by 130%.

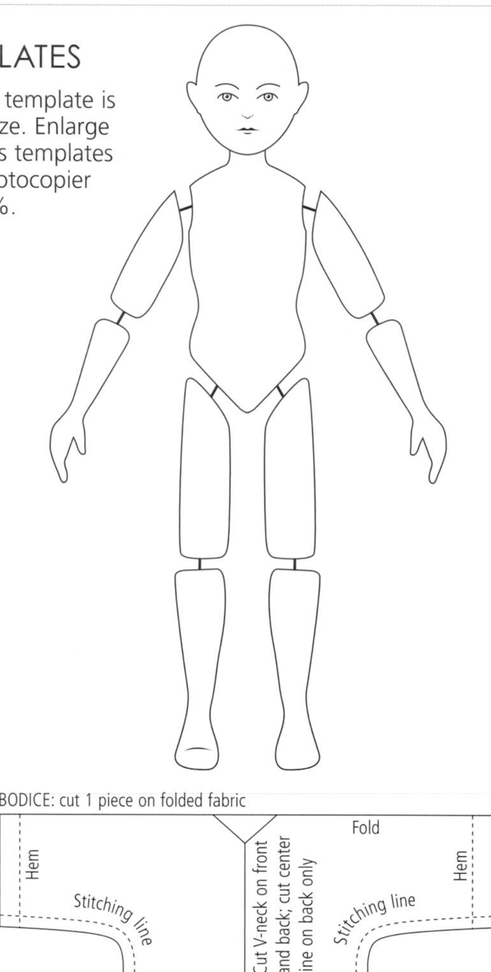

BODICE: cut 1 piece on folded fabric

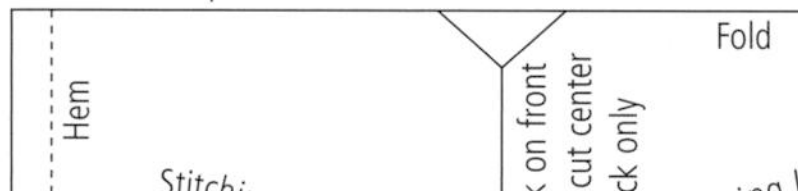

SKIRT: cut 1 piece on folded fabric

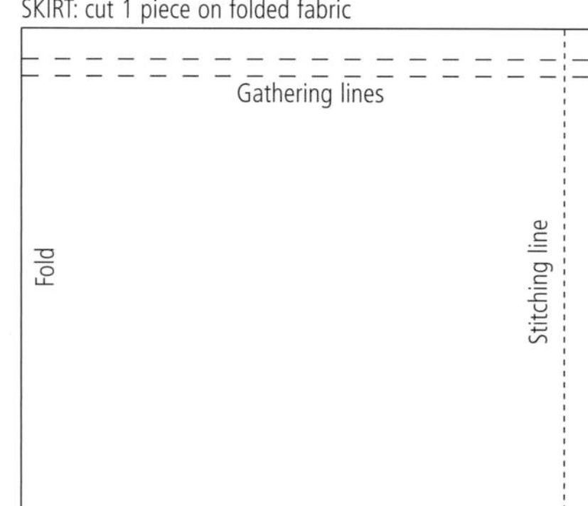

FINISHING TOUCHES

Follow the instructions on page 129 for painting a face, using a very fine brush for the tiny features. Leave the feet bare or paint the feet to suggest shoes and socks. It is best to dress the doll before gluing on the hair.

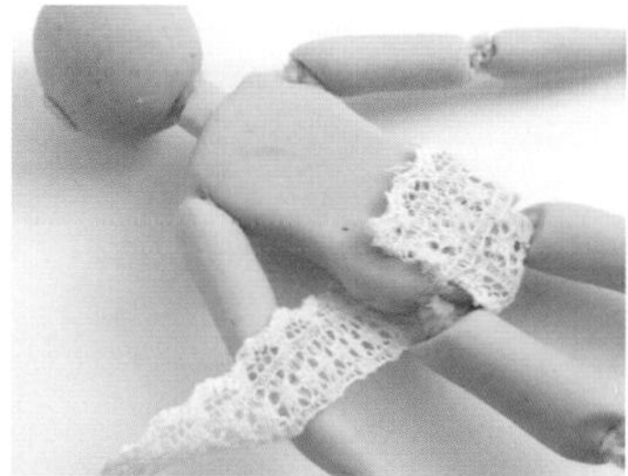

STEP 1

Clothes Glue some white lace around the doll to make simple underwear. Cut out the bodice and skirt using the templates opposite. Use a fine cotton lawn or similar material with a tiny pattern.

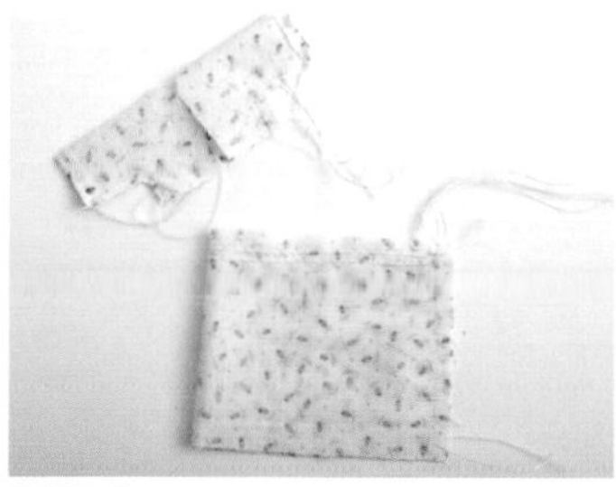

STEP 2

Stitch the sides of the bodice and hem the sleeves, either stitching them in place or gluing with PVA glue. Run two rows of gathering stitch, ⅛in (3mm) apart, along the top of the skirt and stitch the side seam of the skirt. Turn all to the right side.

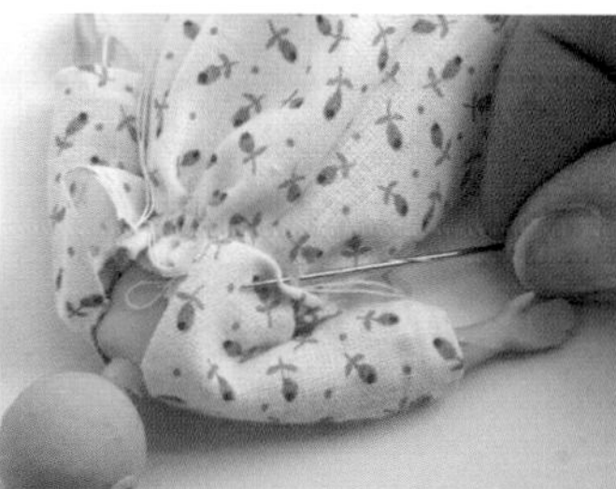

STEP 3

Pull up the threads to gather the skirt and pull it onto the doll with the bodice. Fold under the bottom of the bodice and stitch it over the skirt. Sew up the back opening.

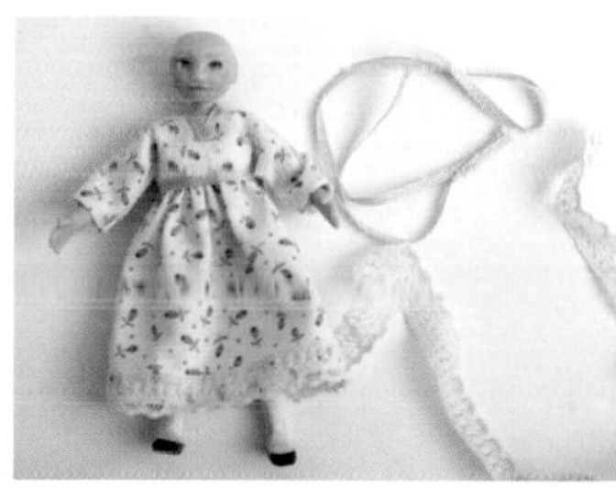

STEP 4

Trim the dress with lace or ribbon to cover raw edges as necessary, glued or sewn in place.

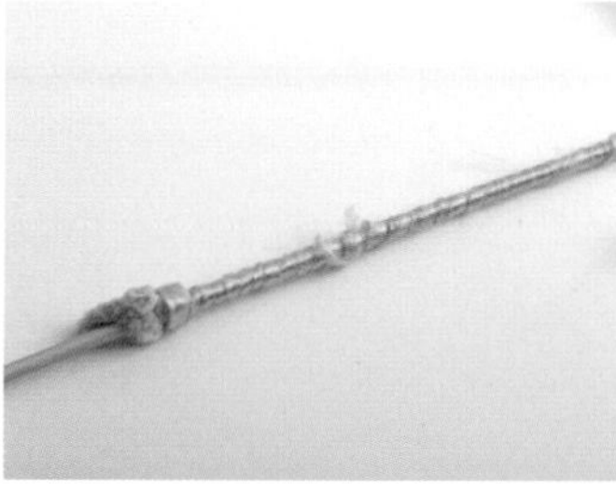

STEP 5

Hair Separate a length of hair, about ⅛in (3mm) thick, from the hank and dampen it. Wind the length around a knitting needle and secure with twisted pieces of pipe cleaner. Allow to dry overnight or use a hair drier. When dry, slip the coil off the knitting needle and cut into ½in (13mm) lengths for ringlets. Cut a longer length for the hair of the crown.

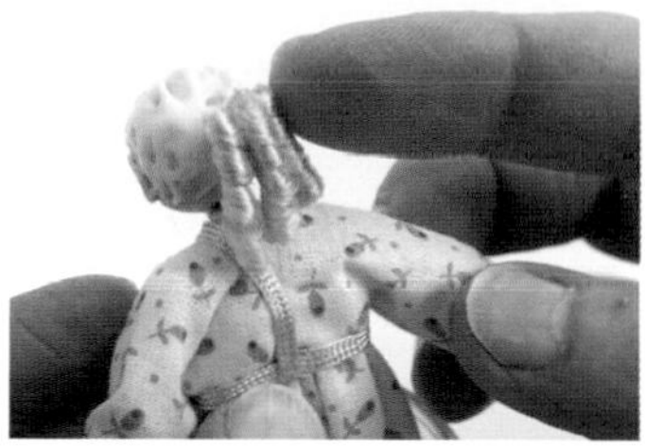

STEP 6

Stand the doll in a jar to hold her upright and apply a cap of PVA glue all over the head. Press several ringlets onto the glue around the bottom of the head.

STEP 7

Tease out the longer length of hair and press over the top of the head, covering the tops of the ringlets. Allow to dry thoroughly and trim away any excess hair.

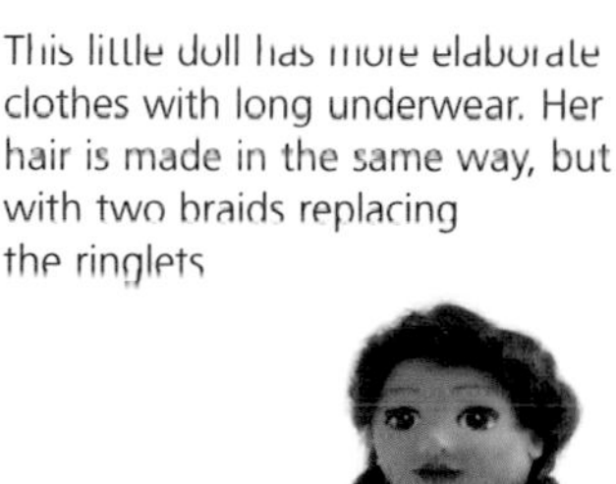

This little doll has more elaborate clothes with long underwear. Her hair is made in the same way, but with two braids replacing the ringlets

50 ARMATURES

Armatures are internal supports that are traditionally used for sculpture of all kinds. The stronger brands of polymer clay can be used without armatures for simple sculpted animals and figures that are 6in (15cm) tall or less. For pieces larger than this or those with unsupported limbs, it is wise to use an armature. Polymer clay sculptures can use armatures of several different kinds. The materials used for the armature should withstand the baking temperature and be permanently stable, because the armature will remain inside the sculpture.

A pair of chickens in different color schemes. Each one was formed around a foil armature.

ADVANTAGES

- An armature is useful for minimizing the amount of clay needed for a sculpture.
- It helps to make the piece lighter than if solid polymer clay were used.
- It supports the sculpture during baking when otherwise the clay may sag in the heat before it hardens.
- Polymer clay can crack during baking when used in thicknesses greater than 1in (25mm); the armature helps to prevent this from happening.

SIMPLE ARMATURE

A seated figure is the easiest type to make, and this example shows a seated fairy that is made by adapting the doll sculpting instructions on pages 130–132. The sculpture is intended to sit on the edge of a shelf or something similar.

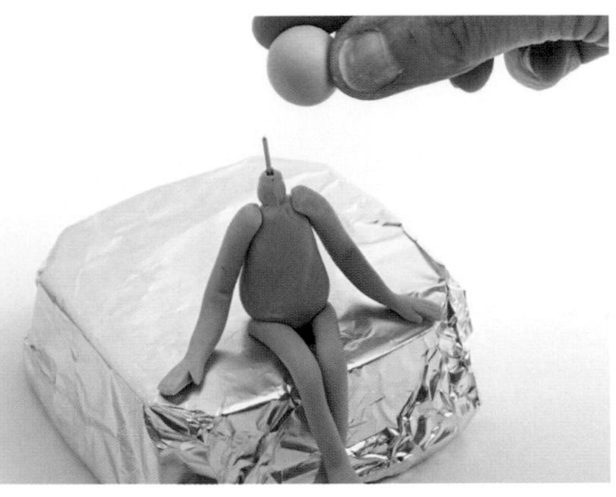

STEP 1
First, model the legs and set them on an upturned foil-covered ovenproof dish to support them, bending the knees and arranging the feet. Press a cone-shaped piece of clay onto the legs for the body. Press the arms on top of the body and add a neck. Insert a piece of wire into the neck and press on the head.

STEP 2
Clothing can now be added as sheets of clay, cut to shape and pressed onto the sculpture. Bake the figure on the support; when cool, apply polymer clay hair (see page 129) and other details as required and bake again. The wings are made from sheets of polymer clay that are dusted with pastel powders, shaped, baked, and then superglued in place.

Transfer the finished fairy to a more decorative seat. Here, she is seated on a glass jar, which could be filled with trinkets or decorative items such as glass pebbles.

FOIL ARMATURE

Aluminum foil can be used on its own for small sculptures that do not have unsupported limbs or parts that need a wire frame.

STEP 1
Tear off a piece of foil—a 12in (30cm) square will make a 2in (5cm) diameter ball—and shape it roughly in your hands into the required shape. Roll the foil firmly on the work surface, adding more layers if necessary to get the required size. Tap with a small hammer to compress the foil and smooth the surface.

STEP 2
Cover the foil with a sheet of clay and add details as required. When using a foil armature, always pierce through the clay into the foil in several discreet places to minimize the chance of trapped air lifting the clay surface during baking.

ARMATURE CLAY

A lightweight polymer clay, such as Sculpey UltraLight, makes excellent armatures. It is much easier to use than foil. It can be shaped into more intricate forms, is lightweight, and has a smooth surface. It can also be carved or sanded to refine the shape before applying the polymer clay covering. Wire can be used to join shapes into a more intricate sculpture.

WIRE AND FOIL ARMATURE

These are ideal for sculpted figures of all kinds. Use only galvanized or coated wire so there is no danger of the wire rusting. For small sculptures of 6in (15cm) tall or less, 18-gauge—1/16in (1.5mm) thick— jewelry wire is suitable and widely available. Larger sculptures will need proportionately thicker wire—galvanized or coated coat-hanger wire works well.

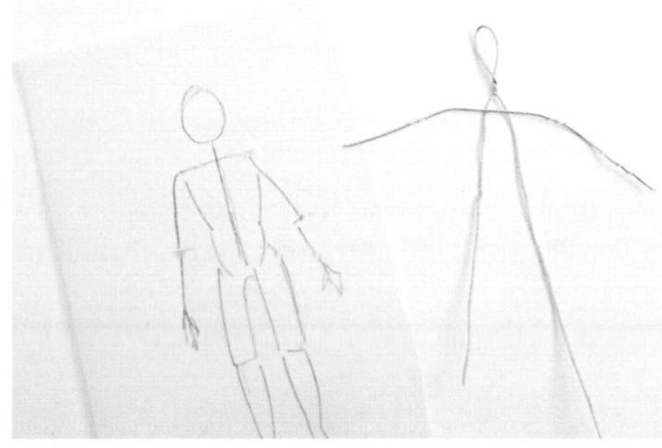

STEP 1
Draw the outline of the sculpture, in this case a standing figure. Bend the wire to make a rough skeleton shape and leave one leg wire 2in (5cm) longer than the other for the figure to be attached to a base later.

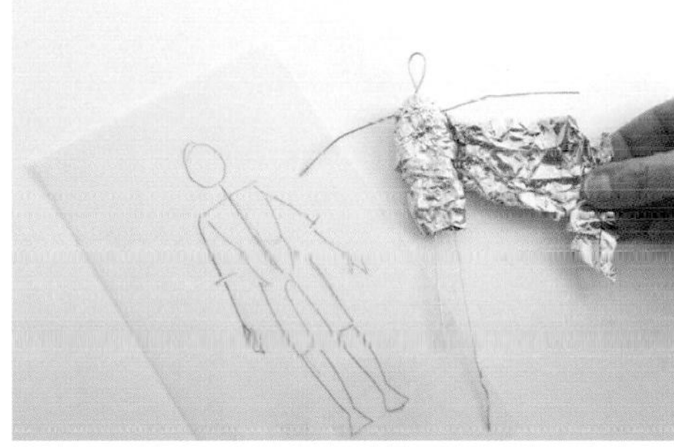

STEP 2
Wind strips of foil round the body of the figure, compressing the foil as you work so that the wire is held firmly in place.

STEP 3
Add polymer clay to the wire and foil frame, building up the figure shape. Details such as the face and hands can then be worked into the clay. The piece can be baked at any point to consolidate the work and then more clay added as required.

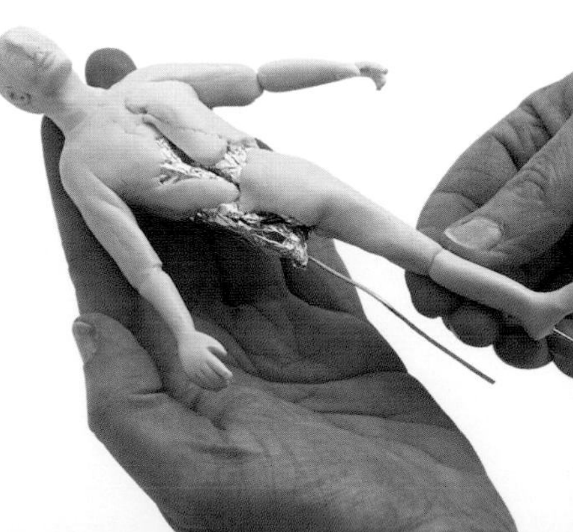

51 FANTASY SUBJECTS

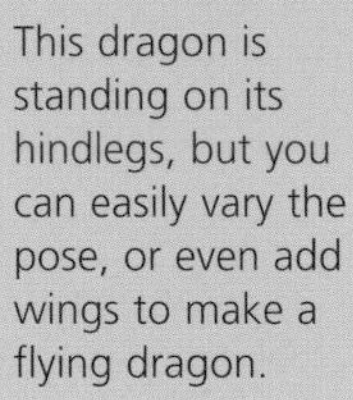

Fantasy sculpture is very popular and is ideal for beginners—nobody can say exactly how a dragon or a goblin should look, so it gives the sculptor wonderful freedom of imagination and design.

This dragon is standing on its hindlegs, but you can easily vary the pose, or even add wings to make a flying dragon.

The head and hands of this wonderfully expressive puppet were sculpted from polymer clay and then painted. Fabric clothing and fiber hair complete the witchy look.

SCULPTING A DRAGON

Dragons are highly popular sculptures and it is great fun to make your own in polymer clay. This example shows in detail how to sculpt a fantasy dragon on an armature of clay.

MATERIALS AND TOOLS

- Armature clay: about 2oz (56g)
- Polymer clay: 1 block gold; scraps of red, yellow, white, and black
- ¼in (6mm) diameter brush protector or circle cutter
- Craft knife
- Pearlescent powder: gold, copper, bronze

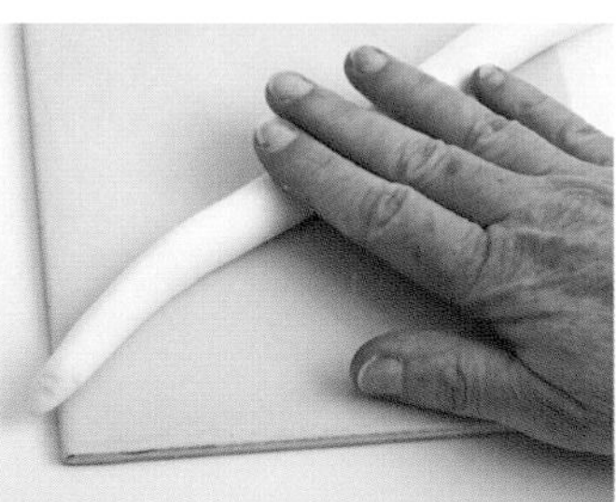

STEP 1

Form the armature clay into a 1in (25mm) thick log and taper it to a point at both ends. It should be about 6in (15cm) long.

STEP 2

Curve the tapered log into an S-shape. Trim the tail; it is easier to make the curved tail in the covering clay only. Bake the armature according to the instructions on the pack.

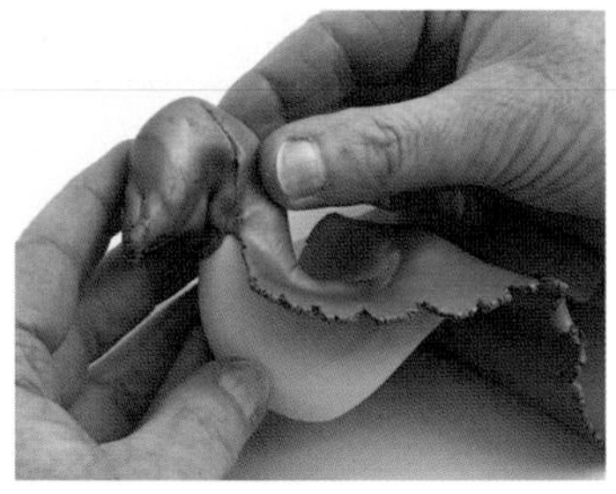

STEP 3

Roll out a 1/16in (1.5mm) thick sheet of gold clay and use this to cover the armature completely, cutting the sheet to fit around the curves and smoothing the joins. This will provide the base for the sculpted details.

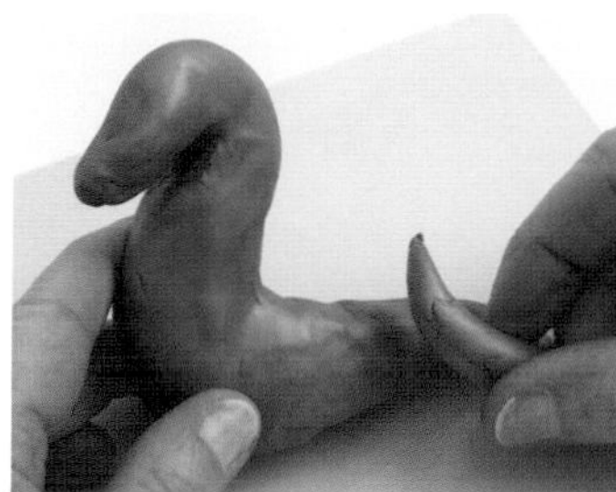

STEP 4
Add a tail of gold clay, taper it to a point, and curve it over the dragon's back.

STEP 5
Use the brush protector to mark scales all over the dragon's sides and tail.

STEP 6
Apply flattened logs of clay to the brow and snout to build up the features. Apply a flap of clay under the snout for the lower jaw. Smooth the edges of the added clay into the clay base. Mark horizontal lines down the dragon's belly.

STEP 7
Form a ⅜in (10mm) thick log of clay, 3in (7.5cm) long, and flatten it on your work surface. Cut one long side into points for the crest. Press onto the dragon's head and back.

STEP 8
Form a ½in (13mm) ball of clay into a log pointed at both ends for the end of the tail. Cut one end lengthwise and open out into an arrow shape. Press onto the end of the tail.

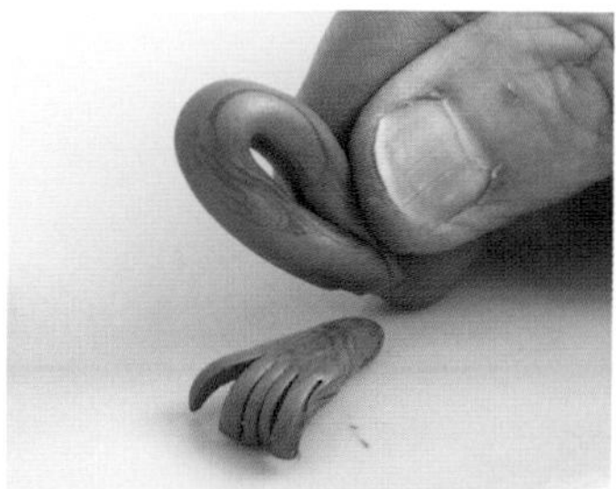

STEP 9
Form two ⅜in (10mm) balls into teardrops and press onto the work surface. Cut the wide end into five toes and curve the ends to form claws. Form two tapered logs from two ½in (13mm) balls and fold in half for the legs. Press one on each foot. Press the legs on each side of the dragon.

STEP 10
Form two logs, each ¼in (6mm) thick and 2in (5cm) long. Round one end of each and press onto the work surface to flatten that end. Cut the end of each into five fingers and curve around to form claws. Bend into a forearm and press one on each side of the body.

SCALES
Try applying cane slices all over a dragon sculpture to imitate scales. The slices used here are from millefiori spiral canes that were shaped into a trianglular cross-section before being sliced.

STEP 11
Make eye sockets and fill with small balls of black clay for the eyes (see page 126). Apply eyebrows and whiskers over the nostrils, all made from thin logs with pointed ends; allow them to fly backward to suggest movement and ferocity. Add a red and yellow forked tongue. Two white fangs on either side of the mouth complete the effect. Brush the dragon with a mixture of the powders. Bake the dragon for 30–40 minutes on a tile. When cool, varnish to protect the powders.

52 NATURAL HISTORY SUBJECTS

The wonderful color range of polymer clay and the fact that different colors can be mixed to form even more colors means that it is an ideal material for making realistic natural history sculpture. The fine texture of the clay and its ability to simulate all kinds of materials adds to the realism.

The pond is built over a polymer clay liner to ensure that there is no leakage when the resin is poured in.

WATERLILY POND

This example shows a naturalistic pond with reeds, moss, waterlilies, and simulated water.

MATERIALS AND TOOLS

- Polymer clay: equivalent of 1 block in a variety of grays, several marbled together to make streaky rock colors; ½ block dark brown; scraps of leaf green, golden yellow, and pale pink
- Armature polymer clay (or use foil)
- Aluminum foil
- Ceramic tile
- Quilt batting for texturing
- Fine-mesh sieve, craft knife, and tapestry needle
- PVA glue
- Clear resin for the water

STEP 1

Pond liner Shape the armature clay into a rough oval about 2½in (63mm) long, 1½in (38mm) wide, and ⅜in (10mm) thick. Bake and cover with foil to use as a former for the pond liner. If you are using just foil, shape the foil into a rough oval and compress with a hammer (see page 135).

STEP 2

Roll out a 1/16in (1.5mm) thick sheet of dark brown clay and lay on a tile. Place the former on the sheet and press the clay up the sides. Trim level with the top of the former. Bake and, when cool, remove the clay pond liner from the former.

STEP 3

Stones Form the gray clay mixtures into a series of irregular shaped balls, ranging in size from 1 to ¼in (25–6mm) diameter, for the stones. Place the pond liner on the tile and press the balls around the sides of the pond, straddling the walls of the pond liner and covering them completely. When all the stones are in place, texture them with batting to give them a rough surface.

STEP 4

Reeds Make some thin logs of leaf green, about ¹⁄₁₆in (1.5mm) thick and of varying lengths. Point both ends and roll flat to make reeds. Bake the reeds with the pond for 30–45 minutes. Make small pebbles from gray clay and press these onto the bottom of the pond. Push the ends of the reeds into the pebbles, squeezing the clay around them to secure. Add a collar of foil around the reeds to hold them upright during baking.

STEP 5

Moss Push leaf green and yellow clay through the sieve with a blunt tool and scrape off the resulting mossy texture. Press this onto some parts of the stones, using PVA glue as a key if necessary.

STEP 6

Waterlilies Form a ¼in (6mm) ball of pale pink clay and make a flower (see pages 58–59). Trim the back of the flower so that it will sit upright. Press a scrap of golden yellow clay through the sieve and apply to the center of the flower. Make a bud as well with pink clay.

STEP 7

Leaves Form several balls of leaf green clay, between ¹⁄₁₆in (1.5mm) and ⅛in (3mm) diameter. Press each of these down hard onto a tile so that they form thin disks. Mark veins on each and cut out a small "V." Bake the pond again to harden the reeds along with the lilies and leaves for 15 minutes.

STEP 8

Water Measure the capacity of the pond by filling it with water and then pouring the water into a measuring jug. Allow to dry thoroughly in a warm place (or rebake) before adding resin. Mix the required volume of resin by combining it with hardener according to the instructions on the pack. Pour the resin into the pond and allow to set overnight; cover with a box to avoid dust settling onto the resin surface. Glue the lily leaves and flowers on top of the set resin.

Try these...

Sea pond Try creating a sea pond complete with seaweed, crabs, and anemones. Tiny polymer clay fish are glued to the pond bottom before filling with resin.

Shell ornament A real cockleshell filled with polymer clay pebbles, an anemone, and a turtle.

Formal fishpond Square stones simulate a Victorian fishpond, complete with goldfish.

53 MINIATURES

Brush brown pastel powder onto miniature pies and roast chickens to color them realistically.

Before the widespread availability of polymer clay, miniaturists used plaster or air-drying clay for making miniature food. All that has changed and today polymer clay has transformed miniature food and doll making as no other material before it. Polymer clay is also superb for simulating many other materials in miniature, sometimes creating a more realistic result than using the actual material. Examples are wood and ceramics, where the finer details possible with polymer clay make the piece more true to scale. Miniature food is great fun to make with polymer clay. The 4in (10cm) wide table shown here is set with a delicious birthday feast.

This birthday tea party display demonstrates both miniature food and ceramics. It would look perfect in a dollhouse, but also makes a delightful and unusual birthday gift. It is made in the most popular dollhouse scale of 1:12—that is, 1in = 1 foot, or 1cm = 12cm.

TEA SET

A tiny tea set in blue and white china sets off the miniature food to perfection.

MATERIALS AND TOOLS

- Polymer clay: ½ block white
- Ceramic tile
- Thick tapestry needle
- Fine paintbrush
- Talcum powder
- PVA glue
- Round cutters: ¾in (20mm), ½in (13mm), ⅜in (10mm)
- Formers for the center of the plates (use the flat ends of a round pencil, pen, or lipstick holder for the different sizes required): ½in (13mm), ¼in (6mm)
- ⅜in (10mm) diameter marble or ball bearing
- Alcohol
- Blue acrylic paint
- Gloss varnish

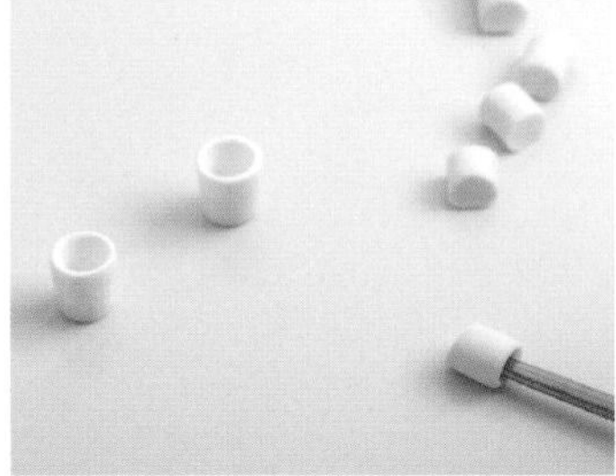

STEP 1

Cups Form a ¼in (6mm) thick log and cut lengths of ¼in (6mm) for the cups. Follow the instructions on page 69 for making pots, using the tapestry needle and the fine paintbrush handle to make little cups about 3/16in (5mm) tall. Stand each cup upright on a tile and bake for 20 minutes.

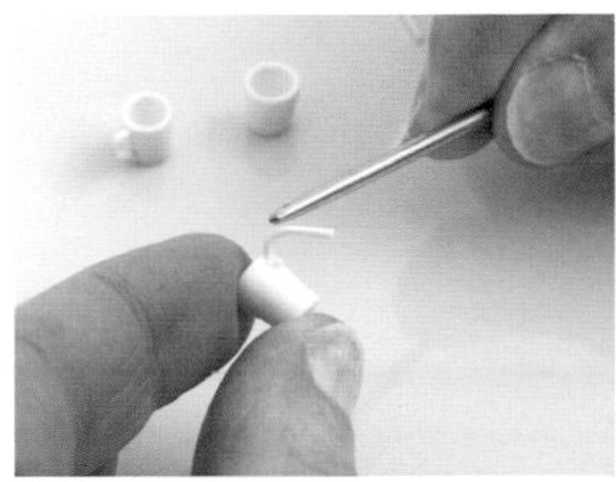

STEP 2

Roll out a 1/32in (1mm) thick log and cut a 3/8in (10mm) length for a handle. Apply a dab of glue just below the rim of a cup and press on one end of the log. Curve the log over and downward, then press the other end to the cup, using another dab of glue to secure. Repeat for the other cups and bake them all again for 20 minutes.

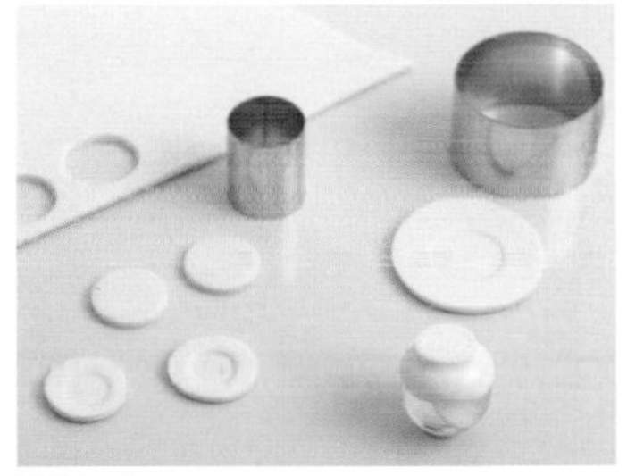

STEP 3

Plates and sugar bowl Follow the instructions on page 68 to make saucers using the 3/8in (10mm) cutter, and serving plates using the 3/4in (20mm) cutter. Follow the instructions on page 68 to make a tiny bowl, using the marble as the former and a disk of clay cut out with the 1/2in (13mm) cutter.

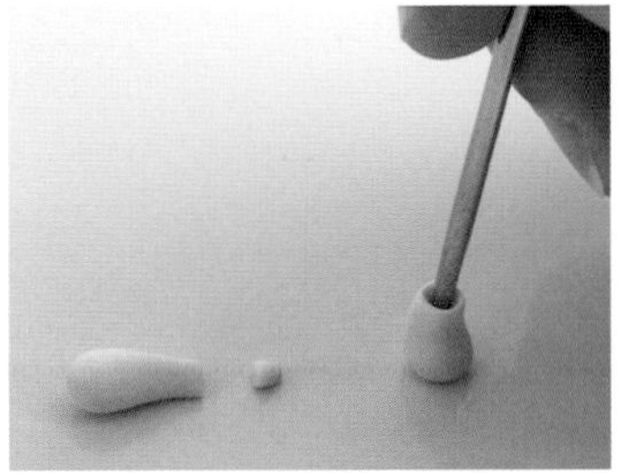

STEP 4

Milk jug Form a 3/8in (10mm) ball of clay into a teardrop and trim off the point. Push the needle into the top and rotate it to open out the top.

STEP 5

Pull out a spout with the needle. Bake the jug as for the cups and add a handle in the same way.

STEP 6

Teapot Form a 3/4in (20mm) ball of clay. Cut a 1/4in (6mm) disk from a thin sheet and press the ball onto this for a foot. Mark the top with the 1/4in (6mm) cutter to suggest the teapot lid.

ARTIST'S TIPS

- Use a firm clay for all miniatures so that the heat from your hands does not make the tiny pieces of clay too soft.
- Keep your hands and working area very clean; small specks of dirt or fluff will ruin a miniature object.

STEP 7

Form a 1/4in (6mm) ball into a tapered log for the spout and cut the thick end at an angle. Cut a small notch out of the pointed end. Press the thick end onto the base of the teapot and curve the spout upward.

STEP 8

Make a handle as for the cups, but a little bigger, and apply a small ball to the top of the teapot for a lid handle. Bake the teapot for about 20 minutes.

STEP 9

Painting Brush over all the pieces with alcohol to degrease the surface. Paint on a pattern with a very fine brush, using tiny spots of color. When completely dry, coat all the china with gloss varnish.

Vary the decoration of miniature china to suit the occasion. This china set is painted with a children's nursery design of running rabbits.

BIRTHDAY CAKE

A classic birthday cake takes center stage on the tiny tea table.

MATERIALS AND TOOLS

- Polymer clay: small quantities of white, translucent white, translucent yellow, translucent blue, translucent leaf green, black
- Ceramic tile
- ¾in (20mm) square cutter
- Craft knife
- PVA glue
- "Happy Birthday" sign printed on paper from a computer or photocopier, ⅜in (10mm) across
- Tapestry needle
- Fabric for texturing
- Silver powder

STEP 1

Press the white clay into a ⅜in (10mm) thick pat and lay on the tile. Use the cutter to cut out a square shape for the cake base. Bake on the tile for 15 minutes.

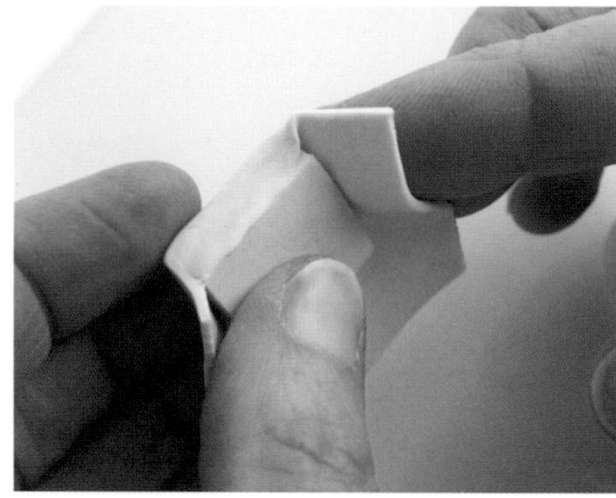

STEP 2

Paint a thin coat of glue over the cake base. Roll out a very thin sheet of translucent white clay—1/32in (1mm) or less—and use this to cover the cake, trimming the edges and smoothing the corners.

STEP 3

Cut out the paper "Happy Birthday" sign and glue to the cake top. Use the appliqué technique (see pages 46–47) to apply tiny flowers and leaves around the sign, using white clay as well as translucent blue, translucent green, and translucent yellow.

STEP 4

Roll out a thin sheet of translucent blue and cut an ⅛in (3mm) wide strip for the ribbon. Press on around the sides of the cake and apply a bow to the front (see page 49). Cut a thin strip from a very thin sheet of translucent white clay and twist into a decorative edging. Apply this all around the top edge of the cake and around the sign as well.

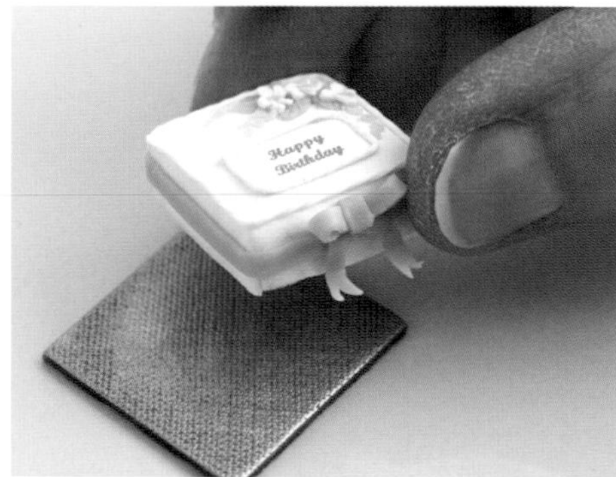

STEP 5

Roll out a sheet of black clay for the cake board and texture the surface with fabric. Cut out a 1in (25mm) square and brush with silver powder. Bake the cake and board for 15 minutes. Glue the cake to the cake board.

MATERIALS AND TOOLS

- Polymer clay: small quantities of ocher, translucent white, translucent blue, translucent yellow, translucent pink, dark brown, crimson, orange
- Ceramic tile
- Craft knife
- Fabric with texture of fine lines

CUPCAKES

Cupcakes have been essential party food for children for more than 100 years. Today, they have become fashionable for adults, too.

STEP 1
Form a ¼in (6mm) thick log of ocher clay and cut 3/16in (5mm) lengths for the cupcake bases. Pinch one end of each to taper it slightly and roll in the fabric to texture with longitudinal lines. Press on a tile to make sure they stand upright and bake for 15 minutes.

STEP 2
Form ⅛in (3mm) balls of translucent white, translucent pink, translucent yellow, and dark brown. Press one onto the top of each cake base, smoothing the icing down the sides a little. Apply a chip of crimson, orange, or dark brown to the top of each as decoration. Bake again for 15 minutes.

MATERIALS AND TOOLS

- Polymer clay: small quantities of beige, white, red, and golden yellow
- Ceramic tile
- Fine grain for texturing (semolina, ground rice, or cornmeal)
- ⅜in (10mm) square cutter and craft knife

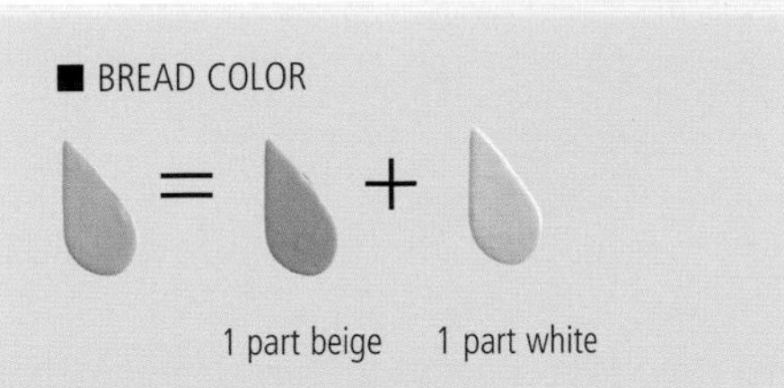

SANDWICHES

These are cheese and tomato sandwiches, but you can vary the clay colors inside the sandwiches to suggest other fillings.

STEP 1
Mix about 1 teaspoon of grain into a walnut-sized ball of bread-colored clay. This will make a realistic texture for the miniature bread. Roll into a 1/32in (1mm) thick sheet and cut out several squares with the cutter.

STEP 2
Cut tiny slices from the red and golden yellow clays and apply to one of the squares. Lay another square of bread clay on top and cut in half diagonally to make sandwiches. Repeat to make more sandwiches. Bake for 15 minutes and arrange on a serving plate.

GALLERY

Polymer clay has rapidly become an art medium in its own right, and the range of artists who now use polymer clay is enormous, from jewelers and sculptors to illustrators and animators. As artists continue to experiment with the material, the vast range of techniques continues to expand. One of the best ways to learn about the possibilities of polymer clay and develop your own ideas is to look at the work of other artists for inspiration.

VALERIE AHARONI
LENTIL
The finely textured pattern on this 2½in (6cm) diameter hollow lentil is achieved with rubber stamps. The texture was then laid over a simple Skinner blend. The technique echoes that of the Korean slip inlay style of pottery known as mishima.

PAMELA ANNESLEY
BOOK WITH POLYMER CLAY COVERS
The colorful and lively images on the book's covers are created from baked sheets of liquid clay that have been screen printed, painted, and then backed with a thick clay sheet.

PAT BOLGAR

NECKLACE WITH LEAVES (LEFT)

Polymer clay using millefiori and gold leaf techniques is combined with silver metal clay for this unusual necklace.

BRACELET WITH METAL CLAY CLOSURE (RIGHT)

The handmade silver metal clay closure adds a lovely detail to millefiori polymer clay and peridot beads.

HELEN BRADLEY

GREEN TEXTURED BRACELET (ABOVE)

Thin layers of green, white, and red clay have been stamped, baked, and then sanded to reveal the layers in this striking piece. The red accents are added extrusions.

COVERED BOX (LEFT)

A papier mâché box covered with faux jade polymer clay and stamped with black ink.

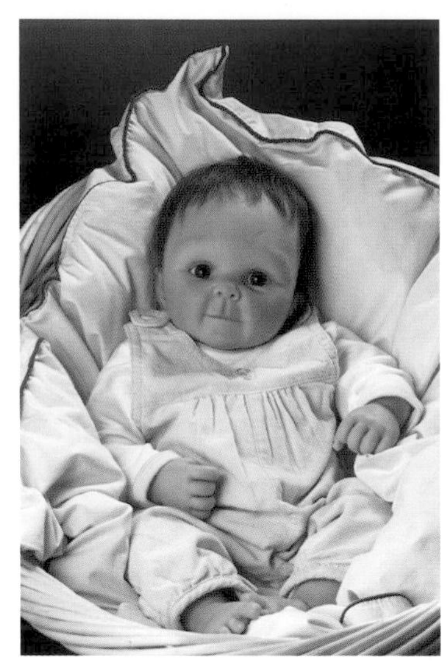

CHRISTEL BRENNER

YANNICK (LEFT)

This lifelike boy doll is 20½in (52cm) tall and has sculpted polymer clay head, arms, and legs. The body is made of cotton filled with granules, and the doll is finished with blown glass eyes and a human hair wig.

ANNIKA (RIGHT)

This larger female doll is 28½in (72cm) tall and made in the same way as Yannick, but with longer sculpted arms and legs. The dress is selfmade.

KEVIN BUNTIN

DAME KAMAYAHOO, THE PINE SPIRIT (RIGHT)

Mixed media has been combined with polymer clay head, hands, and feet to create a wonderfully imaginative art doll. The costume is hand-stitched fabric embellished with natural materials; the body is posable fabric and wire.

NERVOUS JITTERS, THE PINE SPRITE (FAR RIGHT)

As with Dame Kamayahoo, this mixed media sculpture combines polymer clay head and hands with a fabric body over a wire armature to make a posable fantasy figure.

JEANETTE CANYON
SLOTHS
This excitingly textural illustration, from the children's picture book *Over in the Jungle: A Rainforest Rhyme*, combines many polymer clay techniques, including sculpting, extruding, blends, and marbling.

SCOT CONNOR
GILBERTIMUS, THE GLADIATOR GRASSHOPPER
This delightful sculpture is 3½in (9cm) high and made with polymer clay over an armature of soldered copper wire, aluminum foil, and epoxy putty. It is painted with liquid acrylic applied with an airbrush and in washes.

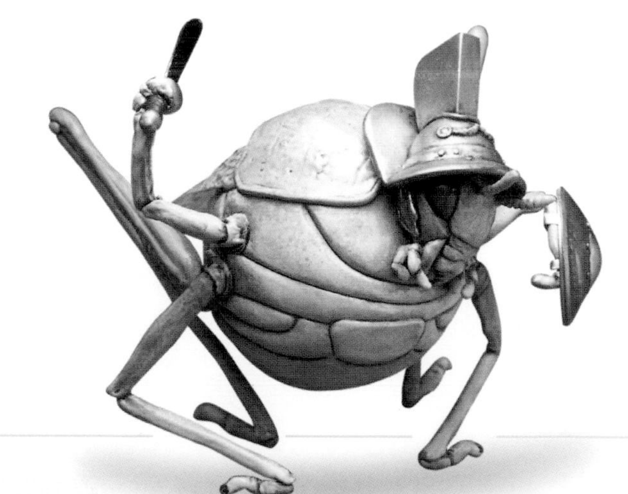

GERA SCOTT CHANDLER
SALMON WOMAN
Many different techniques have been used to decorate this glorious piece of imaginative sculpture over an armature: texturing, powders, liquid clay, inclusions, and painting.

ELIZABETH COOPER

HONEY THE FAIRY (RIGHT)

Flesh-colored polymer clay built over a wire and foil armature gives a highly lifelike effect in this 4in (10cm) tall figure. Other media used include feathers for wings, glass beads for eyes, and red mohair tied up with a silk ribbon for hair. The cheeks and shoes are colored with acrylic paint. The bee is also sculpted from polymer clay and is attached with a wire.

MIMI THE MOUSE WHISPERER (FAR RIGHT)

The artist has achieved an appealing pose in this 4in (10cm) tall sculpture. The same techniques and mixed media are used as for Honey, but this time with a flower petal cap. The polymer clay mouse is colored with acrylic paint.

ROBERT DANCIK

BRICK PIN (LEFT)

Polymer clay is combined with mixed media for a sophisticated result. The rectangular section of the sterling silver mount is inlaid with polymer clay, with an antique button and a carnelian in the circular section.

JUST OFF NORTH (RIGHT)

Polymer clay is inlaid in a sterling silver bezel and combined with mixed media, including a carnelian in the spiral attachment; black pearl, amber, and carnelian beads at the bottom; and an electric-etched silver background.

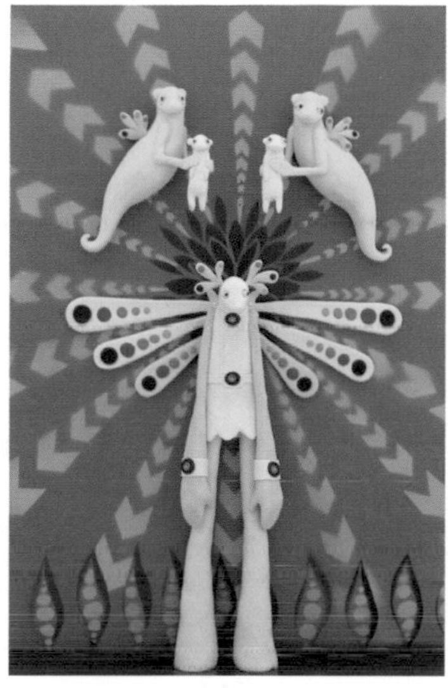

MEREDITH DITTMAR

LET'S BE (LEFT)

This unusual polymer clay wall hanging is mounted on an 18 x 15in (45 x 38cm) sheet of Plexiglas that is stenciled with acrylic. Sculpted mainly by hand with little use of tools, flexible clay is used on parts that protrude and some of the clay is reinforced with wire armature to reduce breakage.

I KNOW (FAR LEFT)

This wall hanging was created using the same techniques as Let's Be, but uses a vibrant rather than pastel color palette.

DAYLE DOROSHOW

THE WAYFARER'S TENT (LEFT)

An unfolding pyramid made with faux ivory polymer clay decorated with photocopy transfer and etching. The sides flap down to reveal a decorative interior containing a mystical book.

BLOSSOM BEADS (RIGHT)

These large and colorful beads, 2in (5cm) in diameter, are made using clay blends and decorated with cane slices and silver wire embellishment.

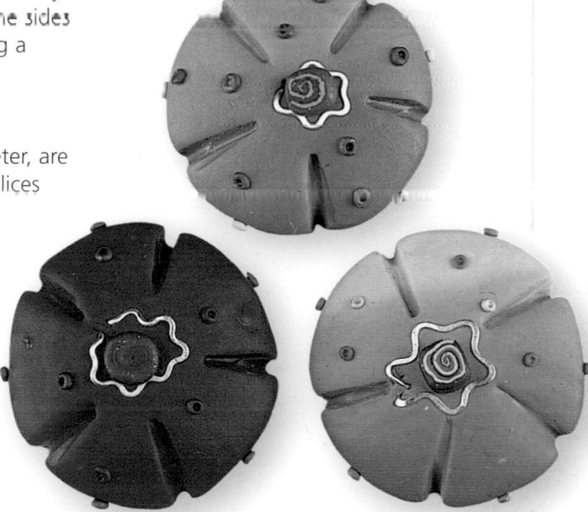

ANNETTE DUBURG

INRO (TOP)

Polymer clay caned spirals have been used to create a shining gold and blue veneer for the walls of this traditional Japanese hanging case, known as an inro. A silk cord and matching beads complete the piece.

PIN (ABOVE)

A striking pin made with polymer clay that has been stamped and backfilled with gold acrylic paint.

CELIE FAGO

CARVED NEEDLE CASE (BELOW)

The needle case has a threaded closure baked into the clay, a technique developed by the artist. It is decorated with carving and paint.

FAUX IVORY CUFF (BOTTOM)

The cuff is formed from faux ivory clay that has been impressed with a texture and then baked. It was then aged by rubbing with dirt and paint.

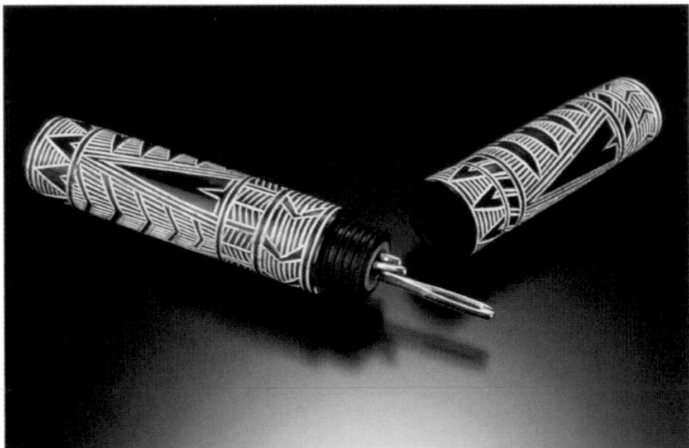

CHRISTI FRIESEN

A RIVER RUNS THROUGH (LEFT)

This fluid and appealing sculpture shows wonderful grace and movement. It is made from polymer clay with added beads and gems, and has been antiqued with acrylic paint.

AH, SPRINGTIME (RIGHT)

A glorious asymmetrical sculpted necklace using blends for subtle color variations and incorporating pearls, 23K gold leaf, beads, and antiquing.

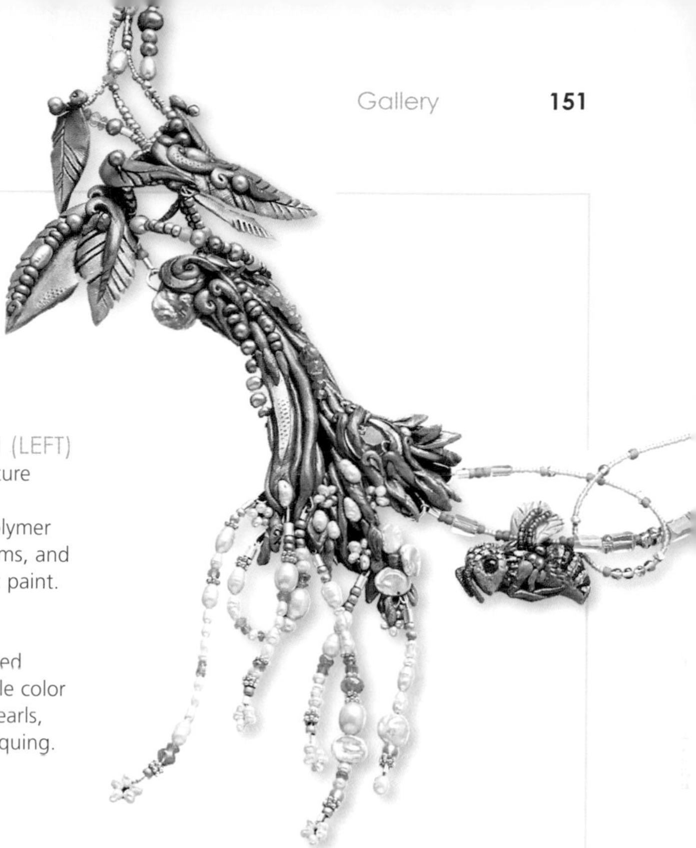

DOREEN GAY-KASSEL

A COUPLE OF BRIGHT CHICKENS

These delightfully humorous sculptures demonstrate a variety of techniques. An armature was made from wire and tissue paper, covered with polymer clay, and then decorated with cane slices.

JUNE HUNTER

GRANVILLE ISLAND PENDANTS

Atmospheric pendants using a photographic image transferred onto polymer clay and coated with a glassy acrylic finish.

SUZANNE IVESTER

FLAMINGOS (BELOW LEFT) & CAFE BOSSANOVA (BOTTOM)

These paintings were built from small pieces of colored polymer clay combined into a thin veneer. This was then textured, cured, and assembled onto a board.

LONDON ROOFTOPS (BELOW RIGHT)

This painting has added details using cane slices. Brick patterns and wrought iron were created by stamping into the clay and highlighting with acrylic paint.

JUDY KUSKIN

ODE TO PELE

This striking piece of jewelry combines traditional metalsmithing techniques with polymer clay. The spacers between the clay pieces are African heishi beads.

LORETTA LAM

AUTUMN VINES NECKLACE

These beautifully finished large beads have aluminum foil cores and are decorated with a variety of techniques, including metallic effects and canes.

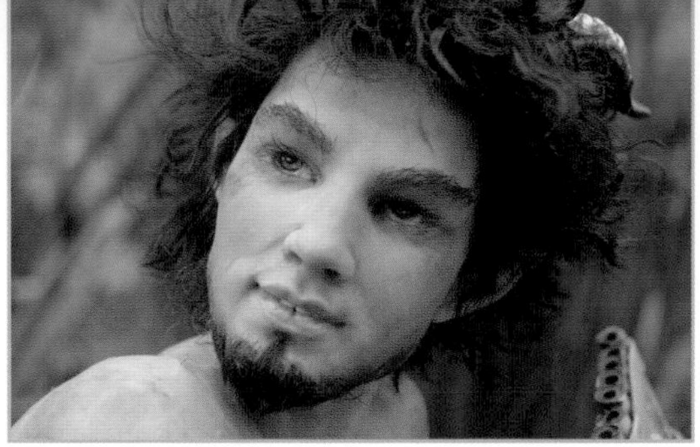

JULIE MANSERGH

PAN (ABOVE & RIGHT)

This remarkably lifelike mythical creature would be 11in (28cm) tall if standing. He is built on a strong armature of wire with brass rods and tubes and is removable from the base. His hair is soft Tibetan lamb and his eyes are inset into the clay.

AUTUMN FAERIE (FAR RIGHT)

Built using the same techniques and materials as Pan, and 7½in (19cm) tall if standing, the skin of this faerie is the natural clay color with a hint of blush and freckles painted on. Her bodice is clay with dainty lacing, and her skirt is sheer fabric edged with glass beads.

LISA PAVELKA

ASIAN COLLAGE PENDANT (LEFT)

The techniques used to make this polymer clay pendant include image transfer, stamping, and a millefiori accent combined with mixed media embellishment. Measuring 1in (2.5cm) square, it is set in sterling silver and strung on a beaded helix cord.

COLLAGED BUSINESS CARD CASE (RIGHT)

This 2½ x 3½in (6 x 9cm) metallic-based card case features antiqued stamped clay with image transfer, millefiori embellishment, and sliced inlay.

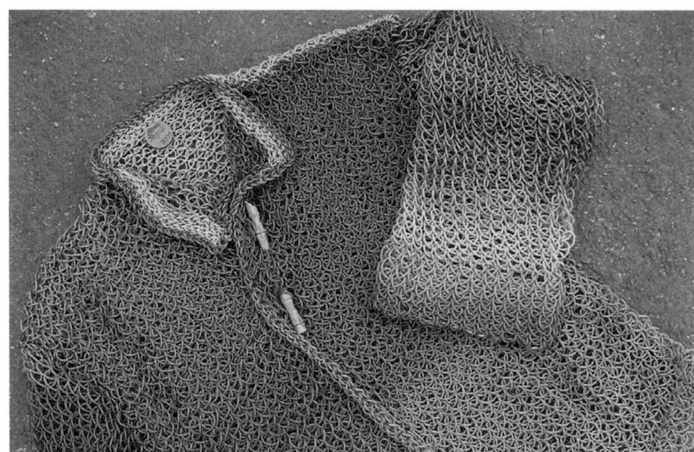

MARIE SEGAL

ASIAN CLAYMAIL

This chainmail-style jacket is made from a 50/50 mix of flexible and standard polymer clay. The mixture is extruded in long strands that are baked and then knitted on a knitting loom—the entire process taking 100 hours.

KENSHIRO SUZUKI

NEKO RYU (ABOVE)

This large fantasy dragon is 29in (73cm) tall. It was made with polymer clay on a galvanized steel armature with brass tubes to connect the different parts. The superb detail and texture were enhanced with acrylic paint after baking.

MINOTAUR, LORD OF THE LABYRINTH (RIGHT)

This fabulous fantasy creature has a removable polymer clay helmet and is 23in (58cm) tall. Constructed in a similar way to the above piece, the artist has used real hair for the minotaur's fur.

MARTIN AND CHARLOTTE WILLMOTT

GREENGROCER'S SHOP (LEFT)

A miniature shop in the scale of 1:12, or 1in to the foot, which is the most popular dollhouse scale. The shop front is constructed from wood and mixed media, and displays a wonderful array of tiny polymer clay fruit and vegetables.

BOWL OF PEAS (ABOVE)

Miniature peas made from polymer clay in a ceramic bowl and in the same scale as the shop. Mixing accurate colors in polymer clay is vital when making miniature food.

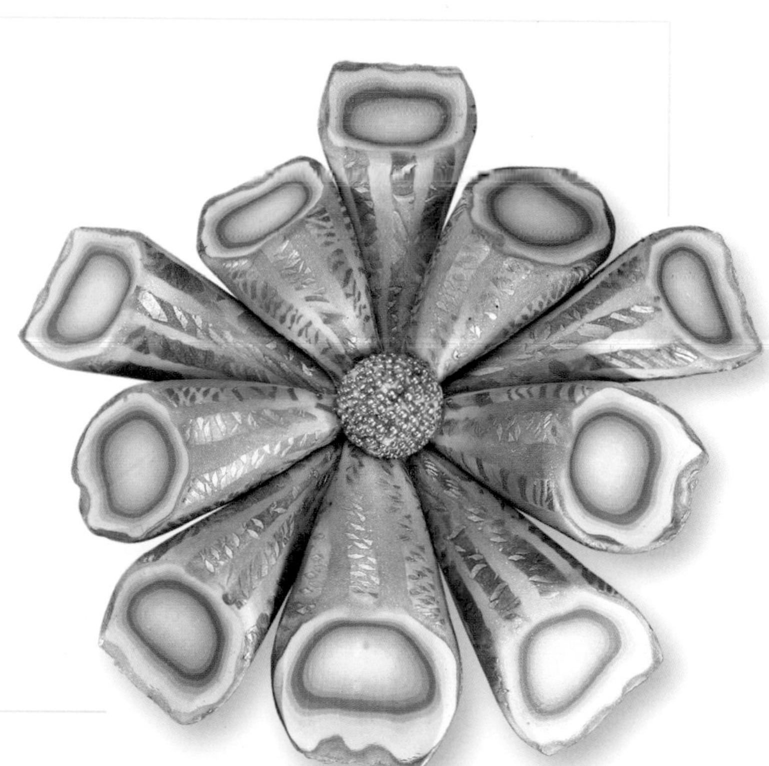

ELISE WINTERS

PINK PENTALA PIN (ABOVE)

This solid pin has layers of painted clay laminated over a scrap core. Mica is incorporated into the clay.

SKINNER INNER PIN (RIGHT)

This dramatic pin is also composed of painted layers, but this time laminated over a Skinner blended core. The cores were then sliced open to reveal the Skinner blend inside. The center is embedded with tiny glass beads.

RESOURCES

CLAY PROPERTIES

The main brands of polymer clay listed here have been tested for their attributes in use and their baked strength. Please note that this is a guide only, and there may be variations within brands due to the different color pigments used and the age of the clay.

FIMO CLASSIC
Manufactured in Germany
Conditioning: may crumble at first
Baked clay strength: ***
Color range: 24
Smoothable: partly
Good for: jewelry, caning, miniatures, dolls (doll clays), general hobby

FIMO SOFT
Manufactured in Germany
Conditioning: slight crumbling
Baked clay strength: ***
Color range: 48+
Mica clays: yes, but subtle effects
Smoothable: yes
Best for: jewelry, caning, miniatures, general hobby

PREMO SCULPEY
Manufactured in US
Conditioning: rapid
Baked clay strength: ***
Color range: 32; colors mix true
Mica clays: yes; strong effect
Smoothable: yes
Best for: jewelry, caning, miniatures, sculpting, general hobby

SCULPEY III
Manufactured in US
Soft clay; matte surface after baking
Conditioning: very rapid
Baked clay strength: *
Color range: 48
Smoothable: yes
Best for: children's projects, general hobby

CREALL-THERM
Manufactured in the Netherlands
Conditioning: crumbles at first
Baked clay strength: *** (needs to be well baked for full strength)
Color range: 25
Smoothable: yes
Best for: jewelry, miniatures, sculpting, dolls (doll clays), general hobby

CERNIT
Manufactured in Germany
All colors have a porcelain effect
Conditioning: slight crumbling; hand heat makes the clay floppy
Baked clay strength: ****
Color range: 32
Smoothable: no
Best for: jewelry, advanced doll making (doll clays), general hobby

DU-KIT
Manufactured in New Zealand
Glossy surface after baking
Conditioning: slight crumbling at first
Baked clay strength: ****
Color range: 25
Smoothable: yes
Best for: jewelry, miniatures, general hobby

KATO CLAY
Manufactured in US
Conditioning: crumbles at first
Baked clay strength: **
Color range: 17
Mica clays: yes
Smoothable: partly
Best for: jewelry, caning

RATINGS

- **Softness:** In the past, polymer clays varied widely as to softness and ease of conditioning. All polymer clay manufacturers have addressed this issue in recent years and the clays listed here are normally soft and easy to condition. If clay is too firm, it may be old stock.
- **Baked clay strength:** Most clays remain quite soft until they reach room temperature, and baked clay strength varies between brands. Some clays are brittle after baking and will snap like a biscuit; others are always flexible, even when cool, especially thin parts. The strength rating is based on 1⁄16in (1.5mm) sheets flexed into a U-bend after baking. Fragile clay breaks immediately; very strong clay can be flexed many times. * = fragile; **** = very strong
- **Smoothable:** The smoothable rating is for sculpting and indicates if added clay can be smoothed in without trace.

MODELENE
Manufactured in Australia
Conditioning: firm at first, softens quickly with kneading
Baked clay strength: ****
Color range: 28
Smoothable: no
Best for: jewelry, miniatures, general hobby use, doll making

SUPPLIERS

AUSTRALIA
Over the Rainbow
P.O. Box 246
Mt. Eliza, Victoria 3930
Tel: 03 5971 5502
www.polymerclay.com.au
Fimo, Sculpey, Premo, tools, and accessories

NEW ZEALAND
Zigzag Polymer Clay Supplies
8 Cherry Place
Casebrook
Christchurch
Tel: 03 359 2989
www.zigzag.co.nz
Fimo, Premo, Sculpey, Du-Kit, tools, and accessories

UNITED KINGDOM
The Polymer Clay Pit Ltd.
3 Harts Lane
Wortham
Diss
Norfolk IP22 1PQ
Tel: 01379 890 176
www.polymerclaypit.co.uk
Fimo, Premo, Sculpey, Creall-Therm, metal clays, doll making, resin, tools, and accessories

UNITED STATES
Clay Factory Inc.
P.O. Box 460598
Escondido, CA 92046-0598
Tel: 760 741 3242
www.clayfactoryinc.com
Cernit, tools, and accessories

Polymer Clay Express
9890 Main Street
Damascus, MD 20872
Tel: 301 482 0399
www.polymerclayexpress.com
Fimo, Premo, Sculpey, Cernit, Kato Clay, tools, and accessories

PMC Supply
225 Cash Street
Jacksonville, TX 75766
Tel: 903 586 2531
www.pmcsupply.com
Metal clay products

OTHER MATERIALS
Deluxe Materials
www.deluxematerials.com
Solid Water, glues

Lazertran Ltd.
www.lazertran.com
Lazertran Silk transfer paper

Environmental Technology, Inc.
www.eti-usa.com
Resins

SOCIETIES AND GUILDS

AUSTRALIA
Aussie Polyclayers Guild & On-line Group
http://groups.yahoo.com/group/aussiepolyclayers

NEW ZEALAND
New Zealand Polymer Clay Guild
www.polymerclay.co.nz/nzpcg/index.html

UNITED KINGDOM
The British Polymer Clay Guild
www.bpcg.org.uk

UNITED STATES
National Polymer Clay Guild
www.npcg.org

FURTHER READING

There is a wonderful variety of polymer clay books and magazines available on all aspects of the craft. This is a small selection.

JEWELRY AND FINE ART BOOKS
Belcher, Judy
Polymer Clay Creative Traditions: Techniques and Projects Inspired by the Fine and Decorative Arts
Watson-Guptill, 2006

Blackburn, Carol
How to Make Polymer Clay Beads
A&C Black/Interweave Press, 2007

Heaser, Sue
Making Polymer Clay Jewellery
Cassell, 1997

Heaser, Sue
The Polymer Clay Techniques Book
North Light Books, 1999

McGuire, Barbara
Foundations in Polymer Clay Design
KP Books, 1999

Semanchuk Dean, Irene
Faux Surfaces in Polymer Clay
Lark Books, 2006

SCULPTURE, DOLL-MAKING, AND MINIATURES BOOKS
Carlson, Maureen
How to Make Clay Characters
North Light Books, 1997

Dewey, Katherine
Creating Life-Like Figures in Polymer Clay: A Step-By-Step Guide
Elvenwork Press, 2003

Heaser, Sue
Making Doll's House Miniatures with Polymer Clay
Ward Lock, 1997

Heaser, Sue
Making Miniature Dolls with Polymer Clay
Ward Lock, 1999

MAGAZINES
PolymerCafe Magazine
www.polymercafe.com
US magazine dedicated to polymer clay art and craft of all kinds

Art Jewelry Magazine
Kalmbach Publishing Co.
www.artjewelrymag.com
US magazine with regular high-quality polymer clay jewelry

INDEX

Page numbers in *italic* refer to illustrations of pieces by named artists

CREDITS

Quarto would like to thank the following artists and photographers for kindly submitting images for inclusion in this book:

Key: *a* = above, *b* = below, *c* = center, *l* = left, *r* = right

Valerie Aharoni 144*l*
www.vaharoni.com
Pamela Annesley 144*r*
www.textileworkshops.com
Pat Bolgar 145*al* & *ar*
www.patbolgar.com
photographer Jerry Anthony
Helen Bradley 145*bl* & *br*
www.http-design.com
Christel Brenner 146*al* & *ar*
www.christels-puppen.de
146*al* photographer M. Ketz
Kevin Buntin 146*bl* & *br*
www.kevinbuntin.com
Jeanette Canyon 147*al*
photographer Jeff Rose Photography, Inc., from children's picture book *Over in the Jungle: A Rainforest Rhyme* by Marianne Berkes, Dawn Publications © 2007
Gera Scott Chandler 147*ac* & *r*
www.gerascottchandler.com
photographer Genevieve Jenkins
Scot Connor 147*bl*
www.gloryartstudios.com
Elizabeth Cooper 148*al* & *ar*
www.cooperdolls.com
photographer Dan Neuberger
Robert Dancik 148*bl* & *br*
www.robertdancik.com
and www.fauxbone.com
photographer Douglas Foulke
Meredith Dittmar 149*al* & *ar*
www.corporatepig.com
Dayle Doroshow 149*bl* & *br*
www.dayledoroshow.com
149*bl* photographer Daniel Neal
149*br* photographer Don Felton
Annette Duburg 150*al* & *bl*
www.annetteduburg.nl
Celie Fago 150*ar* & *br*
www.celiefago.com
photographer Robert Diamante
Christi Friesen 151*al* & *ar*
www.cforiginals.com
photographer Bernard Wolf
Doreen Gay-Kassel 151*bl*
www.doreengay-kassel.com
photographer Lewis Kassel
June Hunter 151*br*
www.junehunter.ca
Suzanne Ivester 152*al*, *ac* & *bl*
152*al* photographer John Black
Judy Kuskin 152*ar*
Loretta Lam 152*br*
www.lorettalam.com
Julie Mansergh 153*a*
www.faeriesintheattic.com
Lisa Pavelka 153*b*
www.heartinhandstudio.com
Marie Segal 154*a*
www.clayfactory.net
Kenshiro Suzuki 154*b*
www.dreamsorcerer.com
Martin and Charlotte Willmott 155*a*
Elise Winters 155*b*
www.elisewinters.com